"Telford Work invites us to follow him [...] vantage points where new vistas of Christ can be pondered. Like studying a photograph's negative, contemplating Jesus as the omega and alpha draws disciples deeper into the unmeasurable richness of Christ's beauty, provoking us to grapple with our rehearsed Christologies and compelling us to explore afresh what it means for Jesus to be the center of Christian faith for us today. This book will not just provide you new frames of reference, but most importantly it will prod you to reconsider if Jesus is or can be your omega and alpha."

—**Brian Lugioyo**, Azusa Pacific University

"A dynamic and engaging vision that proclaims Jesus Christ as the answer to everything. Simple but not simplistic, Work's book shows that Jesus can transform every dimension of human life from individual salvation to civic life and international relations. Work's focus on biblical theology and specifically on Jesus as the Omega and the Alpha makes this an effective book for classroom teaching and discussion."

—**Steven M. Studebaker**, McMaster Divinity College

"This is a wonderfully fresh approach to Christology—or, better, to the pivotal place of Jesus in the entire Christian vision. From multiple angles, Work guides readers in apprehending the concrete difference Jesus makes for all creation. Attentive readings of Scripture abound in this book, and they are shaped by deep engagement with the Christian tradition. Work's prose is a joy to read—it is simultaneously lively and precise, shining new light on familiar themes. Particularly well suited for classroom settings, this volume is a gift to all who seek a coherent and compelling account of the centrality of Jesus."

—**Doug Koskela**, Seattle Pacific University

"In his accessible, often witty, yet theologically deep way, Work retells the scriptural story from the perspective of Jesus as the disruptive turning point of history. Examined from this Christ-outward perspective, God, the cosmos, Israel, humanity, the nations, and even our own lives all have fresh light shone on them. Deeply scriptural and orthodox yet culturally current, *Jesus—the End and the Beginning* is a wonderful way to know more deeply and to be challenged by Jesus, who is at the nexus of all things."

—**David Stubbs**, Western Theological Seminary

"As a slogan, 'Jesus is the answer' can be found in a wide range of mediums from songs to bumper stickers. As a theological truth, many Christians struggle to appreciate it. Telford Work's latest book unpacks this truth to reveal Jesus as the key to understanding God, the cosmos, humanity, etc. He is skilled at weaving together Biblical passages and modern examples to explain the centrality of Jesus for everything. Work deftly navigates different and differing theological traditions to paint a coherent picture of Jesus as both the ending of the old and the beginning of the new, the Omega and Alpha. Work's text is an invitation to Christian discipleship. He warns believers throughout of ways Christ could be displaced as the Omega and Alpha in their own thinking before ending with a call to a richer understanding of a Christ-shaped life. This book is profound and quotable. I took notes of examples and explanations that would help my students to better grasp what I have been teaching for almost twenty years. *Jesus—the End and the Beginning* will be required reading in my classes."

—**D. Allen Tennison**, College of Church Leadership, North Central University

"What if Christ were all in all? What if Jesus truly were our beginning and end? Drawn by these questions, Work presents the reader with a vision of life enfolded by Jesus Christ. A scriptural imagination engages here with matters of faith. This lively book opens up questions of the Christian faith to show their root and resolution in Jesus. All things, Work reminds us, are gathered up in Christ. Here is the engine that propels him through his consideration of numerous issues of faith and contemporary life. Jesus discloses to us our beginning and end, and life is found in the midst."

—**Stephen Wright**, Nazarene Theological College

# Jesus—the End and the Beginning

## TRACING THE CHRIST-SHAPED NATURE OF EVERYTHING

## Telford Work

**Baker Academic**

*a division of Baker Publishing Group*
Grand Rapids, Michigan

© 2019 by Telford Work

Published by Baker Academic
a division of Baker Publishing Group
PO Box 6287, Grand Rapids, MI 49516-6287
www.bakeracademic.com

Printed in the United States of America

Library of Congress Cataloging-in-Publication Data
Names: Work, Telford, author.
Title: Jesus—the end and the beginning : tracing the Christ-shaped nature of everything / Telford Work.
Description: Grand Rapids, MI : Baker Academic, [2019] | Includes bibliographical references and index.
Identifiers: LCCN 2018018007 | ISBN 9781540960542 (pbk.)
Subjects: LCSH: Jesus Christ—Person and offices. | Jesus Christ—History of doctrines. | Theology, Doctrinal.
Classification: LCC BT203 .W667 2019 | DDC 232/.8—dc23
LC record available at https://lccn.loc.gov/2018018007

19  20  21  22  23  24  25          7  6  5  4  3  2  1

To whom else could I dedicate this book than its subject?
With fear and trembling, I present it to Jesus of Nazareth—
my end and my beginning—as well as
to his Father and the Holy Spirit whom
he so graciously shared with us.

◇◇◇

# Contents

# Acknowledgments

This book's core structure is indebted to the many theologians and preachers who have formed me over decades by honoring and teaching the centrality and universal relevance of Christ's life, death, and resurrection. They are too many to name here, but I appreciate each deeply—for inspiring the book, to be sure, but much more so for shaping so many into more faithful disciples.

In 2005, All Saints-by-the-Sea Episcopal Church in Santa Barbara, California, invited me to deliver a Lenten series. I was grateful for the opportunity and even more grateful that the resulting presentation, "Omega and Alpha: Jesus, the Center of Christian Faith," became the embryo from which this book grew. I had the privilege of teaching an expanded version at El Montecito Presbyterian Church, which has graciously hosted me for a number of teaching series over the years.

This book was written while I was on a sabbatical leave courtesy of Westmont's provost office. My esteemed colleagues in the religious studies department covered for my absence.

I spent that year abroad, writing while volunteer teaching in remarkable institutions of Christian learning: Ethiopian Graduate School of Theology in Addis Ababa, Ethiopia; St. Frumentius Theological College in Mekele, Ethiopia; LCC International University in Klaipèda, Lithuania; Ukrainian Catholic University and Lviv Theological Seminary in Lviv, Ukraine; Asia Pacific Theological Seminary in Baguio, Philippines; Trinity Theological College in Singapore; Torch Trinity Graduate University in Seoul, South Korea; and South Asia Institute of Advanced Christian Studies in Bangalore, India. Each place's spirit worked its way into these pages somehow or other. That was the year of a lifetime, and I can't fully express my gratitude for it.

My wife, Kim, and younger children, Junia and Benjamin, accompanied me on most of that adventure and extended grace and support then and back at home while I wrote, thought, edited, and edited some more. My older children, Jeremy and Daniel, and our extended family endured our yearlong absence, and it wasn't always easy.

Westmont students patiently read my draft, suggested improvements, and offered critical feedback. Theological colleagues at other institutions kindly read sample chapters and offered assessments that helped this project see the light of publication. Editors Bob Hosack, Melisa Blok, and John Simpson patiently and wisely made or suggested further clarifications and improvements. I so appreciate their careful and insightful reading. Any flaws that remain are solely my own.

Thanks to all of you!

Telford Work
May 2018

# Preface

## Am I Writing to You?

Nowadays books are pitched to particular audiences. Am I pitching to you or to someone else?

I'm pitching to you if you have some familiarity with the Bible—not necessarily a lot, but enough to know your way around—and are looking for insight into how the parts relate to the whole. I'm especially pitching to you if you aren't totally satisfied with the formulas and paradigms you've already been taught. Not because they're necessarily wrong, but perhaps you've found them too hard to understand or use or too unwieldy and complicated. Perhaps these paradigms seem like round holes for which too many parts of the Bible are ill-fitting square pegs. Or it may be that those formulas and paradigms are fine but need fresh illumination or explication.

If this is you, then I'm pitching to you, whether you are a student new to this, a Bible study leader looking for a more powerful framework for understanding the big picture, or a pastor or academic colleague whose deep experience needs fresh energy. I've tried to keep my writing accessible. The tone may be a stretch for some and yet too casual for others, but I aim to straddle these different walks and seasons of life.

I'm pitching to you if you have some familiarity with the big topics of Christian theology—salvation, incarnation, Trinity, church, and our hoped-for future (theologians call this "eschatology")—but are struggling with them. Whether you have absorbed these doctrines in church or have taken formal courses in theology doesn't matter to me. I'm pitching to you if you want to see more clearly how they all fit together, or how one or more of them applies to your life, or how it functions, or even whether it's true at all. Maybe your understanding of things like the Trinity, the church, the cross, and creation's future are compartmentalized, standing alone like silos on a farm. Or maybe one of them is weak and could use strengthening.

I'm pitching to you if you have a hard time relating the first thing I mentioned (the Bible) to the second (church teachings or theologies). Maybe you find church doctrines tidy and clarifying—many people in my field do—but the Bible frustratingly messy, unorganized, and apparently contradictory. Or maybe you find the Bible full of vivid narratives, pithy guidance, and delightful surprises but theology cold, abstract, predictable, and distant. Or maybe *both* of them feel foreign, whereas Jesus is real and alive and present to you, and worship and prayer are the life-giving ways the Holy Spirit draws you to him. Or maybe you're in that dreadful place where the church's Scriptures and doctrines are the familiar things, and it's Jesus that seems distant and unreal. If you suffer from any of these disconnects, I want to help.

I'm also pitching to you if when you hear (or repeat) the grandiose claims Christians make about Jesus, salvation, or whatever, voices of dissent are crying out from inside you: *Really? Jesus is the answer to* all *of creation's challenges? Jesus is the hope of* every *nation in the world? Jesus is the source of life when Christians I know are stagnant, hypocritical, and corrupt?* Too often theology ignores these complaints, and that just encourages them to grow. I want to honor some objections by giving them a fair hearing along the way.

I've been in all these places and more in my years as a new Christian, a new churchgoer, a seminary student, and an academic who likes to teach and preach what I call "the good stuff." I'm still looking for clarity, simplicity, answers to stubborn questions, and new energy. If you are too, I hope you find some here.


### Jesus, Center of Everything?

Here is my focus: Christians claim all the time that Jesus is the center of everything. And we genuinely mean it. Still, we need to improve at understanding and explaining *how*.

> In what ways is Jesus the *center* of everything? What does that really look like? How does it play out in life and in history?
>
> And how is it that Jesus is the center of *everything*—not just the things we naturally associate with him, but the whole world, all creation, and our entire lives?

One sign that we need to do better is our struggle to expand on the formulaic ways we confess this claim. There's nothing wrong with formulaic answers. All my significant relationships can be named neatly in a word or two: wife, son, mother, boss, Lord and Savior, student, pastor, colleague. These terms are powerful because they are *packed.* So if someone asks me what I mean by one of them, I can *unpack* it. I can explain what being a husband means, expand on it, illustrate it, and demonstrate it. And if I can't? Well, I may just be inarticulate or unreflective: a person who loves his wife but needs a Hallmark card to say it, or who hasn't stepped back to consider just what she means to him. But at some point people will begin to wonder whether anything really *is* packed into that term. If I keep insisting that "she's my wife" when pressed to describe her, a thoughtful friend might suspect a poor or strained relationship. A psychologist might perceive an empty one. A skeptic (perhaps an immigration officer) might gather that our marriage is a sham.

*Are* those confessional formulas packed and rich, maybe even beyond our capacity to unpack? Or does our reliance on them indicate that we really don't know Jesus well? Or is Jesus a sham—a socially constructed illusion?

Sometimes the answer to each question is yes. There are Christians whose terms for Jesus are just Hallmark cards that they trust—sometimes rightly—more than their own words. Others are just mimicking the faith of a parent. Others use them as a balm to bring comfort during tough times. For still others, these words are a cultural vestige that is likely to fade with time.

We *can* do better. In fact, we who grasp how rich and dependable our Scripture, liturgy, and dogmas are can still do better than merely repeating them back to God. I buy Hallmark cards too, but I'm not going to just sign my name and seal the envelope. I'm going to write something of my own.

This book works toward a deeper appreciation of Jesus as the center—and specifically, since the Bible puts it this way, as *the end* and *the beginning*—of everything. My core focus is that slogan: the end and the beginning, *the omega and the alpha.* It deserves a lengthy unpacking and repacking. I want it ready—full, compact, organized, and familiar—so I can take it everywhere I go and use it well. That's how a good formula ought to work.

**Why Write This?**

I have a list of writing projects, some years old. Why did I write this one, and why might you want to read it? A few stories will help me answer this.

First, until middle age I never flossed my teeth. I didn't see the point. Fluoridated water, advances in dental care, and good genes have all given me good teeth and few cavities. I found the little boxes of floss too inconvenient anyway. That changed one day during a visit to my hygienist.

"Do you floss?" she asked.

"You tell me," I said. "I assume you can tell."

"I can tell," she said.

"Then why do you ask?"

"Just to see whether people will be honest."

I would have told the truth anyway. "No, I don't floss much," I admitted.

"You should," she told me. "It can put six years on your life. And not just years, but *good years*."

That got my attention. "Why is that?"

"Gum tissue is similar to heart valve tissue," she told me. "When you get gum disease, the bacteria can migrate to your heart and weaken it."

That was enough for me. That and the little plastic flosser she handed me, which I use instead of wrapping the stuff around my fingers like a tourniquet. I've flossed more or less faithfully ever since, thinking about the chance for those six extra years to live, serve the Lord, and maybe see my grandchildren, which is something my father didn't get to do.

*The connection made the difference.* That morning in the dentist's office I learned that something I hadn't cared about was related to something I cared about. And that made me start caring. My circle of interests has widened again and again as I have learned that something I had shrugged off or ignored turned out to matter after all. I hated backpacking as a kid but embraced it as a parent as I learned that Scouting could help children grow up well (and that backpacking could be light and comfortable). Now I look forward to getting on the trail. I grew frustrated with philosophy as an undergrad and set it aside but found it interesting again as a graduate student after seeing how it has shaped the Christian tradition I cared so much about.

This book explores *connections* among Jesus Christ and our lives, our communities, our nations, the people of Israel, the human race, the world, and God. You care about at least some of these already. The more we learn about their connections, the more we'll care. And yet caring isn't the whole challenge we face.

Now for my second story. One morning while I was teaching a general Christian doctrine course, my students were suddenly staring back like deer in headlights. I had asked them to discuss how their responsibilities as citizens of their countries relate to Christ's reign and victory. This was a Christian theology class at an evangelical liberal arts college. A number of these students studied political science, history, philosophy, and sociology. They were all constantly prodded to think about matters of social and political involve-ment, often for the sake of Christian faithfulness and responsibility. And I had just taught them in detail about Jesus's primacy as the crucified, risen, and reigning King of kings. They already cared about these things. Yet when it came time to connect the dots, they were still dumbfounded. One student even dared to say what others were surely thinking: "How are we supposed to answer that?"

My classic question is an important one in our age of powerful nation-states. Why had it blindsided my students? Because they had segregated the kingdoms of this world from Christ their King. Caring apart from connecting leads to *compartmentalizing*. It's not enough to show *that* all things relate to Jesus. We must begin to understand *how* they relate.

This leads to my third anecdote. Ten years ago, a nearby Episcopal church invited me to teach a Lenten series at a retreat. Since Lent is a season of prepa-ration for celebrating Passion Week, I wondered how I could help the class grasp the sheer significance of Jesus's life, death, and resurrection. It's one thing to say and hear that Christ's love reaches great "breadth and length and height and depth" (Eph. 3:18). It's another thing to *display* all that. Beyond listing the usual titles, abstractions, and all-encompassing claims about Christ, I wanted the vivid *specifics* of his impact to reach our finite minds. I wanted the people of this church to see not just a confessional forest but individual trees. Moreover, I wanted them to see how each shapes the other, how the Christian faith is a forest *of* trees.

We often operate in detail mode, analyzing pixels rather than the image they render, threads rather than the pattern of the tapestry. Then we turn around and do the opposite. We proclaim the pattern without showing how the pattern (forest) is made up (of trees), which turns the pattern into an irrelevant abstraction. This can happen with essential theological formulas such as "justification by grace through faith," "one being in three persons," "the fellowship of saints," and "Christ died for our sins." It can even happen with Jesus's own name:

> The Sunday school lesson for the day was about Noah's Ark, so the preschool teacher in our Kentucky church decided to get her small pupils involved by playing a game in which they identified animals.
> "I'm going to describe something to you. Let's see if you can guess what it is. First: I'm furry with a bushy tail and I like to climb trees."
> The children looked at her blankly.
> "I also like to eat nuts, especially acorns."
> No response. This wasn't going well at all.

"I'm usually brown or gray, but sometimes I can be black or red."

Desperate, the teacher turned to a perky four-year-old who was usually good about coming up with the answers. "Michelle, what do you think?"

Michelle looked hesitantly at her classmates and replied, "Well, I know the answer has to be Jesus—but it sure sounds like a squirrel to me."[1]

*The answer has to be Jesus.* The apostle Paul said so: "Christ is all, and in all" (Col. 3:11). But the kids in this story have no clue as to *how* or *why*. My dazed college students were in the same position. They knew that everything summarizes to Jesus and resolves in Jesus. Both their churches and our lecture notes said so! They had learned the rules of how to throw his name around among evangelicals. Just don't ask them to explain how *this* tree—their national citizenship, for instance—is part of *that* Passion-shaped forest. And don't expect academic theology to teach them how to do it since the same problems often appear there.[2]

The answer *does* have to be Jesus. But the answer doesn't have to be trite. It doesn't have to be idealized or forced. It can be *shown*. It can be developed. It can even be derived. When we do that, it becomes clear that screens and tapestries are too rough as metaphors. An image doesn't modify a screen's pixels as Jesus transforms his collective bride. A forest context affects its trees, and Jesus changes us far more than that. So it won't do to just teach a macro view of "Jesus as all things" alongside a micro view of the things as such. Paul's metaphors are better, which might be why he chose them: a body of members, a temple of cut stones, a cultivated field, a household, and so on. The parts of these things owe their character to the whole and vice versa.[3]

1. Susan Webber, *Chicken Soup for the Christian Soul*, ed. Jack Canfield and Mark Victor Hansen (New York: Simon & Schuster, 2012), 176.

2. Forests dominate in some traditions of systematic theology, while trees dominate in others. In "forest" theology, dogmatic or ideological claims drive theological visions and dominate biblical and later texts that supposedly support them. Contrary texts tend to be explained away or simply ignored. Movement primarily runs from the top down, from the abstract to the specific. In "tree" theology, by contrast, biblical and other passages are sorted into theological categories such as Christology, soteriology, eschatology, and so on. These compilations are then generalized, producing categories that are treated as doctrines. This movement is primarily bottom up, from specificity to abstraction.

Champions of each approach tend to find the other side's productions unsatisfying and end up talking past each other. The situation in theology might be improved through greater attention to the genuine interaction happening across these levels, both in the formative eras when the biblical and patristic texts were being written and freshly read and broader Christian sensibilities were taking shape, and in later settings when both the texts and sensibilities were in wide and increasingly stable use.

3. The term *organic* is worn out, and *emergent* seems more or less ruined, but these terms are closer to capturing the relationship.

I did come up with an approach for the Lenten series I was invited to preach. The omega-and-alpha trope that structures this book struck me as a promising way both to get across the absolute relevance of Jesus's death and resurrection for every aspect of Christian life and to indicate some familiar as well as unfamiliar specifics. This book grew out of that Lenten challenge. It aims to demonstrate formative and essential ways that Jesus's human life, death, and resurrection shape many areas of Christian life and thought and vice versa. Jesus as omega and alpha isn't just a formula to memorize for a test or a catechism. It's something to take in, to learn to love, to see in Scripture and in action, to glimpse in far-flung settings, and to stand on when we desperately need things in our lives to end and better things to arrive.

My reflections stress biblical texts, for these are molten with the energy of prophetic and apostolic imaginations dazzled by the fresh realization of Christ's implications for everything. The book's chapters don't fall into the usual theological categories, because they are exploring the common pattern underneath them. But basic theological categories unavoidably recur and mingle throughout: Christology, eschatology, creation, soteriology, Trinity, and ecclesiology.

It's a blast to see students discover that the all-purpose Sunday school answer is no cliché but a kind of theorem that comes to life as we use it. They see how the whole structure fits and works together, and they find they're in on something even better than they had realized. I hope these pages enact the same reaction in you.

# ONE

# Introduction

> For in him all the fulness of God was pleased to dwell, and through him *to reconcile to himself all things*, whether on earth or in heaven, making peace by the blood of his cross.
>
> Colossians 1:19–20

"The Quest is achieved, and now all is over. I'm glad you are here with me, Sam. Here at the end of all things."[1] J. R. R. Tolkien puts these apocalyptic words in Frodo's mouth just after the destruction of the Ring of Power in *The Return of the King*. Frodo immediately perceives that everything will change, even his remote and cherished Shire. (The books make that clear. Sadly, the film does not.) With the Ring's destruction, Middle Earth's reclamation and restoration are at hand. It takes time to unfold, bringing the demise of elves, dwarves, wizards, and even hobbits, and the rise of "the Age of Men." Tolkien perceptively reckons the end of the Third Age and the beginning of the Fourth two years later to the day: March 25 on our calendar.

March 25 is the Feast of the Annunciation, the day that commemorates the conception of Jesus Christ as described in Luke 1:26–38, a decisive event at the *true* end of all things. The annunciation was the moment God invaded his own rebellious world and began to take it back from within. As March 25 began the denouement of Middle Earth's Third Age and the dawn of its Fourth, so March 25 began, in essence, the Age of the New Adam. All

---

1. J. R. R. Tolkien, *The Return of the King* (1955; repr., New York: Ballantine, 1986), 241.

the elements of the old age would still exist—for a while anyway—but totally rearranged, "fall[ing] and rising" (Luke 2:34). Jesus put an end to "all things"—a biblical term for all creation[2]—and brought a new beginning for them. Do you believe that? You might not. Look out the window, at a newspaper, or even in a mirror. What's so new? Sadly for Tolkien, "the Age of Men" would prove too depressing to write about. He soon abandoned his attempt to imagine the Fourth Age. Human hearts were the same as before; not enough had changed after all.

When 2 Peter was being written, skeptics were making similar observations. Creation seemed to be creaking along just as before (2 Pet. 3:4). Those skeptics were underestimating Jesus's transformative power. Countless others have ever since. Even many Christians have traded the apostles' far-reaching vision of total transformation for the much more modest claim that our *souls* were all Jesus renewed. Salvation was *spiritual*, they supposed. The material part of creation hadn't changed and wouldn't. Human families, cultures, histories, and politics were not the Lord's focus and would last only until his return, to then be consigned to the lake of fire or unceremoniously dropped into history's rubbish heap. This pattern of thinking was powerfully reinforced whenever the mood of the times ran in a pessimistic direction.[3]

But Christians face an opposite temptation: to overestimate the transformation. The apostles had expected the old world's kingdoms to topple like dominoes at the Messiah's coming to "restore the kingdom to Israel" (Acts 1:6). That obviously didn't happen, as it had not happened in Middle Earth or the Shire. Christians have reconciled themselves to this disappointing development for the most part, but we haven't entirely abandoned the dream. Our perceptions of Christ's renewal can get carried away into wishful thinking. When the signs seem to be pointing in the direction of a Christian Rome, a Christian Russia, a Christian America, a Christian Korea or Africa or China, or when the zeitgeist shifts global consciousness toward justice or prosperity or freedom, we who would love to see such breakthroughs can extrapolate the trend too optimistically and imagine the Lord's hand in it.[4]

Our day offers plenty of warrants for both pessimism and optimism. One of this book's purposes is to untangle the apostolic faith from both and to examine Jesus's transformation of all things for what it really is.[5] If you're

---

2. Richard Bauckham, *The Bible and Ecology* (Waco: Baylor University Press, 2010).

3. In Republican circles in 2009 and in Democratic ones in 2017, for instance.

4. In Democratic circles in 2009 and in some Republican ones in 2017, for instance.

5. I don't know whether to be optimistic or pessimistic about our times. I've been on the pessimistic side for some time now. My pessimism may be as much a function of bad information as a reflection of reality. Bradley R. E. Wright's *Christians Are Hate-Filled Hypocrites*

turned off by Christian visions that are excessively modest or grandiose, don't dismiss this one too quickly. I try to be carefully realistic and to put biblical claims about Jesus's vast ministry in honest conversation with the twenty centuries of often sobering and occasionally intoxicating reality that follow it. To do that in a simple and memorable way, I've taken the liberty of inverting a biblical trope.

## Jesus—the Alpha and the Omega

In the book of Revelation, the Lord—God the Father and Jesus Christ as well—is described several times as the "alpha" and the "omega."[6] That might be familiar language to you. You might have heard it in sermons, in songs, or in people's prayers, or you might have seen it on a banner in your church sanctuary. Alpha and omega are the first and last letters of the Greek alphabet. So Jesus Christ is the beginning and the end and everything in between.

The Gospel of John begins with the same startling claim that Jesus was in the beginning with God. He's the alpha. The church had to defend this claim against a heretical school of thought called Arianism, which claimed that only God the Father was the true alpha. Arians considered Jesus the "beta," so to speak, a second-class deity whom the only true God created and then worked with to create everything else. Fourth-century church leaders labored to convince even many of their fellow Christians that Jesus wasn't a second-tier archangel, but that he along with the Father and the Holy Spirit was and is the one, coeternal God of Israel.

Jesus is time's omega as well. His Kingdom will have no end. Jesus lasts, and anything else that lasts does so in and because of him. His life is eternal life. The church had to defend this claim, too, against those same Arians, who treated the incarnation of the Word as only temporary. Arians thought of the divine Word shedding Jesus's human body on the cross and returning to its earlier spirit form. Trinitarians eventually convinced their fellow Christians that Jesus was the Z, not just an X or Y; that his human existence was

---

. . . *and Other Lies You've Been Told* (Bloomington, MN: Bethany House, 2010) provides a refreshing statistical corrective to widespread conventional wisdom that Christian faith makes little or no difference to the way Americans live. He shows that active Christian faith makes a broad and significant difference. It hardly matters if my pessimism is unwarranted though, because Christ's transformation doesn't depend on passing feelings or minor historical trends. If we stand on the precipice of doom, it'll pass. If we stand on the threshold of technological singularity or a great awakening, it too will pass.

6. To get a sense of how the writer of Revelation associates this language with both God the Father and Jesus Christ, see Rev. 1:4, 8, 17; 2:8; 4:8; 11:17; 16:5; 21:6; and especially 22:12–13.

eternal, so that we can have an eternal existence too; that the same one who died and rose reigns today from heaven and is coming to bring all creation to the perfection that the Father has always intended.

That is the way that we normally use the phrase "alpha and omega." You can see how vital this compact claim from Revelation 1:8; 21:6; and 22:13 is. Those chapters begin and end the book; they are its *A* and *Z*. Jesus Christ frames and dominates the imagination of John, the prophet who wrote the book of Revelation. John isn't simply coming up with a clever structure. He is passing on the whole structure of his life and thought, which he received from Jesus himself (Rev. 1:1).

And yet, that alpha implies more than *just* the source of creation's beginning, and that omega implies more than *just* the eternity in which creation finds its eternity. Here is what else we hear in Revelation along with alpha-omega language:

> 1:18: "*I died,* and behold *I am alive* for evermore."
>
> 2:8: "The words of [him] . . . who *died* and *came to life.*"
>
> 11:17–18: "You have taken your great power and *begun to reign.* . . . Your wrath has come, and *the time for judging the dead . . . and for destroying those who destroy the earth.*" (NRSV)
>
> 16:5–6: "You are just *in your judgments.* . . . It is their due." (my translation)
>
> 21:5–6: "Behold, I make *all things new.* . . . *It is done!* . . . To the thirsty I will give from *the fountain of the water of life.*"
>
> 22:12–14: "Behold, *I am coming soon, bringing my recompense.* . . . Blessed are those who wash their robes, that they may have the right to *the tree of life and that they may enter the city.*"

Those alphas are generally *new beginnings*, not some lingering original past. And those omegas are generally *definitive endings* of things that never make it into that new and eternal future. This is why this book switches the order. Jesus Christ is also the *Z* and the *A*, the last and the first.

### Jesus—the End and the Beginning

After all, the biblical story doesn't unfold smoothly from beginning to end like alphabets do: *a, b, c, d, e.* History doesn't follow an orderly sequence right to the end. It is punctuated by disruptions in which an old order is swept away and a new order is begun. And Jesus is the fundamental disruption of all cosmic history.

Let me suggest an analogy. Geologists for the past two hundred years or so have debated two visions of the earth's history. Did the earth come to be what it is through extraordinary dramatic events such as massive volcanic eruptions[7] and meteorite and comet collisions? The "catastrophists" thought so. Or has the earth been shaped primarily by gradual processes such as sedimentation, erosion, and continental drift? "Uniformitarians" insisted on it. Each side made valid observations over the course of their long academic conflict. Most geologists today refuse to wholly endorse one side or the other. Both gradual processes and extraordinary events interact to shape our planet.

History, too, has elements of continuity, gradual change, and shattering disruptions. Return to a place you haven't visited in years and you may be shocked by the change that happened day by day—perhaps the locals barely noticed. But some dates are etched into the world's collective memory because nothing could be the same afterward (Z) and people had to pick up the pieces and start again (A, B, C).

The crux of the biblical story is one of those catastrophes. Indeed, *crux* means cross. Jesus's crucifixion was an omega: an end of the sequence. "It is finished," he said when he breathed his last. Yet it wasn't *just* finished. After that Z came a new A. Not just a return or revival of some past A, but a *whole* new A. Many philosophies and religious traditions think of history as a great wheel that turns, placing the world back in a spot it had occupied before. That is not what happened on the third day after Jesus was murdered. God answered Jesus's demise by creating something totally new: Christ's risen, eternally embodied life. The resurrection's new beginning marked the ushering in of a whole new order. This was so staggeringly unprecedented that, as theologian Lesslie Newbigin notes, the apostles had to retrieve Israel's word for the *first* unprecedented beginning: creation.[8] Jesus's resurrection had inaugurated a new creation (2 Cor. 5:17).

Inverting the letters captures another element of Jesus's central role in everything: his indispensable role in putting an end to whatever doesn't belong in the new creation. The Bible's creation stories portray God originally granting humanity a privileged role in further developing creation—in moving from A to B to C, so to speak—and equipping human beings for the task. In making all things, God had a mysterious goal in mind. That goal, it turns out, is Jesus (Col. 1:15–20), the wisdom of God (1 Cor. 1:24). As Wisdom says in the book of Proverbs:

7. The highest category on the eight-point Volcanic Explosivity Index that geologists use is termed "apocalyptic," which tells you something.
8. Lesslie Newbigin, *The Gospel in a Pluralist Society* (Grand Rapids: Eerdmans, 1989), 11.

> The LORD begat me, the beginning of his way, his acts from eternity.
> Forever I was appointed, at the first, from before the earth.
> When there were no depths I was brought forth,
> when there were no springs abounding with water . . .
> when he established the heavens, I was there, . . .
> when he assigned to the sea its limit, . . .
> when he marked out the foundations of the earth,
> then I was beside him, like a master worker;
> and I was daily his delight, rejoicing before him always,
> rejoicing in his inhabited world and delighting in the human race.
>
> (Prov. 8:22–31, my translation)

A beautiful picture of God's alpha and ours. Wisdom then beckons us not to miss out on this golden opportunity to become full partners in the Lord's project. In fact, Wisdom hints at something beyond partnership: we are called to be *sons*, her full heirs, who stand to inherit their mother's wisdom somehow in some unprecedented way:

> And now, my sons, listen to me:
>     happy are those who keep my ways.
> Hear instruction and be wise,
>     and do not neglect it.
> Happy is the one who listens to me,
>     watching daily at my gates,
>     waiting beside my doors.
> For whoever finds me finds life
>     and obtains favor from the LORD.
>
> (Prov. 8:32–35 NRSV alt.)

Sometimes we hear Wisdom's call and answer back: "How many are your works, LORD! In wisdom you made them all" (Ps. 104:24 NIV). Sometimes we are humbled by this unparalleled and undeserved vocation, and we are moved to jubilant worship and to insight into God's deeper purpose in crowning us with glorious dominion (Ps. 8:4–6). Sometimes.

However, Genesis 3 depicts a more common contrary. The story of the Garden of Eden portrays a *coup d'état*, a hijacking, a human commandeering of God's project (Ps. 14:1–3) just as the human task was ready to get under way. God had laid out a space and then commissioned us to be its developers (see Gen. 2:5, 15). In that garden we humans put our own goals ahead of the Creator's goal. We asserted our own glory rather than his. We grasped at wisdom as if it were something we could usurp (Gen. 3:6) rather than finding it by faithfully waiting, listening, and watching. Having received unique authority on God's earth, we made ourselves the earth's tyrants. And we have kept doing so to this day.

The story of Eden closes with the man and the woman ejected from the garden and facing harsh consequences, leaving the garden unmaintained and undeveloped. We have attempted to invert things, and in a sense we have succeeded, if only in ruining them. Our irresponsibility has spawned three challenges, not just one.[9]

God's creation goes undeveloped, and is even ruined, because the servant-rulers have refused the task that God has created them for. Someday Jeremiah will prophesy a sadly similar future:

> Many shepherds have destroyed my vineyard,
>     they have trampled down my portion,
> ................................................
> The whole land is made desolate,
>     but no one lays it to heart.
>
> (Jer. 12:10–11 NRSV)

This is the first problem: God's project has stalled because his workers have walked off the job and been banned from the premises.

The workers themselves are the second problem. As Paul puts it, although creation's caretakers knew God (not necessarily well), "they neither glorified him as God nor gave thanks to him, but their thinking became futile and their foolish hearts were darkened. Although they claimed to be wise, they became fools" (Rom. 1:21–22 NIV). God's designated agents prove themselves to be both incompetent and malevolent. The man and woman are distrustful of God, one another, and God's other creatures (Gen. 3:7–19). We who are "crowned with glory and honor" are also "foolish, faithless, heartless, ruthless" (Rom. 1:31). This has to stop. God has to rectify his appointed servants and reconcile them to their roles in his creation so they "image" or point to him as he intended. Theologians call those acts *justification* and *redemption*, respectively.[10]

Third, work has to get back on track. God has to bring creation to its goal. That's called *perfection* or *consummation*, and it involves more than just a building-out of creation's original potential. Even if humans had not rebelled, more needed to happen than the original creation's smoothly unfolding

9. This is the case whether one reads Gen. 1–3 literally or figurally. If these chapters use imaginative literary devices, they still depict a promising beginning that we have ruined.

10. Redemption of creation and its creatures can also be used as a broader category that includes justification of its sinners.

*A-B-C.* This is only hinted at in Genesis's opening chapters—for instance, in the not-quite-redundant parallelism between "image" and "likeness" in 1:26, and in 2:9's two mysterious trees. What they signify becomes clearer in the course of God's reclamation effort, because that effort brings much more than just justification and redemption. Jesus's ministry did not return him or his followers to where Adam and Eve were in Genesis 2. His transfiguration introduced *glorification* into creation, and his bodily resurrection introduced a new and eternal imperishability.

The following chart relates the distinct tasks involved in salvation:

Figure 1.1

### Biblical Creation, Fall, Redemption, and Consummation

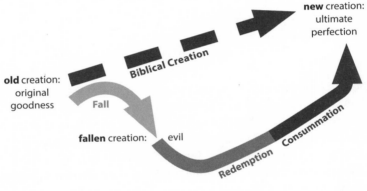

Jesus's coming is an alpha in that it both *reverts* creation and *converts* it. It ends all that's wrong with original creation, inverting our earlier inversion so to speak, and ends all that was never meant to last anyway by inaugurating its long-awaited new version. Jesus is the Z and the A. The author of Hebrews, too, cannot help but see Jesus as the resolution of the contradiction between humanity's calling and humanity's condition:

> It is not to angels that he has subjected the world to come, about which we are speaking. But there is a place where someone has testified:
>
>> "What is mankind that you are mindful of them,
>>     a son of man that you care for him?
>> You made them a little lower than the angels;
>>     you crowned them with glory and honor
>>     and put everything under their feet."

In putting everything under them, God left nothing that is not subject to them. Yet at present we do not see everything subject to them. But we do see Jesus, who was made lower than the angels for a little while, now crowned with glory and honor because he suffered death, so that by the grace of God he might taste death for everyone. (Heb. 2:5–9 NIV, quoting Ps. 8:4–6)

Isn't that marvelous? What Psalm 8 celebrates in advance, we get to celebrate in review. Jesus the Son of Man met our end, took on our humiliating omega, and thereby authored and pioneered our glorious alpha. And he did it in a way that we can see and appreciate even in the midst of an old world still tumbling toward its omega.

That's how this logic works. You'll hear it all through the New Testament. "I died, and behold I am alive for evermore," Jesus tells John in Revelation 1:18. *I ended, and behold, I am begun.* The goal of this book is to examine some ways that Jesus alone brings about the end of the world's evils and sufferings and frustrations, and begins eternity's new creation.

## The Ends of the Ages

Paul is utterly convinced that Jesus has done all this. In 1 Corinthians 10 Paul warns the church in Corinth by appealing to a horrible event in Israel's early history: the day the Israelites lost their patience with God and Moses on Mount Sinai and turned to a golden calf (1 Cor. 10:7, quoting Exod. 32:6). Reminding them of the plague that followed their idolatry, Paul says, "These things happened to them as a warning, but they were written to instruct us, upon whom *the ends of the ages have come*" (1 Cor. 10:11, my translation). That last phrase is the tip of an iceberg. Few Bible translations honor the plural *ends* in that verse. Paul's imagery is that of two coinciding ages, and we stand at the hinge. We live in the meeting place of the new and the old. Paul doesn't develop that point in this passage, but elsewhere it's developed very well indeed (e.g., Rom. 8:18–25; 1 Cor. 7:29–31; 2 Cor. 5:16–17).

The figure on page 10 depicts the two overlapping ages, which Ephesians terms "this age" and "the age to come" (Eph. 1:21 NRSV). Both ages have to do with the same creation. Each age has an alpha and an omega, and Jesus is both alphas and both omegas, as the verses from the book of Revelation affirm.

We live in the time marked by the bracket in the following figure, in the midst of the old and in the midst of the new. We occupy a moment of history—two thousand years long so far—where the new is breaking in on the old, the old is suffering its omega, and the new is undergoing its alpha.

Figure 1.2

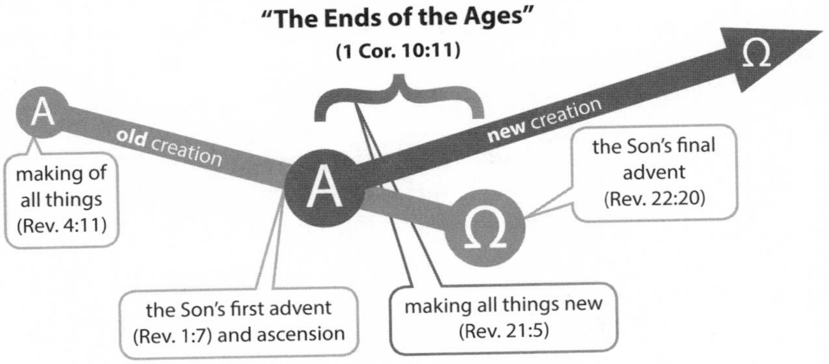

## "The Ends of the Ages"
### (1 Cor. 10:11)

A

old creation

new creation

Ω

making of all things (Rev. 4:11)

the Son's final advent (Rev. 22:20)

the Son's first advent (Rev. 1:7) and ascension

making all things new (Rev. 21:5)

**Between Times**

I've been sketching the forest. The same passage in 1 Corinthians 10 zooms in on one of its trees. It demonstrates how being at "the ends of the ages" guides Paul as a church leader in specific situations and ways. Paul reminds the Corinthian church of the episode recorded in Exodus 17 when "our fathers," camping in the wilderness and lacking water, quarreled with Moses and with God. God graciously answered by offering himself: "I will stand there before you by the rock at Horeb. Strike the rock, and water will come out of it" (Exod. 17:6 NIV). Our fathers, Paul says, "drank from the spiritual rock" (1 Cor. 10:4 NIV).

From his apostolic vantage point, Paul sees a deeper significance in this scene, something Moses and the Israelites could not: "the Rock was Christ" (1 Cor. 10:4). As the alpha of both ages, the Messiah was sustaining even those who preceded his incarnation. And the Corinthians now faced their common omega. "With most of them God was not pleased; for they were overthrown in the wilderness . . . destroyed by the Destroyer. Now these things happened to them as a warning, but they were written down for our instruction, upon whom the ends of the ages has come" (10:5, 10–11). Christ, the Lord who judges (11:32) and who destroys every enemy (15:25–26), was already putting abominations to an end in the wilderness. So will he do in Corinth.[11]

11. Ever wonder why "biblical" disasters don't happen today like they used to? Paul's analogy suggests an answer: the Hebrews in the wilderness had to learn without an example. Like children today who suffer the mixed blessing of being firstborn, they had to live under stricter rules and live out the consequences of breaking them. In the old age, God proved again and again that he was serious. He thereby acquired a lasting reputation among those who will pay attention. Rules backed by real-life examples are more compelling than rules alone, so the stiff-necked Hebrews became the powerful example for their younger siblings to remember and heed. Perhaps one reason the church age is not marked by the same spectacular plagues is that

To us this may not feel like an everyday example, but to Paul it sure is. It frames all his pastoral actions, in 1 Corinthians and elsewhere. What distinguishes the old and new ages is the same as what links them: the Lord Jesus Christ and specifically his comings. He is the first one to inaugurate the age to come and to put the present age on notice and the final one to end the present age and to fully establish the age to come. Paul immediately connects the dots between ancient Israel's wilderness wanderings and the Corinthians' struggles: "*Therefore*, my beloved, flee from idolatry" (1 Cor. 10:14 NKJV). Old Testament Israel shared the Lord's altar; Christians now share the same Lord's one bread and cup. Both privileges make idolatry—sharing with demons, Paul calls it—unthinkable, provoking our ever jealous Lord (10:16–22). Israel's old life is of pressing relevance to the church's new life, because Christ is their common currency.

Paul expects his readers to connect these dots themselves, and he's disappointed when they don't. First Corinthians 10 is full of rhetorical questions and appeals to the Corinthians' common sense (vv. 15–16). Paul is thinking, "Why don't they *get it*?" Many Christians today scratch their heads at Paul's reasoning. We can't even follow it, let alone assimilate it, if we, like the Corinthians, don't understand *how* Jesus is the omega and alpha. But once we *get it*, we'll be able to do more than just follow puzzling New Testament passages. We'll be able to discern Jesus's relevance to matters ranging far beyond the Bible's original concerns.

This book aims to help you really *get* that Jesus is the omega and alpha of all things: of God (chap. 2), of the cosmos or "world" (chap. 3), of humanity (chap. 4), of Israel (chap. 5), of the nations (chap. 6), and of individual lives (chap. 7).

## A Nuptial Analogy

Paul can be hard to understand (2 Pet. 3:15–16). Scripture's more brilliant authors can just be a challenge. Ordinary life offers illustrations of omega-alpha logic that are more intuitive for many of us.

One everyday example of what it's like to be at the hinge of two ages is the drawn-out events that make up a wedding. American weddings often involve a rehearsal, a rehearsal dinner, bachelor and bachelorette parties,

---

ancient Israel's example is enough. Jesus suggests as much, in the punch line of his story of the rich man and Lazarus (Luke 16:27–31). We are blessed in ways our fathers were not. (And as the youngest of three siblings and the father of four, all I can say is that life isn't fair. My heart goes out to the world's firstborn, along with my admiration and appreciation.)

day-of preparations, the tradition of bride and groom not seeing each other before the ceremony, a ceremony, a reception and first dance, toasts and blessings, cutting of the cake, a send-off, the couple's exit, and the wedding night. Regardless of a culture's particulars, though, a wedding is an omega to the individuals' old lives ("forsaking all others") and an alpha to a new and even more intimately shared one ("to have and to hold from this day forward"). Both ages hang over the whole occasion. In fact, old and new both exert a strong pull not just during these intense few days but throughout the whole stretch of time from engagement to the honeymoon and newlywed year and, indeed, over the years or decades that follow. Those days now loom over the couple's courtship and earlier lives in singleness, which turn out to have been preparations for their own end in marriage.

Of course, it is no accident that a human marriage is an analogy to Christ's redeeming and consummating work: "We are members of his body. 'For this reason a man shall leave his father and mother and be joined to his wife, and the two shall become one flesh.' This mystery is a profound one, and I am saying that it refers to Christ and the church" (Eph. 5:30–32, quoting Gen. 2:24). Sometimes people fail to remember the *leaving* of the old family that's involved in the *cleaving* that brings into being a new one. The old comes to an end, and the new comes into being "at last" (Gen. 2:23). So "do not stir up or awaken love until it is ready," the Song of Songs warns us (Song 8:4 NRSV). Yet once it comes, why delay? "Make haste, my beloved" (8:14). "Our Lord, come!" (1 Cor. 16:22).

### A Constitutional Analogy

Let me give you another concrete illustration of what it means to be at a hinge like this. Consider living in the final months of 1787, between the writing and the ratification of the Constitution of the United States.

The Constitution had a prehistory in the abuses of George III and American fatigue with kings in general. The backstory of tyranny is essential if you're going to understand why the Constitution limits power so deliberately in each branch of government and then sets them over one another in relationships of checks and balances. It structures American government so there is never one top dog. This strange feature mystifies people from nations that have parliaments and prime ministers, as well as Americans who don't know their own history. Why do we structure frustration and gridlock right into our system? Because our founding fathers were afraid of top dogs. They had had their fill of monarchs and didn't trust people with that kind of power. The Constitution is meant to put an end to it.

The Constitution was also the result of the failure of the United States' *first* constitution. After gaining independence, America's leaders were so averse to dictators that they drew up a loose confederation of states, with weak federal power. It wasn't enough to hold the country together against its enemies and to get things done internally. So the Constitution is also meant to be an end to the kind of weakness that happens when power is fragmented and dispersed. How can we have it both ways? How can a people organize itself around a center without that center becoming a tyrant? That dilemma, keen and fresh in the founders' minds after years of experiencing both evils, is the root of the Constitution.

Our Constitution, then, is an ending and a beginning. Its omega is the ending of the first unsuccessful draft of the American project, and its alpha is the beginning of the second draft of the American project. Its ratification sums up and closes earlier events that led up to it and begins a whole new trajectory of all that proceeds from it. This account in which the Constitution is a decisive turning point is how we learn American history. In fact, as a turning point, it focuses American history like no other event, not even the 1776 Declaration of Independence.

This may seem hard to believe. We celebrate July 4, but Americans don't have a big day to celebrate the Constitution. Yet July 4 is only something to celebrate because the founders' project has succeeded. I'm not that excited about Bastille Day—not so much because I'm not French, but mainly because the French Revolution didn't go all that well. Nor is March 8, the date of the February Revolution in Russia in 1917,[12] an inspiration to me. That day feels more like Genesis 2, forever overshadowed by the October Revolution it preceded. The significance of American independence from England all depends on what follows it. The Constitution is our turning point. *It* is the focus of American loyalty, not just independence. It's what the president, the military, the judiciary, and our legislators all swear to uphold. The Constitution is America.

To live at the end of 1787 was to live "between the times"—in the unraveling of America's first union and the approach of the second. The old arrangement was still formally in force, but its days were numbered; the new one already ordered the imaginations and preparations of the states that were ratifying it one by one.

Other peoples around the world have similar turning points—perhaps even more than one.[13] The exodus is the Jews' omega and alpha: Passover is the

12. The February Revolution began in March?! Not by the reckoning of the "Old Style" Julian calendar in use in Russia at the time. For them it was still late February.

13. My analogies of American history apply to Christian history as well. Historian Donald McKim treats the development of the core convictions of Christian theology, from the Trinity to

day on which Israel remembers both its emancipation—its July 4—and its constitution at Sinai. Both make up God's covenantal arrangement, which makes Israel the people it is. Muslims have a similar omega and alpha in the *Hegira*, when Muhammad gained political power in Medina. Other communities have no such omega and alpha. Some indigenous peoples know a kind of beginning in primordial mythological history. They have an alpha, and at least as far as they remember, they have always lived in that beginning without turning points.

If we take the Constitutional sensibility, which is intuitive to Americans who grow up with it, and use it to grasp this far more important event—the coming of the King, the eternally reigning Son of David, the only Son of the Father—we can see how it really is *the* turning point of the ages. Many Americans can't imagine a world without the United States of America. But the world without the United States wouldn't be a *speck* as different as the world without the Messiah. I don't know how many Americans really believe that. Sometimes we act as if the Constitution's ratification is more important than the coronation and ascension of the risen Jesus Christ as King of kings.[14] But the fact that Jesus really is the hinge of the ages puts all other stories in perspective. In light of Jesus's Z and A, the Constitution's ratification is more like a *J* and a *K*: a significant event, to be sure, but not the fundamental turning point of human history that some of the founders envisioned.

This is good news for Americans because it puts all other events at the disposal of Jesus's overriding end-and-beginning. His story conditions and humbles the American story, awakening us to the realization that our rather brilliant republic is just a wrinkle, just a blip. The apostles reacted that way concerning their own heritage: they came to realize that the exodus from Egypt, as significant as it was in its own right, was much more significant in pointing forward to the true exodus at Calvary (Luke 9:31). If the Constitution has any *lasting* glory, it lies in its relationship to the world's true turning point.[15]

---

the incarnation to the character of both the church and salvation, as a series of decisive turning points. Of course, the foundational turning point of Jesus's death and resurrection dominates and drives them all. See Donald K. McKim, *Theological Turning Points: Major Issues in Christian Thought* (Atlanta: Westminster John Knox, 1988).

14. Some of us do, anyway. Others, going back at least a century (for instance, Woodrow Wilson's progressives), have viewed the Constitution as an inconvenient relic. They're ready for a new omega and alpha. While they generally do not have Jesus's Kingdom in mind, Wilson saw his own progressive policies as "a practical scheme to carry out [Christ's] aims," as Jesus had neglected to supply the means himself. See Patricia O'Toole, *The Moralist: Woodrow Wilson and the World He Created* (New York: Simon & Schuster, 2018), 347.

15. Perhaps a sign of such eternal significance is the Constitution's refusal to grant absolute power to any human institution, including a church—and even itself, since it provides a process for it to be amended—out of respect for the conviction that human beings are incapable of

The gospel has similarly affected all people who truly appreciate its import, including communities that had no turning point—because in Jesus's cross and resurrection they now do. Now that their identities are secure in the identity of Christ, they regain a human purpose that can line up with God's purpose.

## "All Things"

You will find the phrase Tolkien appropriated, "all things," occurring again and again throughout the Scriptures.[16] "Behold," Jesus says, "I am making all things new." That proclamation of his alpha is in Revelation 21, at the canon's very end. His church *has* beheld and has faithfully reported what it has seen in joy and hope. *All things* are reconciled to him. That means nothing is detached from Christ's reign. He is not the Savior of *part* of creation, even the "spiritual" or "religious" part. He is the *whole* creation's Savior. Israel's. America's. France's. Russia's. Even heaven's (Rev. 12:7–11)! There is no other name, no other domain, and no other comprehensive omega and alpha.

I still find it striking that the New Testament witnesses say this about a human being—and one from an obscure family in ancient, small-town Galilee at that. Jesus is just, as one writer puts it, a marginal Jew[17] in a marginal town of a marginal area of a Roman Empire that was on its way out anyway. It's astonishing that Christ's life receives such a sweeping interpretation. Either these writers are right, or they are the greatest exaggerators of all time.

Allow me to draw your attention to some of the places where this core conviction surfaces in Scripture. Let this tour help you recognize it in the worship of our churches, the fabric of our lives, and the substance of our mission. Hear the astonishing claims that are being made again and again. If you've heard them already, then hear them afresh, because many of us have heard them so many times that we have forgotten how shocking and renewing they are meant to be.

Chapter 2 explores the extraordinary development at theology's heart: Jesus ends and begins God. Sure, this is true of our *opinions* of God: our

---

wielding such power as well as we imagine, even when we do it in God's name. Some Americans may idolize the Constitution, but in its modest genius the Constitution refuses to idolize even itself. This leaves at least theoretical room for implicit acknowledgment of a true God above all political idols.

16. Tolkien, *Return of the King*, 241, 244.
17. John P. Meier, *A Marginal Jew: Rethinking the Historical Jesus*, vol. 1 (New York: Doubleday, 1991).

old ones put Jesus on the cross, so they suffer the Father's verdict that we misjudged his Son. The resurrection kindles new and truer opinions of God. But Jesus ends and begins God in more radical ways. A "god" is what we call one end of a certain kind of relationship. Since Jesus's coming terminates our old relationship with YHWH and pioneers a new one, Jesus changes who God is to us. In taking on our relationships as his own—"my God, my God," he says on the cross (Matt. 27:46, quoting Ps. 22:1)—his coming does more than just *express and reflect* his own eternal triune relations. It takes our relationships and makes them his own. The three persons of the Trinity are one another's eternal beginning and end, and Jesus's ministry expresses this, as well as fulfilling and transforming—ending and beginning—it by including us. Through him the Father becomes the Father of many and the Spirit the resident of a whole multitudinous temple. So the Son is the omega and alpha of all three persons: the end of their relational exclusivity (Matt. 11:27) and the beginning of them as Father, Bridegroom, and Spirit of the church. Jesus is how the God of old has chosen to be God anew. This is heady stuff, and liable to being misunderstood and poorly articulated, so we'll need to be careful.

Chapter 3 describes a change in the cosmos—our world—the created older that we're a part of, which we interpret and indwell according to our many different understandings of it. Jesus has been concluding the old one—the whole order, and our cloudy "worldviews" of it—and has inaugurated the new one. At the eye of this revolutionary storm is his engagement with the mysterious "ruler of this world" who acts decisively in the events leading to Calvary, and who is overthrown with his realm as the Son is lifted up.

Chapter 4 narrows our focus to humanity. Jesus's coming brought the end of what it meant to be human "under the sun" (a futility that Ecclesiastes describes, which rose out of humanity's original traits, divine calling, and then sinful depravity) and the beginning of what humanity will mean forever: a life characterized by the Holy Spirit's eternal presence, gifts, and virtues. His mother, Mary, exemplifies both old humanity at its best and new humanity at nearly its earliest, so her life will help us sketch these two pictures with more detail and specificity.

God's chosen people were a fresh start for old humanity, so chapter 5 highlights Mary's nation, Israel. Jesus travels, then blazes, its tortuous path to glory. God promised Jacob's descendants the gifts of belonging to God and vice versa, enjoying earthly power and prominence, and displaying God's wisdom. Israel did truly receive a measure of these gifts but not the wholesale rescue humanity needed. Jesus was, is, and will be its necessary renewal. Each gift comes into its own in the Messiah's ministry, bringing about a surprising new way to be God's people. We will focus on the apostle Paul as an exemplar of Israel on both sides of Christ's transformation.

Israel's fellow nations are the topic of chapter 6. "All flesh is grass" (Isa. 40:6), and human flesh comes in communities and ethnicities that rise and fade like grass patches. They don't perish and rise like individual human beings, and they aren't unique as Israel is, so the pattern here is different. However, Jesus is still the omega of their old rivalries and oppositions to his reign. They simply will not domesticate or defeat him. And Jesus is the alpha of new ways of life and nationhood—*international* ones—that spring up within them. Timothy's mixed ancestry (Acts 16:1) anticipates the gospel's revolutionary impact on nationhood and on contemporary identity politics.

Last but certainly not least, chapter 7 takes up the most obvious way that Jesus is an omega and an alpha. Our world of humanity, Israel, nations, and families is composed of *persons*—beautiful, beloved, wretched, sin-ridden persons. Their only true end and new beginning is Jesus Christ. By every biblical measure, he himself personifies the good life that God intends for human creatures. He took on the so-called life that we have fashioned that gift into, ended it in the only way that wouldn't take us down with it, and began a new resurrection life that he's made available to us. What this looks like in practice is every saint's baptismal life. For brevity's sake we will focus on Simon Peter, a figure who dramatically portrays both that doomed old life and that astonishing new one, sometimes in the very same scene. Yet we will cast sideward glances at the many lives that don't look so exemplary.

I want a question to haunt you throughout these chapters: What is the turning point of *your* life? What is the hinge and identifier of your story, your people, your world, your solemn commitments? Is *your* omega and alpha Jesus Christ?

> What has Christ put to an end? Or what are you holding on to that needs to go?
>
> What has Christ begun in you? Or what are you trying to prevent him from bringing to life?
>
> Into which unconsidered places of life and which unimagined dimensions of reality are Christ's life, death, and resurrection reaching?

I hope the following chapters spark some fresh thinking, new awareness, and deeper appreciation. They have for me.

# TWO

# Jesus—the End and the Beginning of God

For Jews demand signs and Greeks desire wisdom, but we proclaim Christ crucified, *a stumbling block* to Jews and *folly* to Gentiles, but to those who are the
called, both Jews and Greeks, *Christ the power of God and the wisdom of God.*

1 Corinthians 1:22–24 RSV

In a flash, his familiar surroundings were washed away and his eyes disabled.
A *literal* flash, like a lightning bolt that strikes so close that it fills your field
of vision and shocks your eyes out of their ability to perceive. Now all was
white—a blinding snowscape, an empty page. The hunter froze in the light
of his prey, trapped out in the open, his protective power drained, in fact now
turned on him and pressing in.

"Who are you, Lord?" he asked. He knew enough to know—and to know
now that he knew nothing. That flash was exposing his life and his deepest
convictions as one grand error. Horror and fear swelled as the consequences
began to hit him. His mission and destination no longer mattered. No, that
was far too kind. They now condemned him and the faith that had led him to
persecute his own Lord. What awful fate awaited him? A fate, it turned out,
that was nothing like either his present fears or his earlier hopes.

Let's start with the most daring claim of all: Jesus is the omega and the
alpha of *God.* I could mean two things when I say this. I might mean that
Jesus Christ is the source of revelation that puts an end to "God," meaning

our *perception* of God, and begins a new one. Or I might mean that the
career of Jesus Christ really ends and begins the eternal Lord, the God of
Israel. I mean both, together—but not in the heretical ways that someone
might infer.

We will start with the more straightforward meaning: that Jesus ends and
begins our knowledge of God. If that seems too obvious for a long treatment, consider how deeply invested our pluralist culture is in denying it. The
notion is too threatening to the common impression that God is sufficiently
and generally accessible: in many if not all religious traditions, in nature, in
unaided reason, in history, in interior personal experience, and in meditation.
We members of the societies that depend on that axiom are well trained not
to mention or even notice that Jesus is that God's omega too. Some retraining is in order.


## "God"

The overall human response to Jesus's ministry came down to increasingly
intense misunderstanding, polarization, and scorn leading to crucifixion.
Why?[1] For clues, let's page through just one of the Gospels.

Jesus taught with authority that surpassed the formally authorized teachers
of God's law (Mark 1:21–22). He touched the unclean. And rather than history's so-called untouchables contaminating him, the contact cleansed the ones
he touched (1:41–42). He even had one newly cleansed man go and sacrifice

---

1. I don't believe that modern Western culture has a coherent answer. Consider the impression that has somehow taken hold in the West of Jesus of Nazareth as a stereotypical Christian
cleric—innocuous, meek and mild-mannered, clean and well dressed, introverted and other-
worldly, and scrupulously religious—and the idea that the God whom Jesus represented mainly
wants the rest of us to be a little more all of those things too. Who would have bothered to
reject and crucify such a figure? It doesn't add up.

Doesn't it, though? For centuries Christianity has been singled out for ridicule by the very
same Western "cultured despisers" who hold those stereotypes, and today Christians are the
world's most widely persecuted group. Perhaps these meek and churchy representatives of their
supposedly saccharine Lord represent a similar, inexplicable threat—lions in lambs' clothing,
so to speak.

I grew up with that modern caricature of Jesus in my head, and *I* directed my scorn at his
meek and churchy followers. I dismissed fundamentalists, even though I didn't know any. I
made fun of my Mormon girlfriend's faith (and was surprised when she didn't back down). I
remember the day my ninth-grade English class was taking turns reading passages from *Inherit
the Wind*, and I relished the chance to read the part of Clarence Darrow dismantling William
Jennings Bryan. What provoked these behaviors? I'm still not sure. It was like an allergic reaction I didn't understand. But watching Franco Zeffirelli's *Jesus of Nazareth*, particularly its
crucifixion scene, drew me in and kindled a new attitude. I remained an atheist for some time,
but an increasingly chastened one.

as the old arrangement mandated—but now not *in order* to be cleansed but rather to *testify* (1:43–44). The old arrangement was now consigned to a place *within* the new one—indeed, a secondary one. He forgave people's sins, even those of people who weren't asking for it, by his own authority—when only God had that kind of authority (2:5–12).

Jesus appointed disciples for himself not from among Israel's spiritual A-list of people who were widely regarded as righteous but from ordinary people and even sinners—starting with a tax collector, a sellout to Roman occupiers who was hated among his own people (Mark 2:14–17). Jesus's sheer presence overrode the traditional Jewish rules of religious observance. This was true of both the rules of Pharisees and the rules of John the Baptist's circle of followers (2:18–20) from whom Jesus drew his own first disciples (John 1:35–42). He likened himself to a piece of new cloth that cannot be sewn onto an old garment—meaning his own culture and religion—and to fresh wine that cannot be aged in old containers (2:21–22). If you were one of those old containers, how would *you* react? Yet the disruptions have only begun. We aren't even through chapter 2 of Mark's Gospel.

Jesus allowed his disciples to break conventional Sabbath rules, and when confronted about it, rather than defending their lawfulness, he proclaimed himself above the Torah (law), and his followers with him (Mark 2:23–28). That same day apparently, in front of the increasingly irritated religious authorities, and grieved by their lack of compassion, he healed a man with a withered hand. This provoked the Pharisees to begin planning to destroy him (3:1–6).

While these new enemies plotted, massive crowds began to follow Jesus. They weren't only from his home in northern Israel but also from the religious center in Judea and Jerusalem, and even from Samaritan and gentile territories. This violated the old boundaries that defined and stabilized his volatile religious, political, and cultural world (Mark 3:7–10). Unclean spirits that dominated other people fell down instantly before him, confessed that he was the Son of God, and fell silent at his command (3:11–12). He appointed (and sometimes renamed) disciples as he desired, and gave them the same unprecedented authority that he had (3:13–15).

Jesus's outrageous behavior convinced his own family that he was out of his mind (Mark 3:21), and his opponents that he was demonized (3:22). On the contrary, he replied: that was the Spirit's power! He had bound the devil with it, and now he was plundering the devil's house (3:27–30). The captives had so internalized their slavery that they couldn't even recognize either their own kinsman-redeemer or his redeeming God. Then when his family came and called for him, he compounded the outrage by redefining his family in terms not of blood and loyalty—the bonds on which his culture depended for survival in a poor and hostile world—but of obedience to God's will (3:31–35).

*What on earth was going on?!*

According to Jesus, what was going on is that the long-promised reign of God was finally coming into view. Jesus's words and deeds announced a whole new order, a revised set of terms for both God's covenant people and that old arrangement's outsiders.[2] A new arrangement had been forged, and the shock of it was arriving with Jesus. His associations, his eating habits, his Sabbath practices, and even his touch were all demonstrating altered relations with God, with fellow subjects of that arrangement, with subjects of the old arrangement, and with people on the outside. Jesus called this new arrangement the Kingdom of God. It was here and available to all comers, and they were already accountable for how they responded.

What shocked so many people wasn't that this was happening now instead of some future time. That would have been an understandable surprise, like a sudden earthquake or a loved one from far away showing up at your door totally unannounced. What bowled people over wasn't the Kingdom's timing but its *character*.

To every rival, the Kingdom has seemed to pose a mortal threat; to every subject, an unfathomable challenge. John the Baptist merely heralded its arrival from the outside. Jesus brought much more than even the Baptist had announced. He was a new presence *of* God. He wasn't just the Kingdom of God's designated emissary; he was its King, "the Kingdom in person."[3] If we don't see how disorienting and unnerving all this was, it's because we are so used to hearing these stories that we no longer actually listen to them. Mark is describing a revolution. And revolutions are terrifying to live through. They're the end of the world.[4]

God was allegedly assuming power in a new way in and around Jesus. *God* was assuming power. This is what God's power looked like. So this is what *God* was like. His reign's approach was yielding a clearer picture of his character than people had ever seen before, even through Israel's Scriptures and traditions.

The Kingdom as Jesus described it and lived it struck people as compelling but strange. Perplexing. Frustrating. Among the people who had done relatively well under the old arrangement, it seemed scandalous, dangerous—and blasphemous. If the Lord had become visible, he was unrecognizable.

2. See Christopher J. H. Wright, *Knowing Christ through the Old Testament*, 2nd ed. (Downers Grove, IL: IVP Academic, 2014).

3. The Greek term for this, *autobasileia*, comes from Origen.

4. The next chapter focuses on the world's end and new beginning.

Unrecognized, anyway. Jesus took those reactions in stride. Using parables, he explained to his audiences "the secret of the kingdom of God" (Mark 4:11)—what was really going on under the surface phenomena of his ministry. He disclosed to them that the good news of God's coming reign is always met with a variety of reactions (4:3–9).[5] Each soil's reception of the Word implies a distinct understanding of God.

Among those who do not immediately take the gospel to heart, the enemy comes and devours it. They will remember what they have heard, of course, but they will remember it as implausible, offensive, and hostile, and the so-called God behind it as an irrelevant curiosity, if not an opponent to be defeated. At all costs, it turns out.

Among those who do receive Jesus's good news, there are still a variety of outcomes. Some, when they encounter hardships because of it, drop it like a burning coal. For these the good news will seem unpleasant, traumatic, and their memories of embracing it will be bitter and embarrassing. The "God" of such a menacing message will come across as unfriendly, untrustworthy, and even duplicitous—to be avoided for safety's sake.

Still others lose their original interest. To these people the good news cannot compete with life's other attractions. So it withers. It just isn't worth that much. These ex-fans will move on, and if they remember the good news and its messengers at all, it will be with apathy, disappointment, dissatisfaction, or worldly cynicism about fantastic schemes that don't live up to the hype. And the "God" they shrugged off will appear uncompetitive, impotent, and ultimately boring. Finally, some hearers accept the good news in a lasting way and bear its fruit (Mark 4:14–20). For these, the God of the gospel will be—well, I don't want to get too far ahead of myself.

One gospel, four or more distinct Gods of Israel's imaginations and natural observations. When the good news reaches a person, that person's God encounters someone other and higher. The encounter leaves nothing as it was. Those who receive God's Word sacrificially, keep what's planted, and pass it on will receive far more in return. Those who let it go will lose even what they had at first (Mark 4:25).

Jesus's critics seemed to grasp that his gospel meant a revolution. They could see the wake of disruption that followed wherever Jesus went. They resorted so soon to plotting his destruction because he jeopardized their projects to bring purity, holiness, and renewal to Israel. How could God *not* be against him? His movement threatened the fragile, mediocre peace they had

5. The final chapter will reflect more on these as they characterize the individual lives that end and begin anew in Jesus Christ.

worked out with the Romans at the cost of all that blood risked and shed. Moreover, his actions and teachings were encouraging the people to cross moral, spiritual, and ethnic boundaries their God made essential to their well-being and even their national survival.

Jesus's critics were right: he *was* going to put an end to all of those things. Not because he was a fraud or a false prophet, but because he is the real thing. And he would put an end to the old God as well.

Jesus is as baffling up close as he is from a distance. His opponents aren't the only ones who failed to understand what they were seeing. His disciples did too, again and again.[6] The Gospel of Mark communicates their bewilderment to us readers by being nearly as baffling as Jesus himself. It holds back on the longer introductions that Matthew, Luke, and John all add. Mark writes the way some contemporary filmmakers direct, withholding explanatory material so that audiences have to watch the film again to come to a clearer understanding.

Some scholars see a clue to Mark's scheme in his telling of Jesus healing a blind man from Bethsaida, just before the narrative's turning point: "When he had spit on his eyes and laid his hands upon him, he asked him, 'Do you see anything?' And he looked up and said, 'I see men; but they look like trees, walking.' Then again he laid his hands upon his eyes; and he looked intently and was restored, and saw everything clearly" (Mark 8:23–25). At first, this story seems unique: nowhere else in the Gospels does a healing come in stages like this. But nearly the opposite is true. Mark seems to suggest that the disciples, and we readers, are like the blind man. Right after this episode, Jesus asked his disciples who they thought he was. Peter gulped and answered that Jesus was the Messiah. And he was right. But the whole last half of the Gospel is proof that Peter was actually wrong—not wrong that Jesus *is* Messiah but wrong about *how* Jesus is Messiah (8:33). Peter and the others saw, but saw a walking tree. They got it; but they didn't really. You might say that they were legally blind. To see everything clearly, to see and believe, would take further grace.

The blind man's restoration is a parable for Christian discipleship. We will never be the same after we read Mark's Gospel for the first time, because we will have reacted in at least one of the ways Jesus specified in his parable of the sower (Mark 4:2–20). He brings our old perceptions to their omega. But that doesn't mean that we understand Mark's Gospel, receive it, or bear its fruit. We have to go back to the beginning and read again to be truly restored.

I know I did.

6. See, for example, Mark 4:10–13; 6:51–52; 7:17–18; 8:21, 31–33; 9:6, 30–32; 10:13–14, 26.

## The Blind Man from California

I grew up in a supposedly churchgoing liberal Protestant family that didn't go to church all that often. We had a good family, and our Christianity was real. But it was awfully thin. My family considered itself religious, but we never talked about God. We were well trained and obedient pluralists. We had a number of Bibles, but we brought one out only once a year, at Christmas. As the grandparents demanded, we would read Luke 2—the Christmas story from *A Charlie Brown Christmas*—while the kids practically died waiting to open our presents. As far as I can recall, my early childhood belief in God had faded away by the fourth grade.

With high school came stage one of my healing. A friend's mother was one of those apocalyptic fanatics who believed Hal Lindsey's claims that the rapture would come in 1982 at the latest. It was 1981. She fed her son books such as *The Late Great Planet Earth* and turned us into apocalyptic true believers too. To my teenage brain it all made sense: Jerusalem was part of Israel again, a huge computer in Brussels knew everything about us, Visa cards were being printed with sixes all over them, the ten nations of the European Community were adopting a common currency. And we needed to belong to Jesus to avoid being left behind.

I was seeing something, all right. Walking trees. God used Lindsey to teach me some truths: that I couldn't take a free ride to heaven on my family's cultural Christianity, that Jesus is coming again to judge the world, that God demands a personal commitment.

However, I don't think affirming these truths made me a Christian. What did Lindsey's Jesus ask of me? What I took away was that I had to say the Sinner's Prayer, count the earthquakes and wars, and be ready for the rapture. I did this not for God but to save my own skin. I didn't know who God was. I didn't know Jesus. I just didn't want to be left behind. My belief was a superstition.[7] I had put my faith in a walking tree.

That might have been the last I "saw" Jesus. But providentially, a couple of years afterward, I read another apocalyptic fanatic's book: the Gospel of Luke. I was home from college for Christmas vacation, and I was bored. All my stuff was locked away in my dorm hundreds of miles away. So before bed I fished around for a book in the new nightstand in my room, which my parents had redecorated and rearranged in the three months since I had left home. What I found there was the New Testament my godparents had given me when I

---

7. I'm not saying that Hal Lindsey's disciples were superstitious non-Christians, only that I was. There was precious little Christian formation in my life for Lindsey's eschatology to come alongside. In Jesus's parable, I was rocky and weedy midadolescent soil.

was a year old. I did not even remember having it before. So I opened it up, for the first time, to Luke's Gospel and spent the next few hours in terror.

Luke's Jesus wasn't like either my family's Jesus *or* Lindsey's. This Jesus wanted a lot more than sporadic church attendance, rote prayers at meals and bedtime, or even the Sinner's Prayer. He wanted it all. He wanted my family loyalties, my friendships, and even my money. Worst of all, he didn't want all this for my sake, just to make me "saved." He wanted it for his Father's glory. I had to do more than acknowledge Jesus as Lord and Savior; I had to treat him as Lord and Savior.

Like the blind man Jesus healed, I "looked intently" through the Gospel of Luke, and what began coming into view was the Lord himself instead of a walking tree. He is not just a means of personal fulfillment. He is not even just the way to escape damnation that I took him for at the time. The Lord is Jesus of Nazareth, killing our old perceptions of him to spawn new ones, coming slowly into view as our sight of him replaces our blindness. That encounter with him in the Bible was the new alpha of my meaning of the word *God*.

I had a lot to learn, of course. My picture of Jesus was still two-dimensional, focused on cost and sacrifice rather than blessing, and on dying to self rather than rising to life. My understanding of God needed a beta, gamma, and delta, and in due course those came. But none of those epiphanies have ever compared to that alpha. Mark was right.

### Foolishness and Wisdom

When Jesus appeared to Paul on the road to Damascus (Acts 9:5) and Paul asked, "Who are you, Lord?" it was more than just a terrified greeting. It reflected the omega of Paul's old way of seeing the Lord. In turn, the Holy Spirit provided the alpha for his new one (9:10–20).

The turn defined Paul's whole ministry. He reminded the Corinthians that "Christ did not send me to baptize but to preach the gospel, and not with eloquent wisdom," not the old stuff, "lest the cross of Christ be emptied of its power. For the word of the cross is folly to those who are perishing" (1 Cor. 1:17–18)—that is, to those loyal to old arrangements. The Corinthians were still too inclined to think that way themselves, to their church's peril.

In Jesus's coming, Paul saw Isaiah 29:14's eclipse of the wisdom of the wise. Jesus's arrival turned it into folly. After all, who foresaw his revolution or understood its arrival in him? Who was there rejoicing at the cross because they were seeing the plan unfold just as they predicted? No one. Not only that but, as Mark's opening chapters already proved, the wisdom of the wise put

Jesus on the cross. Condemning him was common sense. Shrewd political and social strategy. The prudent theology of Paul's old "God."

The true God wisely ensured that the world didn't come to know him through its conventional wisdom. "Greeks seek wisdom," Paul summarized—but old wisdom, wisdom that's already known to them and intuitive to them. They wanted Jesus to align with their expectations. They wanted him not to be an omega of this age but to support and extend it, to affirm and advance their philosophical convictions and instincts.[8] In Christ's parable, the first three Gods of the soils bear an unsettling similarity to the deities who haunt the world's imaginations from which they sprang (cf. Mark 4:4–7). How does God's arrival undermine them?

I traveled recently to Kyoto, Japan. That old capital city boasts beautiful ancient shrines that pay tribute to nature; to nature's spirits, who bless and curse the living; to Confucius and other masters who taught respect for their cosmic hierarchy; and to the Buddha, who turned their negated Hindu forms into supporting characters in his new spiritual order. Shinto isn't the only nature worship in Japan; the whole place is a temple to nature. Japanese are world leaders at what I'll call "augmented nature." Their Zen gardens, bonsai, graceful temples, and nature walks are almost never nature as such, but nature processed through a remarkable aesthetic that highlights and engineers beauty. This is also true of their automobiles, electronics, bullet trains, cityscapes, and cinematic worlds. They are awe-inspiring glimpses of nature's brilliance, reminiscent of the highlights of Hellenism's golden age and the Renaissance that rediscovered it.

But nature augmented, engineered, perfected, and deified is still just nature. Even nature negated is still just nature. The gods of our imaginations and observations are constrained by our imaginations and observations. They necessarily fall far short of the God who approaches us from beyond all that in his invasive seed. The Creator of all things is super-natural, "above nature" rather than in it. He doesn't abide in creation's perfections, or even beyond them in the direction of the superlatives we might use to construct even grander "theologies of glory." He is off creation's every scale. His arrival humiliates nature and exposes even its most brilliant worshipers as fools.

Islam grasped that truth and has steadfastly championed it, while failing to perceive how our Creator isn't *just* hyper-superlative. While Muslims did often sense the need to do that, what resources did they have for it? Islam

---

8. We still do. Every age and every ideological camp tends to identify with the aspects of Jesus that it finds most intuitive and to let those swamp the others. Jesus becomes a sign-bearer and advocate of our old wisdom rather than a prophet and judge. The persistent appeal of classic Christian heresies demonstrates the dynamic.

formally regards humanity as no more than a kind of pet. Yet with no solid thing on which to ground its theology except "divine" words with human referents, it couldn't help but press humanity and especially Muhammad into service as the creation's microcosm and essentially the measure of all things. So Islam ironically confesses a creator who feels all too human: humanly strict and vengeful, but also humanly compassionate and sentimental. And as it matured, it absorbed Greek philosophy like a sponge, using it to justify a dual affirmation of God's paradoxical dissimilarity (*tanzih*) and similarity (*tashbih*) to his creation.

The God of Israel isn't like the gods of the nations, and he said so repeatedly. The Hebrew names "Michael" and "Micah" are rhetorical questions— *Who is like God? Who is like YHWH?*—meant to trigger Jewish memories of his holiness and keep God's people from answering with confident analogies. Yet Paul lumped Jews and Greeks together in 1 Corinthians 1 because Jesus had revealed how much their theologies actually had in common. "Jews demand signs." The people waiting for their Messiah kept asking Jesus to show them that he was the one they expected (Mark 8:11–12). They demanded data that confirmed their prior hypotheses and watered the God of their soil. Jesus replied: You're thinking old here. It's actually wickedness that's producing this desire to see me meet *your* expectations.

God preferred instead to save through a new, "foolish" message. Jesus said his doubtful Jewish audience would get only one sign: the sign of Jonah, the omega-alpha sign of the Son of Man being rejected and three days later rising.[9] They would see the sign that puts an end to all those old reasons for asking for a sign in the first place. The people who personified the question "Who is like God?" would see the God they failed to recognize.

Paul sure did. "We preach Christ crucified: a stumbling block to Jews, and folly to the nations"—theological omegas clearing ground for the alpha "Christ the power of God and the wisdom of God." The good news of Christ's revolution shames and ends the old that just can't cope with it (Mark 2:22). God's folly is wiser; God's weakness is stronger. The crucified Jesus is more *God* than all the deities our human imaginations set against him—including Israel's old impressions of her formerly invisible God. Paul reminds his readers of how Christ revolutionized God for them:

> Consider *your* call, brothers and sisters. Not many of you were wise, according
> to the flesh. Not many were powerful. Not many were of noble birth. But God

9. That answer is in Matt. 16:4. In Mark, Jesus doesn't give his opponents even that scrap to go on, though he does tell his uncomprehending disciples.

chose what is foolish in the world to shame the wise. God chose what is weak in the world to shame the strong. For God chose what is low and despised in the world, even things that are not [that's alpha language] to bring to nothing things that are [that's omega language] so that no one may boast in the presence of God. He is the source of your life in Christ Jesus, whom God made our wisdom, our righteousness, our sanctification, and our redemption. (1 Cor. 1:26–30 RSV alt.)

Paul was perceptive to avoid the conventional contrast between Jews and gentiles here. Lesslie Newbigin observed that "the experience of Paul is mirrored in that of many converts from the Hindu and Muslim faiths. . . . At the point of crisis Jesus appeared to them as one who threatened all that was most sacred to them. In the light of their experience of life in Christ they now look back and see that he has safeguarded and fulfilled it."[10]

*All of that* is already front-loaded into the first chapter of Paul's letter. The same revolution is erupting from the beginning of Mark. The coming of Jesus is the omega of every so-called God that misses the reality and can only think of Jesus as folly or try to warp him into its image. And it's the alpha of the true knowledge of God that can think of every rival to Jesus's lordship only as folly.

Paul's problem children in Corinth had a lot more to learn, and he would address it in his next chapters. But he put his "theology of the cross" up front because if it were all his readers caught, they'd be okay.[11] And if they didn't catch it, the rest really wouldn't matter anyway.

The picture I have sketched collides, apparently, with two oft-told stories of how certain people come to know God. The first concerns people who grow up outside the Christian tradition and know of "God" through those sources already listed: other religious traditions, nature, unaided reason, history, interior personal experience, and meditation. Some optimistic natural theologies describe these people as faithful insofar as they follow what limited goodness of God they know through creation. In these theologies, that warm reception of God's natural graces might warrant at least provisional hope for their future salvation on the day God judges our secrets (Rom. 2:15–16). God has set eternity in these people's hearts (Eccles. 3:11), and they act conscientiously at least some of the time according to the divine law in their hearts

10. Lesslie Newbigin, *The Open Secret: An Introduction to the Theology of Mission*, rev. ed. (Grand Rapids: Eerdmans, 1995), 177.

11. In Greco-Roman writing style, the beginning is where writers lay out their whole thesis. You can find a decent précis of just about every New Testament writing in the book's first chapter.

(Rom. 2:15). That day brings the end of what was partial and the beginning of what is full (cf. 1 Cor. 13:8–12). We could think of that as an omega and alpha of a sort, I guess.

Yet 1 Corinthians 1 and many parallel arguments across the biblical canon all insist that these outsiders must undergo a much more radical theological omega and alpha. After all, even the best of these "virtuous pagans" cannot find out what God has done from beginning to end (Eccles. 3:11) or truly understand or seek after God (Rom. 3:11). And whenever and however the fuller picture reaches them, the cross is still a scandal (Gal. 5:11). So the stories of the saints do bear a common omega-alpha shape, whether they had been God's friends or foes, and so does their knowledge of God.

The second, seemingly incompatible, story is quite different and poses a problem. What about people who grow up in Christian homes? As children they were dedicated or baptized, and as far back as they can remember, they've known (some of them anyway) only the Triune God as God. They get quiet when evangelicals around them are trading testimonies of dramatic conversions; what are they supposed to say? Are these people really in the same position as a pagan or Jew or Muslim or Deist who sees Jesus as a walking tree (if at all) and only later comes to know him in Spirit and truth? Where is the omega and alpha of their "God"?

I believe that it's there, just not necessarily in such a clean linear sequence. Some of these children have rough spiritual rides as they mature. They are rattled when they learn of other Gods. Some are lured away. The enemy is still a threat, as scared and heartbroken Christian parents well know. Other disciples experience disillusionments and crises decades into their Christian lives.

We who *can* point to a time when we were born again and God's reality broke through to us, are we in such a different position? The old seeps back into my life and starts pulling me into it even after my new being has germinated and begun to grow. A shock of some kind reveals to me that the God I thought I saw so clearly resembled a walking tree more than I knew. I have learned over the years to expect more such shocks. And I've learned to expect that if I open my eyes and look, rather than hide them out of fear, I will find a God truer to reality than the one I was forced to give up.

Warnings against apostasy permeate the New Testament just like the Old. In Matthew, Jesus issues one of them right after his parable of the sower. The farmer plants a field with a new crop, and *then* an old enemy vindictively sows weeds (Matt. 13:24–28). The old Gods do indeed find footholds in the imaginations of believers who are naive, immature, impatient, tempted, ignorant, and unready. The situation is serious enough to call for a thorough sorting out—a judgment—at the end of the age (13:28–30).

None of this jeopardizes the basic schema. In fact, it sets up the material in following chapters, because our inclination toward those old Gods comes from something old in us, lingering even in Jesus's disciples and in their theologies. Something in my rattled students is already there to resonate with an idol, a heresy, or a temptation. Paul calls it "the flesh," and it belongs to the old humanity that cannot inherit the Kingdom of God (1 Cor. 15:50). Both the soil and the weeds that infest it are still old and doomed, whether they take root before or after the good stuff. Whatever the sequence of our lives and whatever God's judgment, Jesus is still every old God's omega and every lasting one's alpha.

So far we have been speaking in terms of perceptions, of "God" rather than *God*. Now let's go further.

## New Cloth

The good news is not just newly accessible information. It isn't just "revelation" or "illumination" of the kind that the Qur'an and so many other holy texts claim to be. The gospel is *news*. It is an account of a happening. One of the reasons for all the perplexity around Jesus and his Kingdom's ambassadors is that God was doing something new. Eternally planned, to be sure, but newly executed (Isa. 42:9; 43:19; cf. Eph. 3:11). And not just something new for us, but something new for God too.

We're always God's creatures. That doesn't change. And God is still what God has always been: our Creator, provider, deliverer, and so on. Those relationships define what it means that we are human beings and that God is God. *God* is, after all, a relational term, like *brother*, *wife*, *Creator*, and *employee*. Nevertheless, if you sum up humanity's relations with God under the old arrangements, God is still simply on the Creator's side of them, and we are merely on the creaturely side.

So when this human being named Jesus comes along and starts doing things like forgiving the paralytic's sins in Mark 2:5, the audiences react in shock: *How can he say something like that? Only* God *can forgive sins* (Mark 2:7). In other words, Jesus does not have the kind of relationship with fellow human beings that would authorize him to forgive their sins.[12] Forgiving, judging, commandeering the Sabbath commandment—it's just impossible. Pigs don't fly. Under the old arrangement, in which humans were merely creatures, Jesus would be a false prophet. He'd be a blasphemer, because he claimed the

---

12. "Well," Jesus replies, "so that you know that I am the Son of Man who does have authority to forgive sins, I'll heal the man, and then you'll know" (Mark 2:8–12).

prerogative to do things that only God is qualified to do. On the other hand, if what was once impossible is happening, then something has changed.

The Kingdom's new arrangement involves a new set of relationships between God and humanity. Here's how the first verses of Hebrews portray it:

> Long ago God spoke to our ancestors in many and various ways in the prophets. In these last days he has spoken to us in a Son, whom he appointed heir of all, through whom he also made the ages. He is the radiance of God's glory and the exact imprint of God's being, and he sustains all things by the word of his power. Having made purification for sins, he sat down at the right hand of the Majesty on high, having become as much superior to angels as the name he has inherited is different from theirs. (Heb. 1:1–4 NRSV alt.)

Hebrews 1 is not about some new appearance of the same old glorious God. It is news of an heir—the Creator of the beginning and the end—who recently restored his fellow human beings to God, received his inheritance, took power, and came into his name above all names. It is about the glorification of a human who is not merely a human.

Rules reflect relationships. So this new development calls for a new set of rules. "He is doing away with the first covenant to establish the second" (Heb. 10:9, my translation).[13] The domain of the "second" extends far beyond that of the "first" Torah to which Hebrews refers. Paul similarly exclaims that "the law of the Spirit of life in Christ Jesus has set you free from the law of sin and death" (Rom. 8:2). The context and rules of the new have freed us from those of the old. In their new context, the old rules are no longer dominating as they had.

Christ's new reign was at once the coronation of God and the coronation of a human. There has been nothing like it before or since—though the writer of Hebrews immediately marshals a list of those old Scriptures that hint at it (Heb. 1:5–13). We will leave until a further chapter how this is humanity's end and new beginning. It is also God's. In Jesus Christ, God has become *God*. If this claim sounds wrong or heretical to you, it may be. By that I mean that there are a number of wrong and heretical ways to interpret it. God has *not* become God in the ways that some religions and some theologians believe. Classical Christian theology developed a technical vocabulary to keep things clear. The *essence* of the one we call God has not changed. Nor have the essential *relations* that constitute the persons of the Trinity as

13. The present tense in the Greek here may be indicating that the new is doing away with the old in the present, and thus that the old is lingering in a kind of extended twilight. A whole range of New Testament texts express the same conviction.

Father, Son, and Holy Spirit. God is not shifting from one kind of being to another as Jesus takes his place at the Father's right hand. God is not engaged in some quasi-creaturely process of development. And Jesus is not becoming the Son of the Father at some point in time, brought in as God's partner (as the Qur'an worries), progressing from humanity to divinity. All this should be clear from Hebrews 1:1–4.

What *nonheretical* thing could it mean, then? Remember that God is a relational term. If I may quote from an ordinary online dictionary, *God* in common usage means "the supreme or ultimate reality: such as . . . the Being perfect in power, wisdom, and goodness who is worshipped as creator and ruler of the universe."[14] These words are shot through with relationality: *supreme*, *ultimate*, *perfect*, *worshiped*, *Creator*, *ruler*. And all of these relational terms mean something new following the Son's incarnation, life, death, atonement, resurrection, and ascension. All of them. For instance, *supreme* no longer means what it did, because now the Lord is not merely above his creation; he is also with it and in it and for it and from it. Supremacy's old meaning can no longer be adequate. It ended and a new one began, the good news redefining the term as its eternal promise is realized. This is not just a new revealing or a new perception but a new reality for revelation to disclose and with which perceptions have to catch up. The same is true of the other terms.

So how could the word whose meaning involves all these relationships, that *means* all these relationships, not end and begin with them too? Jesus is their omega, and so God's omega: he accomplishes the demise of those old and doomed meanings. Jesus is also their alpha, and so God's alpha: he authors and pioneers their new and lasting meanings. The Lord is new wine, new cloth, new being, new creation.

So the cross represents, in a way, the necessary response of the old arrangement to Jesus's coming. It can't help but tear away like old cloth sewn together with new. That is why Jesus says the Son of Man must suffer, be rejected and crucified, and on the third day rise again (Matt. 16:21). *It is necessary*—because he comes as Immanuel, introducing a new set of relationships alongside the old. Once he arrives, God is no longer merely our Creator. God becomes one of us, our brother, and that means his Father becomes our Father. Once the Holy Spirit conceives a temple, Jesus's body (John 2:18–22) becomes God's earthly dwelling place, and we along with him (1 Cor. 6:19).

14. *Merriam-Webster*, s.v. "god," updated March 15, 2018, http://www.merriam-webster.com/dictionary/god. Incidentally, the common definition can take the "theology of glory" approach that Martin Luther rejected and the previous section objected to, but that is not the only way to construe supremacy, ultimacy, and perfection.

In Jesus Christ, God has granted us new relationships with God alongside those old relationships, which makes us creatures God's companions and God's friends. It makes God our God.

## Same God?

If Jesus's original detractors missed that God was *newly* our God, God's vast newness caused some later interpreters to miss how it was that *God* was newly our God. Marcion, a second-century Christian, concluded that the God of Jesus Christ was too different from the God of the Old Testament to be the same being at all. He alleged that the Father had sent his only Son to overthrow YHWH, the capricious and inferior god of the Jews who created the universe that held us captive. To maintain this position, Marcion had to reject the whole Old Testament and much of the New. The church condemned him along with other gnostics who could not identify YHWH as the Father of the Lord Jesus Christ. All that newness pertained to the same being.

This bit of ancient history relates to an ongoing debate over whether Christians and Muslims worship the same God. Reputable and honorable evangelical schools have taken different sides on the issue. Some people say that we don't, we can't worship the same God, because Jesus Christ is God. Since Muslims deny that Jesus shares the Father's essence, the two groups can't be referring to the same being.

The stark contrast here gets something right. The word *God* must mean something different for the two camps. Those who say there's no major distinction are either naive, willfully ignorant, or misled by their pluralist cultural assumptions.

Yet here's the problem with that line of reasoning: you can apply every one of those contrasts to the question of whether *Jews* and Christians worship the same God. And there is no indication or claim in the New Testament to the effect that Jews and Christians worship different gods.[15] Jesus never suggested anything like it as he taught Jews. The apostles didn't treat Jews that way. Paul didn't treat nonmessianic Jews that way in the synagogues where he preached. Christ's disciples never testified that they used to worship one god and now worshiped another. Then what is the difference? The Gospel of John puts it well: "The Torah came through Moses, but grace and truth came through Jesus Christ" (John 1:17, my translation). To understand what that passage means, consider Jesus's conversation with the Samaritan woman in John 4.

---

15. Jesus's claim that his opponents are from their father the devil (John 8:42–44) is saying something other than that Jews as a whole worship a different god.

Samaritans shared a lot of elements of Jewish faith, but they reorganized those elements around Samaritan rather than Judean nationhood and religion. Where Jews focused on Mount Zion and its ruined temple, Samaritans focused on *their* mountain, Mount Gerizim (see Deut. 11:29), and on its ruined ancient temple that they had built. Both groups do this to this day. Each group has thought of itself as the true Israelite religion (*Samerim* means "guardians," meaning guardians of the Torah) and of the rival group as corrupted. Incidentally, for Samaritans to shift their geographical focus in this way resembles what happened in the first days of Islam. The first Muslims worshiped facing Jerusalem. It was only after Jews rejected Muhammad's prophetic claims that the direction of prayer was changed to face Mecca.

Jesus's encounter with the woman at the well set the stage for an interreligious dialogue. And sure enough, after Jesus intrigued her with talk of living water from a well other than rival patriarch Jacob's well, she tried to draw him into the age-old controversy between their peoples. That way she'd determine which side he was on, and maybe even determine which side was right. "Our fathers worship on *this* mountain; and you all say that the place where it is necessary to worship is in Jerusalem" (John 4:20, my translation). *You have your national religion; we have our national religion. Where do you stand, prophet?*

Jesus answered in a fascinating way. He didn't answer the way a lot of people nowadays might. A religious pluralist might reply, "Well, Jews have their story and Samaritans have theirs, and whatever your story is, that's fine." Jesus didn't go in what we might think of as a "liberal" direction. Nor did he refrain from weighing in on the issue. He made an authoritative pronouncement. He said, "You worship what you do not know; we worship what we do know, for salvation *is* from the Jews" (John 4:22). However, he didn't say this just to condemn her stance and insist on his own tribe's tradition. He didn't go in a "conservative" direction and say, "You're wrong and we Jews are right," as she may have suspected he would. He certainly didn't claim that Samaritans worship a different god. Instead, he told her, "The hour is coming, and now is, when the true worshipers will worship the Father *in spirit and truth*" (4:23).

Worshiping in spirit and truth is apparently different from both "worshiping what one knows" as Jews do and "worshiping what one doesn't know" as Samaritans do. Jesus affirms that salvation is from the Jews. But what he means by that is, *I am from the Jews*. And the time has come when the Father is worshiped not in the old way but in a new way of spirit and truth—*as* Father, a divine person now known truly and in spirit instead of a thing known, or unknown, from afar.

If you talk to Muslims who become Christians, that's usually their testimony: "Of course I used to worship God. But now I know God intimately. I know God *as* God."

God's old meaning is over. But the new meaning doesn't give us an alternative God. It gives us God's alpha, God in a new way, God anew. God not up on some mountain temple but gushing from below, from within, from the temple of our body (cf. Rev. 22:1). "The one who conquers will inherit these things, and I *will be his or her God,* and he or she will be my son" (Rev. 21:7, my translation).

Jesus did not treat this change in relationship as some kind of enhancement or upgrade to what is already valid and adequate. It is absolutely necessary. "God is spirit, and those who worship him *must* worship in spirit and truth" (John 4:24). So for our worship of God to be true worship, for God to be *our* God, for God's intended relationships with creation to come about, the hour Jesus mentioned in John 4 had to come. It was the hour for which the Father sent him (12:27–28). It was the hour of inheritance and exaltation that Hebrews 1 celebrated. Jesus was and is the man of the hour. It all hinges on him.

### Sower and Sown

Jesus's homespun parable of the sower gestures toward the radical way that he is God's omega and alpha. In the parable, the sower is spreading seed from some other source: last year's harvest, a seed lot, wherever. But that ordinary seed *stands for* the sower's own word. This word powerfully and fruitfully prophesied something new into being (Mark 4:12, quoting Isa. 6:9–10). It is not something the sower got from somewhere else; after all, no eye had ever seen it (Isa. 52:15; 64:3). This word is—or was—exclusive to the sower who invests his very self in it. It expresses and inherits his mysterious authority (Mark 1:27), being, and character (cf. Heb. 1:3), so that all those who finally come to know it come to know him (Isa. 49:23). In this case, then, the word *is* the sower in some way, though the relationship between the two allows us to distinguish them. They stand or fall as one. Furthermore, the speaker's self-expression does not happen out of some necessity beyond his own sovereign covenanting will. The *act* of speaking thus also expresses the speaker's own being and inhabits the utterance in a way that is distinguishable from both the speaker and the word spoken. We are on our way here to an image of the Triune God.

What this parable offers beyond other trinitarian figures such as Psalm 33:6 is its stress on harvest. We know a word by its fruits (cf. Mark 4:20). Not all speech coheres so wonderfully. An unsuitable audience frustrates a speaker's will. When a speaker recites another's words, even in good faith (as Isaiah recites the Word of YHWH), the expression is no longer self-expression but mediation or appropriation, and the harvest it brings belongs to the other, not to the speaker (Luke 10:1–2). And when a speaker is false, the word doesn't express being but nonbeing, and its harvest is willed deception. A speaker may not even will the message's intended outcome (John 11:49–52).

Jesus's parable binds the speaker, speaking act, message, and even the audience together more profoundly—indeed, confusingly. What the sower sows is the word (Mark 4:14)—at first. But then the hearers become what is sown. The word somehow makes *them* "the ones sown" (4:15, 16, 18, 20).

Was Jesus just being careless with his analogy? Not at all. This is how agriculture works. The seed *and* the soil become the crop. Once they meet, their old selves end. Once I hear the word, I am no longer mere soil. I am something new; *I* am sown. On Jesus's account, this is true (and sobering) even if I am a rock that rejects the word that was cast on me and yields nothing; but it's all the more true if I am fruitful and multiply (4:20), bearing the word that is sown afresh (4:21–32). Both reactions are endings and beginnings, and both are necessary to the parable's outcome, which is purposefully delivered to insiders and outsiders alike.

Speaking of being fruitful and multiplying, Jesus reminded John the evangelist of God's creating word and wisdom as portrayed in Genesis 1 and Proverbs 8. (Maybe Jesus's parable had got John thinking.) Jesus's analogy in John 1 seems to run in a different direction. After all, what the Word originally brought into being was not a harvest of God's self-expression but a creation that was profoundly different from the Creator. Its limited goodness was merely *like* God's unique and unlimited goodness.

John's image may at first run in a different direction than Mark's, but the two converge. The Word's old creating work was setting the stage for later when the Word became flesh and dwelt in the earthy creation that had been made for eternal union with him. Then what was made *by* him (John 1:3) and *for* him (16:15) was *made* him (1:14). God's eternal self-expression became God's glorious creaturely self-expression (1:14). His Word was sown and glorified as much through rejection as acceptance (1:10–11; cf. Mark 8:31–35; 1 Cor. 15:42). And through his Spirit-delivered words (John 3:34–35), we mere creatures are remade *in* him (1:16; 3:29) to belong *to* him (1:12–13; 17:6–10).

Since the sower's own being and glory were destined for the word and bound to it, the word's complex reception was an omega and an alpha for all concerned. Whether Jesus is the sower in Mark 4 or the one sown in John 1, the Word's missional ending and beginning are his own as well as the Father's and the Spirit's. All three persons were utterly and irrevocably invested in this realizing of creation's purpose for which the soil was made and the Word was delivered in the first place.

**Heir and Giver**

Jesus is also the end of God in the sense that an end is a *goal*. The term *omega* means an end point. The only begotten Son is the omega of God in that he is the destination of the Father's being and purpose. God's being itself is begotten in the Son. The Son is the point of the Father, the Father's omega. Here the traditional order of alpha then omega applies; but the inverted order applies too.

Marianne Meye Thompson's *The Promise of the Father* examines the Father-Son language throughout the New Testament. Thompson finds that Father-Son language typically refers to inheritance.[16] In first-century Israel, fathers bequeathed their estates to sons.[17] An heir is the destination of your estate, where your property ends up. Over and over, when Jesus's sonship is brought up, it is unpacked in terms of inheritance. This relationship is demonstrated throughout his ministry.

For instance, at Jesus's baptism the voice from heaven proclaims, "You are My beloved Son" (Mark 1:11 // Luke 3:22 NKJV). The voice is quoting Psalm 2:7, which continues: "Ask it of me, and I will make the nations your heritage, / and the ends of the earth your possession" (2:8). All that the Father has belongs to the Son, as Jesus puts it in John 16:15. This was always meant to be so: as Paul puts it in Colossians 1:16, all things were made for him. The Father's promise to the Son is secured at his baptism with a gift: the Holy Spirit, the highest gift of all. Jesus, then, is the omega of the Holy Spirit too.

Jesus is a generous heir. He doesn't head to Rome or Jerusalem after his baptism to rule his acquisitions with an iron rod. Rather, he faces Satan in the wilderness and then returns to Galilee to proclaim the good news that we are invited into his royal inheritance (Col. 1:12–15). Are we ever! As Paul

16. Marianne Meye Thompson, *The Promise of the Father: Jesus and God in the New Testament* (Louisville: Westminster John Knox, 2000), see especially chaps. 2, 5.

17. Mothers didn't bequeath in that culture, and daughters didn't inherit. So the gendered language here is important in its original patriarchal context but in ways that don't apply in our present setting. This is unfortunate because we who hear and use the words *father* and *son* today instinctively attach unoriginal meanings to them. I don't know of an adequate English substitute, however. Functional terms such as *benefactor* or *heir* lack the intimacy and love that are part of the Bible's personal, familial terminology. In my life and teaching I use the biblical terms with asterisks, so to speak, striving to bear in mind and explain their proper connotations.

says, "All who are led by the Spirit of God are sons [that is, heirs] of God. For you did not receive the spirit of slavery to fall back into fear, but you received the spirit of sonship. When we cry out, 'Abba, Father,' it is the Spirit himself bearing witness with our spirit that we are children of God—and if children, then heirs, heirs of God and fellow heirs with Christ" (Rom. 8:14–17 RSV alt.).

We are inheriting the only Son's *full* inheritance. The Father spared nothing, and Jesus spares nothing. As faithful Boaz brought Ruth and her family into his, for the sake of his ancestors and ultimately his ancestors' messianic line, so Jesus bought us at the price of himself for the sake of his Father so that we could be the royal priesthood that he already was. As heirs, we sit on his throne, we have his authority, we can forgive in his name. He brought us into that extravagant omega to glorify his Father with him.

Later chapters will explore what an omega and alpha this all is for us. But dipping into one aspect of it briefly will help set up my next point. The church's inheriting the only Son's full inheritance sheds light on the meaning of the (in)famous language in Ephesians 5 of how husbands and wives are to treat one another. Some think this language makes wives less than husbands or women less than men. That might suggest some of the old Gods that express their power in domination and intimidation. But Ephesians 5 says that the husband provides for the wife: he prepares her to be flawless, robust, and ready. *That* is the direction in which the passage takes the metaphor. And this works wonderfully to describe Jesus's relationship to the church. What does Jesus give the church? Well, what doesn't he? He even gives us the Lord who is the Spirit, the same Lord who took the initiative to drive him into the wilderness (Mark 1:12). The bridegroom luxuriantly empowers the bride, just as the bride handsomely glorifies the bridegroom. This is not a power play or a power struggle. This is about lavishing one another with the highest, most unimaginable gift in order to become powerful and perfect. And it's a sign of *God*—stemming from Pentecost's alpha from, of, and for the God who expressed himself fully and beautifully in Jesus of Nazareth.

We will return to these matters when we speak of Jesus as the omega and alpha of creation and then again when we speak of him as the omega and alpha of humanity. Here, consider what it says about the one creating. If I were to beget my very being exclusively in another, give my name and thus my identity to that other, live sacrificially for that other, bring all things into being with the intent to give them to that other, breathe out my being on that other and in and through him, and glory wholly in that other—and it would never have been otherwise—then apart from that other, and apart from fulfilling all those intentions, I would not be myself. That other would be my very end, and that other's fulfillment would also be my beginning—the way that

I am who I am.[18] That is what it means for the First Person of the Trinity to be the Father. The Son is his omega. The Son is his alpha.

On a side note, if I *were* like this, a therapist would likely worry that I were "enmeshed" in that other person in a toxic way. And I guess I would be, because I am not the Lord. It's a good thing that the persons of the Trinity are healthy givers and receivers of one another's love, and that through them we gain ways of loving that we are not otherwise capable of. Chapter 7 reflects on such love.

Jesus expresses his sonship in taking his people and all peoples to be his very own, and that gives the eternal Father a new and lasting fatherhood. Like a father who asks his new son-in-law to call him "Dad," the only Father of the only Son is now our *Abba*. The Father shares his divine essence eternally and exclusively with his only Son and Holy Spirit, but he has come to include us in the very relations with them that constitute him as Father. If I invite my daughter-in-law to call me "Dad,"[19] it both expresses my fatherhood of my natural son and recharacterizes it according to his action of taking a wife. For all parties involved, it ends one stage of my fatherhood and inaugurates a new one.

The church was careful to maintain the distinction I've drawn here between the "immanent Trinity"—God's exclusive aspect—and the inclusive "economic Trinity," while insisting that these terms refer to the same Triune God, whose actions and nature are always consistent. God's "economic fatherhood" graciously expresses, fulfills, and recharacterizes God's "immanent fatherhood" without duplicating, undoing, or changing it. The same is true of the Son and Holy Spirit. So Jesus's revolutionary work is truly an omega and alpha for all three persons. Just as Paul claimed, when we cry out "Abba," we allude to the whole story of God's gracious being.

Having inherited all things as their omega, Jesus hands them on and hands them back, an alpha now of newly extended and fulfilled relationships. Having

18. Thompson's label for this being-in-relation, coming to pass in the course of creation, redemption, and consummation, is "the eschatological trajectory" of God's fatherhood. It is a way of speaking distinct from the later church's preference for the ontological "creedal trajectory" of Father-Son language, but the two are compatible and, understood correctly, inseparable. After all, for the Father, Son, and Holy Spirit to be fulfilling these intentions is simply to become who they eternally are. Thompson, *Promise of the Father*, 158.

19. Or even informally "adopt" a stranger who needs a family. This actually happened several years ago with my former student Jenny. I took her in, so to speak. Now she calls me "Dad," I call her a daughter, and she hangs out with her adoptive siblings and exchanges Christmas and birthday gifts with them. None of this supersedes or competes with either her loving biological family or ours. It does affect them, though. And it ought to, for it echoes God's gracious inclusion of all of us into his grand family.

received the Holy Spirit at the beginning of his ministry—an infinitely greater gift than the ends of the earth, though many of us act as if we believe otherwise—he poured out the Spirit in his death and resurrection. Through him the Spirit blew on, into, and through his bride, dwelling in her forever. Christ shared the Lord himself with us, and shares him still. He gives freely, fully, naturally, instinctively. Jesus the Spirit-receiver and Spirit-giver is thus the omega and alpha of the Spirit of sonship. He is the way that the Spirit is the Spirit. (This is one reason why it's not a problem for the Western doctrine of the Trinity to have the Spirit proceeding not only from the Father but also from the Son.)

## "Behold the Beauty of the Lord"

Something deep in us seems to revolt against fully affirming these breathtaking deeds. We turn the Trinity into some odd mystery that isn't supposed to make sense, as if our sense of God didn't really need it and therefore our theologies can avoid coming to terms with it. We turn God into someone people all over the world worship with or without Jesus, treating Jesus as just *our* incidental way of describing *our* experience of God rather than the defining nexus of the spectacular love that realized God's very deepest desire. We turn Jesus into nothing but a means for us to gain forgiveness, prosperity, or other things we desire—which makes *us* God's omega and alpha—rather than acknowledge Jesus as an end in himself, indeed the Father's and the Spirit's common end. We turn the Father, Son, and Holy Spirit into nothing more than Creator, Redeemer, and Sustainer—three ways that God relates to God's creation, as if *creation* were God's omega and thus the Trinity's alpha. We turn Jesus into merely an exemplary human being whose perfection sets the standard for human behavior to imitate, making *righteousness* God's omega and alpha. Or we turn Jesus into one of three divine beings in some kind of heavenly council who are more or less independent rather than constituted by relationships of lavishing, self-sacrificial love.[20] When we fail to appreciate Jesus as the end and the beginning of God, then the Father, the Son, and the Spirit all escape our perception. We see walking trees. And one way or another, we miss *our* God.

Not God in every way. But God's real spirit and God's deepest truth elude us—as well as God's *beauty* (cf. John 4:24). The Scriptures are quiet about this; they only rarely acknowledge that Israel's invisible God would have such

---

20. Theology has labels for schools of thought like these. Respectively, we call them mere monotheism, pluralism, Arianism, modalism, adoptionism, and tritheism.

a visible quality (Pss. 27:4; 96:6). God's beauty could only be displayed in visible acts such as creating heavenly and earthly splendor, delivering Israel, and dwelling in the sanctuary. All three happen in Christ's coming.

Even many Christians don't see God as beautiful. I recently graded a stack of student papers that reflected a backdrop of frustration, alienation, and suspicion about God. These students consider God's long-undelivered people all over the globe and wonder whether all the praise we lavish on God in worship is well deserved. Their faulty communities of faith publicize themselves as temples of the Holy Spirit, so the Spirit takes on their unappealing likeness. They shrink back from the world's literal as well as figural ugliness and glance back suspiciously at the God they hold responsible for it. When they experience or witness horrors, they are assured by other believers that everything is part of God's mysterious plan, and God's silhouette recedes further and further into heaven's impenetrable fog.

The students were discomforted by the biblical stories they were reading. Their questions were authentic and searching, not uncharitable or cynical; but they seemed shaken. Where's all the beauty the psalmist sings of? The God of their perceptions seemed more like those three Gods of the parable's three poor soils: a possible opponent, an untrustworthy ally, or an impotent and unhelpful supporter.

You can't prove that something is beautiful. You can only point out its features and help beholders see what you see. Others will disagree (Matt. 23:27; 26:6–10). Not because beauty is just in the eye of the beholder, but because the clash of Gods that plays out at the theological level plays out aesthetically too.

Jesus offends his opponents' taste. Profoundly. Touching the unclean, associating with outcasts and collaborators, and refusing holy customs were all as repugnant to Jewish cultured elites as desecration, sexual license, and idolatry. So they had him dispatched to Golgotha with the rest of the trash.

Jesus totally refused their way of seeing. In John he cast his coming crucifixion as a thing of glorious beauty: the lifting up of the Son of Man (John 3:14; 8:28; 12:32). Its display of God's loving and gracious self-sacrifice totally outshone the worldly ugliness that the rest of us brought to it. No other scene in all creation—indeed, no other deed of God, whether wonderful or terrible—could compare.

It took time for the cross to remake the old world's aesthetics. For centuries, depictions of the crucifixion remained rare in Christian circles (and unheard-of outside, except for anti-Christian graffiti). Isaiah 53:2 spoke truly in describing the suffering servant as unattractive. But a new vision of God had dawned on humanity, and its light grew and grew over the years. Iconography of the crucifixion developed, and the scene flourished in Western art from the Renaissance to the Enlightenment. Nowadays crucifixes are ubiquitous, dispersed into every Catholic and Orthodox home and quite a few rearview mirrors, even recruited into pop culture for their now fading shock value to subvert. And where spectators think to pay attention to a depiction of the crucifixion and even where they understand its horror, love is still what they mainly see: the beauty of its extravagant love that overpowers all its darkness (1 John 4:18).

The cross's beauty is God's alpha-beauty, eternal and yet new in Jesus Christ. It revolutionizes our notions of beauty, including earthly beauty. As perceptions of God's triune nature and character became increasingly clear to Christian visionaries, God's manifest beauty expelled from their hearts the old accounts of the good life, virtue, and sanctification and planted new ones. Their cruciform lives shone with the Lord's familiar light. Onlookers began taking notice of the lives of these saints. Their beauty is alpha-God's beauty communicated. Isaiah had seen the old's demise in the fading beauty of Israel, "God's branch," whereas the Lord's beauty was permanent (Isa. 28:4–5). In Jesus's new arrangement, God was bestowing his beauty on people in lasting new ways through the gift of his abiding Spirit (cf. 2 Cor. 3:7–18).

This is a topic for our final chapter on how Jesus is the end and the beginning of a life, but it's worth noting now that the other chapters' topics are all grounded here, in the Triune God's end and beginning in Jesus Christ. If we fail to grasp the Trinity, we'll lose the whole plot, because all that follows examines how that triune life plays out in old and new creation. Our visceral aesthetic response to God's self-manifestation in the risen crucified Jesus is a rough but illuminating diagnostic of how well we get it.

What do you see? What does your reaction say about you? What grade of soil might you have been? And what will you do with that information?

# THREE

# Jesus—the End and the Beginning of the Cosmos

*The creation was subjected to futility*, not of its own will but by the will of the one who subjected it, in hope that *the creation itself will be set free* from its bondage to decay and will obtain the freedom of the glory of the children of God.

Romans 8:20–21 NRSV

When Frodo speaks of "the end of all things" on the slopes of Mount Doom, he means *the end of the world*, the end of the reality he has known. The world has changed—forever. Christ's coming is the world's *true* end and a whole new one's birth. He is the end and the beginning of the cosmos.

## What's a "World"?

*Cosmos* is a word that John uses often in the New Testament, which we translate as "the world." The underlying sense of the word is of an "order" or "arrangement" with a coherence of its own. Yet the term displays impressive versatility. It takes on distinct shades of meaning in different fields of knowledge. In literature, a "world" is what an author creates. In sociology, it is the outlook of a people or a community. In physics, "world" means the earth or another planet, and "cosmos" means the whole universe. In history, a world is an era—in Greek an *aiōn* or age. In theology, it can refer either to

45

all creation—thus "cosmology" means the study of the structure of creation, angels and heaven included—or to that part of creation that has rebelled against God and resists God's Kingdom, so that being "worldly" means living a doomed life of denying God's sovereignty and love. Jesus uses the word *cosmos* in both senses, interrelating them.

The variety here makes this chapter's topic unwieldy and slippery. But there is a deep reason for these proliferating and messy senses.[1] In each of these uses, a world is an expanse, which from within *seems* limitless. This is true even in the most restrictive senses of the word. A novel may go on and on, spawning sequels and spin-offs and fan fiction as the possibilities of its "narrative universe" are explored. A person or a culture tends to assimilate new events and discoveries into its prior guiding framework or "worldview." Even a planet seems to go on forever when you're on its surface.

Yet a world is also an island. Its limits define it and even set it against others. This is so in each of the senses we just listed. Fiction faces the "narrative paradox" that a coherent story must exclude its audience from genuine interaction—as fan fiction's and Hollywood sequels' proliferating, inferior, and incompatible worlds demonstrate. And cinema's "celebrity paradox" admits that the reality a film supposedly depicts cannot contain the actors depicting it.[2] Even bigger worlds have necessary limits: every person, culture, and worldview has blind spots, if not tunnel vision. And a vast planet's gravity makes it almost impossible to escape.

The students at my school like to disparage their environment as "the Westmont bubble." Christianity is ubiquitous and rich on our one-hundred-plus-acre campus. Yet if we walk ten feet off campus, we are confronted by the reality that our home is also a safe house—a world—hidden away among the Santa Barbara area's utopian estates, gated celebrity mansions, Lotuslands, and Neverlands. And when our students venture farther out to California's multicultural megacities, or travel overseas for a semester in "another world,"

---

1. There are other senses of *cosmos* for which this is not true. The most common use of the term in the Septuagint is for "adornments" that beautify. From that meaning we get "cosmetic" jewelry, makeup, and surgery.

2. "So, in *Terminator*, Arnold Schwarzenegger doesn't exist and is not the governor of California," explains an article on the topic. "In a recent and amusing example, actress Jeri Ryan divorced her husband to play Seven of Nine on *Star Trek: Voyager* (he refused to move to Hollywood with her). The divorce was contentious, and a lot of salacious dirt was spilled. When Jack Ryan ran for the US Senate in 2004, the release of the documents forced him to withdraw, allowing his challenger to win in a landslide against a last-ditch replacement. The landslide victory propelled the challenger, Barack Obama, to a position from which he could then launch a campaign for President. . . . The paradox is, do you think it says that in *Voyager*'s historical database?" "Celebrity Paradox," TV Tropes, accessed March 16, 2018, http://tvtropes .org/pmwiki/pmwiki.php/Main/CelebrityParadox.

as they usually call it, they wonder whether Westmont is a Neverland too, a fantasy world that vanishes once we stop suspending our disbelief.

And those multicultural megacities that might seem so much more real are more isolated than they appear. We evangelical Christians are not the only ones who stay within our comfort zones. Everybody "bubbles": social classes, ideologies, genders, tribes, tongues, and nations; merchants, journalists, professors, politicians, and professions; churches, schools, corporations, industries, and even urban neighborhoods. Social media hasn't created this situation, though it has certainly capitalized on it. Humanity is a lather: a thick layer of bubbly worlds jostling, colliding, seeing others only through the distorting curvature of their own dividing walls, interacting with strangers only at their common surfaces, and generally minding their own business. A world of worlds.

A world's limits are formidable, even in *cosmos*'s most expansive senses. Creation depends on its mysterious Creator, who is metaphysically unavailable except through his own revelatory initiative. The universe is not only vast but elusive, and philosophical accounts of the nature of everything bump up again and again against the rough edges of the stubborn mystery of what they're trying to comprehend. And wherever I go on earth, or any other planet, I perceive horizons: I know there is a beyond, but my knowledge of it is a construction of imagination, memory, or cartography. Even our immense physical universe might merely compose one "plane" that is expansive in one sense but dimensionless in some other way that its inhabitants are ordinarily unaware of, until other neighboring planes (astral, or spiritual, or heavenly— who knows?) intrude somehow into their consciousness.

If that kind of talk sounds too mystical, too quaint and unscientific for our modern *world*, then trade it for the more respectable term *multiverse* and the point still stands.[3]

So it takes three things to make any world: perceivers, their apparently limitless perceptions of order, and the things beyond those perceptions.

Even *the* world, then, is still a world. It includes all three ingredients. Cosmology still misses some things and misperceives others. Likewise, even the smallest world is a *whole* world. G. K. Chesterton characterized the mindset of a madman: "His mind moves in a perfect but narrow circle. A small circle is quite as infinite as a large circle; but, though it is quite as infinite, it is not so

---

3. In fact, the term *multiverse* works rather well to highlight the logic of old worlds made new. *Versio* means "turning"—thus version, inversion, reversion, conversion. Whereas universe means "turned to one," or a totality, a multiverse means "turned to more than one." Living in the overlapping ends of the ages, we *do* exist in a certain kind of hinged multiverse, though not the kind that physicists conventionally envision.

large. In the same way the insane explanation is quite as complete as the sane one, but it is not so large."[4] Chesterton was implying that sanity is circular too, but larger. Its limits are further away, but they're still limits. All worlds, however unique, are still worlds.

## When Worlds Collide

Nevertheless, Chesterton drew a stark contrast between sanity and insanity (including the "madness" of a modern ideology such as materialism): "The madman is not the man who has lost his reason. The madman is the man who has lost everything except his reason. The madman's explanation of a thing is always complete, and often in a purely rational sense satisfactory. Or, to speak more strictly, the insane explanation, if not conclusive, is at least unanswerable."[5] Sanity is more humble, lives at a greater peace with its world's limits, and stays more open to mystery, surprise, discovery, further enlargement, and even revolution. Living in a self-enclosed ideological world is even more confining than being caged in a cell, because it has no window or door. It is a mental grave.

I say that sanity is *more* open because the contrast is not absolute. Human sanity and insanity are ranges in a continuum of contrasts. What lies beyond even the farthest horizon is still mysterious; and a cell with no door can still be broken into with sufficient force. Even a grave can be exited (John 11:43–44). All along that continuum spanning wide open fields and epistemological coffins, surprises still happen. Such intrusions—perhaps from another world, or perhaps from the reality a world is supposed to express—disrupt. They stretch my circle. They may rock my world—or *the* world—or even shatter it.

Even just stretching a world-circle is discomforting. Breaking it is terrifying. We naturally resist. Many defend the world from its threats. We protect our existential status quo either by ignoring the unwelcome evidence of something beyond or by trying to drag it onto our circle and make conventional sense of it. (How quickly we succeed in doing this is, for Chesterton, a measure of our madness.) Others resist surprise by surrendering the world. Nowadays one might protect a world-circle from violent intrusions by treating it as *just* a social construction: a "world" with quotation marks, a rubber band that flexes however it must because it has no shape of its own, or else a Hula-Hoop to slip on or off like a child at play. Some postmoderns treat worlds and their identities in them the way a shopper tries on clothes or a lawyer takes positions

4. G. K. Chesterton, *Orthodoxy* (New York: Doubleday, 1959), 20.
5. Chesterton, *Orthodoxy*, 19.

on behalf of clients. What threatens a circle like that can pose no threat to *me*. After all, I can disown it or retrieve it at any time.

> It is possible to meet the sceptic [*sic*] who believes that everything began in himself. He doubts not the existence of angels or devils, but the existence of men and cows. For him his own friends are a mythology made up by himself. He created[6] his own father and his own mother. . . .
>
> [The solipsistic "panegoist" and the materialist] have both locked themselves up in two boxes, painted inside with the sun and stars; they are both unable to get out, the one into the health and happiness of heaven, the other even into the health and happiness of the earth. Their position is quite reasonable; nay, in a sense it is infinitely reasonable, just as a threepenny bit is infinitely circular.[7]

Thoughtful people need some kind of rationale for an odd stance like this, and relativist and pragmatist cosmologies obligingly supply them. These are the true, behind-the-scenes world-circles of people with only "worlds." They seem boundless and all-explaining, but their limits are severe.


## The World of Worlds

The proliferation of contrasting and colliding worlds makes pluralism—the denial that they have any overarching unity—a tempting conclusion. After all, what does some fictional narrative world, or the thinking of some solipsist who believes that "the outside world" is an illusion, have to do with extragalactic astronomy and cosmology? And what does one novelist's or philosopher's construct have to do with the imaginings of another? It might be that Jesus is the end and beginning of some kinds of worlds but not others.

One answer is obvious: these novelists and philosophers communicate. They have voices. They have ears. They speak and read and think in languages, and thus in communities. They give and take. They observe with their eyes, move on their feet, and grasp with their hands. They are part of things, and things are a part of them. No man is an island, either with respect to others or with respect to other things. No world is an island either.

This is true of even our thoughts, dreams, and hallucinations. "Who among humans knows the things of the human being, except his or her own spirit within?" (1 Cor. 2:11, my translation). Yet even if we keep these things private, they still draw on the images, words, concepts, and impressions of the wider

6. Today we would say "constructed."
7. Chesterton, *Orthodoxy*, 26–27.

world, and they still influence our social conduct. These invisible worlds are still memory banks of that communications network that spans cultures, generations, and ages. Their isolation is only relative, only partial.

After all, while worlds may be our only interface with reality, reality still has a way of breaking into them and forcing revisions. Even when our stubborn Chestertonian world-circles resist adjusting to such forces, they are not completely impermeable. "Life's lessons will be repeated until learned," says a proverb. Over and over in life, my own picture of reality has had to yield to signs of its inadequacy. Sometimes reality intrudes into my picture like rain through a leaky roof, with droplets of inexplicable phenomena; other times it falls down on me in a chaotic avalanche. Either way, accommodating the contradictory evidence is a losing struggle and a growing source of pain until I patch my framework—or perhaps replace it, as if waking from a dream.

That does not mean that our adjustments always improve our world-circles. A person can suffer repeated "reality checks"—an apt phrase—and learn the wrong lesson, coping in self-destructive ways. "Today, if only you would hear his voice, / 'Do not harden your hearts as you did at Meribah,'" the psalmist and then the writer to the Hebrews plead, "'where your ancestors tested me; they tried me, though they had seen what I did'" (Ps. 95:7–9 NIV; cf. Heb. 3:7–9). People's grasps of reality need not progress toward perfection, since they can just as easily spiral into vices and mental disorders. The point here is that whatever the outcome, these encounters show that people are participants in an interactive reality. Their give-and-take demonstrates the interrelatedness of their worlds. After all, even hardening one's heart constitutes a response.

Fictional stories involving the afterlife sometimes imagine hell as a kind of insane asylum where people's lives of self-centeredness have left them totally closed in on themselves. Yet even here—in the horrible abysses of Richard Matheson's *What Dreams May Come*, Christopher Nolan's *Inception*, and C. S. Lewis's *The Great Divorce*—the lost are still reachable. Their hearts are tough and curved in on themselves, distant and small, hardened but therefore brittle and susceptible to cracking. And the water of reality inevitably flows in through those cracks. "'To me every knee shall bow, every tongue shall swear'"—not necessarily happily, but authentically—"all who were incensed against him shall come to him and be ashamed" (Isa. 45:23–24 NRSV).

So reality's constellation of contrasting and colliding worlds is also one shared world, rather than merely a plurality. This sprawling, incoherent meta-world—we'll just call it "the world" or "the cosmos"—has the same three ingredients that make every other world: perceivers, their apparently limitless perceptions of order, and the things beyond those perceptions.

Revelation's alpha-omega trope in its traditional order applies here. The world and all of its constituent worlds have God for their alpha. "For us there is one God, the Father, from whom are all things and for whom we exist, and one Lord, Jesus Christ, through whom are all things and through whom we exist" (1 Cor. 8:6). Any other gods and lords in any lesser realm, however real or unreal, are insignificant in comparison with the God and Lord of our being (8:4–5).

And the Son, as we all know, is the cosmos's omega too. In exalting him, the Father and the Spirit have given him the name above every name, so that *Jesus* becomes the world's common confession of faith (Phil. 2:9–11). "All that the Father has is mine," he told his disciples (John 16:15). "Whether thrones or dominions or principalities or authorities—all things were created through him and *for him*" (Col. 1:16). Jesus is where creation is headed and where creation comes from. He is its reconciliation to God (Col. 1:20), the relationship and the principle of unity that creation is all about.

When people usurped the power that God entrusted to us and seized God's creation like pirates, we rejected his plan to unite all things through a human being (Ps. 8:6; Heb. 2:8–10) and we entangled creation in our rebellion. Because Jesus is the cosmos's beginning and end, "he came to his own" (John 1:11) people and creation to be the world's end and beginning, to make it *from him* and *through him* and *for him* as it was meant to be.

## World Making

No writing has more profoundly displayed Jesus as the world's end and beginning than the Gospel of John. There Jesus refers to the age he was bringing to a close as "this cosmos." In the Fourth Gospel, the cosmos apprehends Jesus in three ways: first, from a unified and coherent perspective, as a single entity;[8] second, through its mysterious "ruler";[9] and third, as individuals.[10]

In the following passage, all three modes of perception coincide. The translation here is wooden to bring out the striking syntax: "Coming, [the Advocate, the Holy Spirit] will convict the world concerning sin, and concerning righteousness, and concerning judgment: concerning sin, because they are not trusting in me; concerning righteousness, because to the Father I go, and you no longer see me; concerning judgment, because the ruler of this world

8. John 1:10; 7:7; 12:19; 14:31; 15:18–19; 16:8, 20; 17:14, 21–23. Also, arguably, John 21:25, if understood as "the world could not *accept* all the books being written" (cf. the use of the same verb in Matt. 19:11).

9. John 12:31; 14:30; 16:11.

10. John 1:11; 3:18–19; 8:12; 9:3–5, 39; 11:9–10; 12:32, 46; 15:20–25; 16:9; 17:6, 13, 20, 24.

has been judged" (John 16:8–11). Let's examine each way the Spirit convicts the perceiving—misperceiving—world.

### Concerning Sin

Wherever Jesus went, he aroused suspicion and opposition. His presence disrupted and threatened the orderly worlds of the people who encountered him. He could not be assimilated into their frameworks. He is those worlds' omega—the definitive reminder of their limits, limits that turn out to be severe. Moreover, in responding to him, his detractors fell back on those same worldviews, like researchers who look away from conflicting data. They retreated from what had dawned on their horizons back into the apparent cover of night. I think this is why Jesus could do so few mighty works at home (Mark 6:5–6): familiarity breeds contempt. It was not because he lacked the will or power—the signs were there to see (6:2)—but because his neighbors couldn't or wouldn't see beyond their given perceptions of him. Rather than reckoning with a destabilized world, they fled into its receding shadows and dismissed him with reassuring rhetorical questions.

The Spirit's coming, like the rising sun, keeps shrinking the available territory in which the world's loyalists seek refuge. Each personal rejection of Jesus Christ, whether past, present, or future, expresses a wider phenomenon of unbelief for which the world will be held responsible.

### Concerning Righteousness

I overreached just then when I said that Jesus aroused mistrust *wherever* he went. The one who sent him in the first place didn't receive him that way at all. The rest of us exit life's stage having delivered performances we aren't entirely proud of, or shouldn't be anyway, and we don't look forward to reading the reviews. We leave uneven legacies that can be hard to face. Our life stories are full of details we would rather keep hidden or forget. So we go to "meet our Maker" with some trepidation.

But Jesus's exit was glorious: a triumphant return to his approving Father. His legacy—unanticipated and unimagined by the rest of us—is what righteousness truly looks like. Jesus's disciples deserved none of the credit for it: his own inner circle misunderstood, betrayed, and deserted him. The Father's joyful reception of his crucified and risen only Son, and of him alone (John 13:36), is the omega of the disciples' perceptions of their own competence. It exposed the limits of not only their righteousness but also their conceptions of righteousness, their many ethical worlds. Therefore, its brilliant light exposed the world as unrighteous, and still does.

### *Concerning Judgment*

The course of the conflict in the first part of John's Gospel, or John's "book of signs," as Raymond E. Brown refers to chapters 1–12,[11] follows a rather classic plotline. In the old American West, when an outlaw rides into town, the sheriff warns him that "this town ain't big enough for the both of us." That's how it was when Jesus came into the world. As Jesus exhibited his signs of the Kingdom, opposition mounted. It intensified. It spread. It hardened and radicalized. Eventually the situation reached a tipping point at which opponents seized an opportune moment to take care of the situation once and for all. But what was unfolding turned out not to be the garden-variety showdown that had seemed to be setting up, to the disappointment of many and the great joy of many more.

After the final sign of Jesus raising Lazarus from the dead, the Pharisees observed helplessly that "the world has gone after him" (John 12:19). Things were clearly going that way. Some Greeks sent word through the disciples that they wished to see Jesus. *Greeks!* Jesus put them off with the cryptic answer that "the hour has come for the Son of man to be glorified" (12:23). Visiting hours were over (12:36). The book of signs had closed. The time had come for its sequel, the so-called book of glory: "Now is the judgment of this world; now the ruler of this world will be driven out. And I, when I am lifted up from the earth, will draw all people to myself" (12:31–32 NRSV).

The Greeks would get their chance to see him. But first there were some things to take care of. John's book of glory begins in chapter 13 with a long parting discourse that includes a preview of what would come next. The Spirit was coming. But someone else was coming first. "I have told you this before it occurs, so that when it does occur, you may believe. I will no longer talk much with you, for the ruler of this world is coming. He has no power over me; but I do as the Father has commanded me, so that the world may know that I love the Father. Rise, let us be on our way" (John 14:29–31 NRSV).

## When the World's Ruler Came . . .

Mysterious language. Who was the ruler of that world, and how was he involved in Jesus's Passion? The players onstage in this coming drama fell into several groups: Pharisees, chief priests, their soldiers and police, Annas, and Caiaphas; Judas Iscariot, Peter, Mary, and the other disciples; Pontius Pilate

11. Raymond E. Brown, *An Introduction to the New Testament* (New Haven: Yale University Press, 1997), 334.

and his soldiers; Barabbas; crowds of people; and Nicodemus and Joseph of Arimathea. All human beings navigating their way through the world's various constituent worlds. The ruler of this world, like the Father and the Holy Spirit, was a player offstage and out of the audience's view. But Jesus saw him. So we who seek to understand how the world changed need to follow Jesus's eyes and avoid our own assumptions. Where did Jesus see the ruler of that world?

He saw it in Judas Iscariot and in his betrayal (John 6:70; 13:2, 21–30).

He saw it in the Pharisees' spiritual ancestry (8:12–59, esp. v. 44), and in their "lifting up" (8:28) and "handing over" (19:11) of him.

He saw it in Judas and the Pharisees coming together to have him arrested (14:30).

And he saw it in the synagogue and temple rulers who succeeded in bully-ing Pontius Pilate into granting their demand for his crucifixion (18:20).

And where did Jesus *not* identify the ruler of this world? Not in his other disciples, even though they had been given to him *from* the world (17:6–8).

Oddly, not in Pontius Pilate (John 19:11). Jesus identified Pilate's authority as coming from above. He did not speak that way about those who handed him over, and he pronounced deeper guilt on them. Pilate's behavior stands in contrast with theirs. Pontius Pilate was indifferent, uncomprehending, su-perstitious, and ambivalent. His attitude changed from dismissal of Jesus's royal claim (18:33–35) to fearful and resigned affirmation (19:22). While the Pharisees were "of the world" like so many others, their sustained and pre-meditated resolve to murder Jesus after hearing the truth of God (8:40) was unique and significant.

Not in the mobs. They played genuine but only supporting roles. They were impulsive and soon moved on.

Also oddly, not in Herod, who is not mentioned in John's Gospel, perhaps because he would complicate the story line coming into focus. Kings mat-ter—and we will attend to Israel's royal line in chapter 5 and Herod in chapter 7. But the Israelites originally got their monarchy after rejecting the God of Israel's covenantal priests and prophets, so God sees them as less fundamental to life than we usually do.[12]

What about Caesar himself? Jesus died on a Roman cross, after all. More-over, the Jews denied that they had any other king (John 19:14–22) and denied

---

12. Incidentally, Jesus's advent as Israel's Melchizedek-like high priest, Moses-like prophet, and heir of David brings an omega to that old tension and a new and eternal, essential harmony to the leadership of God's people.

that they had authority to kill Jesus (18:31). Then could "the ruler of this world" be a veiled reference to Caesar, or the hellish power behind Caesar's throne?

Not in John's Gospel. The Jews' claims of allegiance were disingenuous: they were ready to stone Jesus earlier (John 8:59). Rather than respect Caesar's governor, they criticized him until they got the verdict they were after. And Pilate seemed unintimidated by their warning that "if you release this man, you are not Caesar's friend" (19:12). Caesar comes off as a barely relevant figurehead, more used than obeyed or worshiped, and certainly not someone "coming" into this situation as a ruler. None of these people's behaviors are what real leadership looks like, even leadership of the satanic variety. The most direct confrontation with Jesus ran not through Pilate but through the spiritual leaders of the Jews.

The evil history of Christian anti-Judaism makes it hard for us to hear the voice of the text here. Neither Jesus or John advocated nor justified that kind of treatment. John's Gospel is suggesting something besides blaming or scapegoating: that Jesus died on a Roman cross, but only after Pilate handed him back over *to them* to be crucified (John 19:16).[13] The ruler of this world came primarily through the Pharisees, Judas Iscariot, and the chief priests. Jesus was the priests' unwitting Passover offering in John 19:14–16, just as the proclamation of his death for Israel was Caiaphas's unwitting prophecy in John 11:49–52.

Jesus and John's interpretation of these events is shocking. If we pay attention, it can open our eyes to how Jesus is the omega and alpha of the world, and all worlds.

The priests and rabbis were not the alpha dogs in Jesus's society. Caesar and his minions had the real worldly power. In a few decades, Rome would crush Israel's priesthood in the Jewish War and later abolish its Herodian puppet king in the Jewish War. Not long after, the empire would respond to the Bar Kokhba rebellion by nearly effortlessly crushing the rest of Israel's institutions, all except the Pharisees, remaking Judaism forever. In Jesus's Judea, Pilate was the one who called the shots. He barely knew or cared about his territory's religious affairs. It would have been so easy for a Jewish

---

13. According to the grammar of these verses, it was the chief priests who crucified Jesus. The soldiers who carried out that sentence do not appear until John 19:23, after yet another exchange between Pontius Pilate and the chief priests. The soldiers are not even named as Roman, and there is no centurion on the scene as in Matthew, Mark, and Luke. The scene is bizarre: a Jewish crucifixion! John's Gospel is not denying or contesting the historical details in the other three Gospels. Nor is it engaging in revisionist history; everyone knew crucifixions weren't Jewish. Nor is it being anti-Semitic; testimonies throughout the Fourth Gospel affirm Israel's election (1:11, 47–49, etc.). Rather, John's Gospel is making his point in its characteristic way.

believer like John to blame it all on the Romans and shift the blame for Jewish
zealotry onto the Roman imperialist oppression that provoked it, as many
interpreters reflexively do today.

Instead, John is showing us that these untouchable, dominant elites in
their garrisons and palaces *got played*. *That* is how the ruler of this world
chose to operate. The "powerful" ones were just for manipulating. The rest
of biblical apocalyptic literature reinforces this picture, so counterintuitive
today even to Christians, when it depicts empires as beasts that come and go,
who intimidate and overwhelm the whole known world for a brief season and
then dissolve while the real enemy remains.

John is also highlighting Israel as the center of God's created order. Dante
got it right in putting Jerusalem, not Rome, opposite purgatory in *The Divine
Comedy*. Israel may have *seemed* like a backwater from Rome's imperial
perspective, but the chosen people were the fulcrum in the turn of the ages.
Regional and global empires come and go. They are dispensable. Israel doesn't,
because Israel isn't.[14] So Israel had to be the decisive theater of this war. That
the gospel's early believers were primarily Jews suggests that the gentiles
were secondary. That is an omega for the world-circle of every idolater who
bows down to the usual things that dazzle. Conventional power, strength,
wealth, and cosmopolitanism are not what this world's ruler first reached
for to fight the decisive struggle of all time. He grabbed the clergy, and the
rest fell into line.

Finally, John's Gospel is not de-spiritualizing either the conflict or the world.
Far from it. Outwardly, the power struggle among Jesus, Jewish authorities,
Roman occupiers, and common people looks pretty conventional. It seems
like a project for the political science, history, and sociology departments.
Our legitimate dissatisfaction with traditional "spiritualizing" approaches
that ignore the gospel's ordinary human dynamics has been turning biblical
scholars' attention to those disciplinary perspectives, with enriching results.
Nevertheless, John's Gospel reminds us not to make the opposite mistake of
secularizing the conflict. Christ's passion was no ordinary contest. Its spiritual
dynamics go beyond the merely sociological.[15] Judas Iscariot was not just a
disaffected zealot who finally snapped; Satan entered into him (John 13:27).
The Pharisees in the temple's offering area who would lift him up (8:28) were

14. Much more on this in chap. 5.
15. In countering the widespread error of dematerializing the spiritual (which we usually call
"spiritualizing"), interpreters of the Gospels such as René Girard and Walter Wink have stressed
the human and social dimensions of Jesus's conflict with heavenly powers and principalities.
This tempts some readers to *reduce* these spiritual events to their material human aspects. In
different ways, the Synoptic Gospels and John resist reductionism of both varieties.

not just part of "the system" of power elites; these official caretakers of God's people were doing the bidding of their father Satan (8:44).

The high priests, Pharisees, and Judas Iscariot were all trustees of *holiness*, not just conventional power or authority, nor even religion or "spirituality." Those generalized labels mislead us here. The figures Jesus associated with Satan all came from groups divinely appointed and set apart as ambassadors between God and Israel. They had to (John 12:37–43), for among all the world's nations only one was made, called, and equipped to display and appreciate the one true God's holiness and Kingdom, and they were its earthly governors. They were to God what Pontius Pilate was to Caesar.

Only they weren't. John does not call these opponents holy, because being purposed for holiness is not the same thing as being holy. John's Gospel reserves the word *holy* for the Father (John 17:11), the Son (6:69), and the Spirit (1:33; 14:26; 20:22), and *sanctification* is used only in reference to Jesus (10:36) and disciples other than the betrayer (17:17–19). These spiritual governors somehow, mysteriously, ended up representing a different ruler instead of the true King. The ruler of this world was *unholy*, blasphemous, abominable: present in precisely the last places he should have been.

Those embassies of heaven were thus *part* of the world, and they remain so. Key parts, in fact: far more significant than some fleeting empire, even when they were overrun and enemy-occupied. I am belaboring the point because our relativized modern imaginations are so habituated into denying it. Pharisees, priests, apostles, and their contemporary counterparts are inside the world, not outside, and central, not marginal. Counterintuitive as it may seem, they have shaped the world's character far more than the cultural ephemeralities we magnify. That is the nature of reality. It may sound absurd to you and me, but that's how Jesus and John put it. Émile Durkheim was dead wrong to dichotomize the "sacred" and the "profane." Worldly Judas Iscariot was one of the Twelve—one of the pillars of the church. Worldly Caiaphas prophesied about Jesus, and worldly priests offered him up at Passover, performing their ambassadorial work despite themselves. These figures and their sacral offices *were* profane, in both senses of the word.

The crucifixion was a failed conspiracy. Working through his long-chosen channels (John 8:44), the devil drew together the world's flesh and spirit, its rulers and ruled, its "sacred" and "secular," its Jews and gentiles, Christ's scandalized opponents and disappointed disciple, and whatever other forces there may have been[16] to oust the world's true king. "The world" came together

---

16. Christians have traditionally included angels, demons, nature, and other species in that order and have been comfortable critically embracing different cultures' convictions that the

around Jesus at its unholy ruler's behest, revealing both its true character and his. This town ain't big enough for the both of them. One of them was going to last, and one of them wasn't.

Their unholy actions led to that world's demise.

### . . . And Was Cast Out

Really?! In what sense? Icons of the crucifixion sometimes depict a dark sun and blood-red moon, and stars falling from the sky—the end of the world (Mark 13:24–25). Well, look out your window: the stars are still there, and so is the world. It was business as usual in Jerusalem, Judea, and the ends of the earth as a few witnesses saw Jesus die, rise, and ascend. The scoffers of 2 Peter 3 made a good point when they observed that "all things have continued as they were from the beginning of creation," raising the challenge, "Where is the promise of his coming?" (2 Pet. 3:3–4). Is talk of the end of the world just hyperbole? It's a reasonable assumption. On one of the occasions when King David was delivered from his enemies, his song embellishes the event, to put it mildly:

> The earth reeled and rocked;
> > the foundations of the heavens trembled
> > and quaked. . . .
> > Glowing coals flamed forth from him.
> He bowed the heavens, and came down;
> > thick darkness was under his feet. . . .
> He sent out arrows, and scattered them;
> > lightning, and routed them.
> Then the channels of the sea were seen,
> > the foundations of the world were laid bare,
> at the rebuke of the LORD,
> > at the blast of the breath of his nostrils.
>
> > > (2 Sam. 22:8–16; cf. Ps. 18)

Is this just extravagant praise from a grateful and relieved underdog? That interpretation comes easily; we expect such grandiosity from people caught up in the flush of victory. Or is it a depiction of deeper spiritual realities that are really changing underneath plainer outward circumstances? That better

---

world includes the likes of spirits, ghosts, djinn, gremlins, leprechauns, extraterrestrials, and whatever else—as long as it is clear that Christ reigns over all regardless of their support, opposition, or ignorance of him (1 Pet. 3:22).

honors the sensibilities of God's worshipers as they draw on available ancient Near Eastern military tropes for warring kings and gods.

A third line of interpretation goes beyond mere emotion and cultural religious expression to envision David looking back on Israel's bedrock signs and wonders in Egypt and on Sinai, and framing his deliverance as follow-through on God's foundational actions and promises. That's a common theme in the Psalms. Israel's world *did* end in the Passover and *did* begin at Sinai, and that revolution's repercussions continued to reverberate down the centuries.

In all of these cases the author would be sincere, but in none of them would he be speaking literally. These are not hallucinations. They are not legends that have snowballed over generations of oral folklore, or the superstitious conclusions of prescientific imaginations. They are a warrior's theological interpretation of his own hard-won military success—a success that tapped into God's world-ending and world-making events in the days of Moses and helped bring them closer to fruition.

The extravagant speech of a Deborah, Hannah, or David pulls that earlier supernatural spectacle forward, so that present events share in that earlier victory and anticipate more and greater victories to come. The end of the world is a framework for interpreting the fuller significance of a contemporary moment of deliverance.

But Jesus didn't talk like just another Deborah, Hannah, David, or even his mother, Mary. Not only were his signs and wonders harder to explain away, but they signified a new revolution rather than just the consolidating of an old one. He did appeal to traditional apocalyptic images to help orient his followers, but he rooted Israel's earlier deliverances in the events of *his* life, not the other way around. In him the world was ending and beginning as it never had before.

Just how did the world end when the Son of Man was lifted up?

Recall what makes a world: perceivers, their perceptions of apparently limitless order, and what lies beyond their perceptual limits. Coming, Jesus of Nazareth intruded into the world's order. Its conspiracy to judge him only proved that he and his Kingdom lay beyond its perceptual limit line. It could only perceive him, its absolute omega, by misperceiving him. It could only stumble over the cornerstone (1 Pet. 2:8; cf. John 16:2).

And what a stumble. After the crucifixion, it looked like the old order had won the showdown, but the conspiracy failed. Its attempt to shame Jesus backfired, and glorified him instead. Marvelously, this world's unholy ambassadors were the very ones who lifted him up to the one who did the glorifying. Now their world's limit is more than just exposed; it is further constricted. They and their unholy leader are cast out of the rule they sought to hold on to. To be sure, many of them haven't realized this, haven't acknowledged it, and haven't changed their ways (John 16:2). To them, the world doesn't seem to have changed. The one they serve doesn't seem to have been deposed. Their denial is sincere.

To many audiences then and now, such claims are laughable. Delusional. History is about empires, emperors, and inventions, not pastors, bishops, and Sunday school teachers gone bad. *These* are the evil conspirators through whom the world is unmade and remade? Who even listens to them, besides the dull and superstitious?

Conspiracy theorists are usually crackpots. Is Jesus a crackpot? The test of a conspiracy theory is whether it is later confirmed. At first, this one seems shaky. Israel's authorities survived for decades and even a century, and its institution of the Pharisees remains to this day. The Roman Empire didn't even notice the events in John 18–20 until many decades passed. World affairs go on, seemingly as before, two thousand years later. People are still playing the same games as ever.

Nevertheless, the King of the Jews is now with the Father and reigning, as some can see (John 14:19). The conspirators and their leader have been exposed and identified. The world faces its prosecution because its ruler has been judged (16:11). And a new embassy is now open that offers an alternative to that dreadful future. The world now enjoys human representation in the heavens, and new heavenly representation in faithful apostles (15:19–21).[17] These structures in heaven and earth are still fully human, full participants in reality's one constellation of contrasting and colliding worlds. They are still in that sense part of the cosmos. So Jesus is not just the end of this world; he is also the world's alpha, its cornerstone, available in a new way for the world to build on him.

And what a cornerstone! The spectacle of a lifted-up Jesus is actually drawing people together and freeing them from being slaves of the conspirators. From within the world there has arisen a new body of perceivers with a

---

17. The apostles are still part of the world, but not like they were before. Verses such as John 15:19 are often translated to suggest that Jesus's faithful ones are no longer part of the world. In that case, the word *ek*, which Jesus uses three times, could not mean the same thing each time. However, *ek* can denote an identity deriving from origin—for instance, I am *from* Southern California—and then it can have a consistent meaning: "If you were *from* the world, then the world was loving its own. The reason that the world hates you is that you are not *from* the world; rather, I chose you *from* the world." To be chosen by Jesus is to gain a new identity, a new point of origin that builds on and transforms, rather than negates, the old one. It is a bit like joining the military or a monastic order. Becoming a member of the US Marine Corps wouldn't mean I am no longer *ek* Southern California; but being *ek* Southern California would no longer define me even as I represent and defend my fellow Southern Californians.

new set of perceptions. Their perceptual limits, while still absolute—God's essence remains invisible (1 Tim. 6:16; John 1:18)—are vastly expanded. They see the passing away of the world not only as a future hope but as something that has begun to happen with Jesus's death and resurrection. This new body of perceivers recognizes the light of the world for what it is (John 20:11–18), and in that light they can see the world for what *it* is.

To be sure, they are fragile. They can regress to the old perceptions and need thorough retraining for their new roles in Christ's order.[18] Moreover, the world's old ruler still seeks a comeback and still tempts God's servants to rejoin his cause. However, now he is an outcast (John 12:31), shut out of the world's embassy in heaven (cf. Luke 10:18; Rev. 12:8) and thus permanently exiled from the world's true center of power regardless of how many earthly followers he may attract.

As an aside, does that mean the ruler of this world wasn't shut out and exiled before? John suggests as much. After all, the priests did make their offerings. Caiaphas did prophesy. Judas Iscariot did serve. These all worshiped, just not in spirit and truth. Hostile powers may still maintain embassies in a capital, right until their ambassadors are expelled.

The apostles, their risen and ascended Lord, the Spirit of truth he sends to abide with them (John 14:17; 15:26), and the generations of disciples who join them (20:29–31) are a new locus of perception of the world (14:26; 16:4; 17:6–8). Our words, lives, and even deaths display and proclaim the now open secret of the revolutionary Kingdom of God. Since it takes perceivers and orderly perceptions to make a world, the insight our testimonies make available renews the world as much as the revolution itself does.

## The New World Waits

Over the centuries, a lot of effort has gone into trying to explain (away) this perceptual transformation by reducing it to just some kind of internal shift on the part of the perceivers. It was not. Christians were not visionaries (let alone hallucinators) who constructed a "new" world from old materials. Nor were they "scientists" or explorers or spiritual sojourners who discovered something "new" by observation, demonstration, or reflection that in principle had always been available to anyone. Jesus's resurrection was real, and they were its privileged eyewitnesses. Both the historical event and the new

18. John 21's postscript already anticipates it. There, Jesus appears to his disciples, who seem to have taken time off to go fishing, and reminds them of their mission. The episode anticipates our twenty centuries of Christian failure and restoration.

historical perspectives it spawns are significant; both the revolution and its
heralds do necessary work (Rom. 10:12–15). Encountering the alpha altered
the eyewitnesses' perception and brought them to the new world's threshold.
What they beheld there, above all, was the glorious Word, who had taken on
mortal flesh and ascended to the Father (John 1:14). The disciples saw his
glory; they heard, looked at, and touched eternal life in person (1 John 1:1–3)
as the risen Jesus stayed with them, ate with them, taught them, touched them.

Jesus's eyewitnesses came away from these encounters thinking of him not
as having an immaterial body but as being a new kind of creation that is still
creation—still cosmos. Jesus Christ, creation's originating Lord ("begotten of
the Father before all *aeons*" or *worlds*), had made creation's omega his own
and became its mortal subject, and had been made the alpha of creation's
new and coming immortal self. That new being was a future the disciples were
coming into as well. But they would have to remain patient and persistent.

A temporary break from the Gospel of John can help round this out. God's
lament over Tyre in Ezekiel 27 shows creation's natural beauties and gifts to be
good but also necessarily failed. Natural theology tends to overdo the praise
of nature, and disavowals of it by the likes of Karl Barth tend to overreact
by minimizing nature's glory.[19] Paul avoids the dilemma when he characterizes the universe as having been "subjected to transience"—to the futility of
passing away (Rom. 8:20)[20]—and groaning for a change. I recalled this verse
some time ago when we were spending our last day with our family dog,
Violet. Only hours earlier we had learned we would have to put her down
because of cancer at too early an age. Paul's phrase played over and over in my
mind as she and our family suffered the end of her life. All creation has been
subjected to impermanence and emptiness. We all know the heartbreak of
that. "Even we who have the firstfruits of the Spirit . . . even we groan," Paul
says (8:23, my translation). This subjugation was not of creation's own will
any more than it was our dog's will to pass away, or yours or mine when our
time comes. It's not a future we typically embrace, unless we are in desperate
physical or mental health.

Yet Paul sees our horrible unwilled destiny as having come about "by
the will of the one who subjected it, in hope" (Rom. 8:20). God is not aloof
or detached from our plight. The Father is the one behind creation's being
bound to pass away. Not with indifference or resignation: he did it *in hope*
of what would come after. And not as a spectator: Jesus entered *into* that

19. Robert W. Jenson, *Ezekiel* (Grand Rapids: Brazos, 2009), 217.
20. The word in this verse translated "futility" and here "transience" has both senses in the
Septuagint, especially in its Wisdom literature. Both senses are relevant in Rom. 8.

transience. He took it on as his own. The only God-begotten Son took up residence in the world of futile human bodies, passions, and wills, and he passed away. Then the Spirit raised him to life and to glory, and he ascended to sit at the Father's place of honor as Lord of creation in a whole new way. Jesus, who was made to suffer with us as part of creation's death throes, now reigns over all creation, including sin and death. He is past its transience. He is its alpha: Lord of the cosmos, and himself the cosmos renewed and made eternal.

Jesus's casting out of the ruler of this world and his ascension to the Father's right hand constituted the most consequential regime change in cosmic history. Humanity is ruled differently, whether or not we acknowledge it. A new world with a new ruler has erupted in the midst of the old, and his people are following him out of the old one they still carry in their mortal bodies and into the future he literally embodies.

The Kingdom of God is God's arrangement. The Father initiated its terms and bequeathed it to his ascended eternal Son as trustee. That arrangement stands: "His Kingdom shall have no end" (Luke 1:33). And all human arrangements stand under it. I am a citizen of a political arrangement structured under the Constitution of the United States of America. *The people* made that arrangement, and the people can alter it. Other people live in autocracies ruled by the people who came to power, however they managed to do it; the leaders did the arranging, and they hold the power to change the arrangement as they see fit. Yet all these arrangements stand under God's new arrangement, consciously or not, willingly or not.

I work in an oligarchy: a college ruled by a board of trustees. They have the power to change the arrangement in accordance with my school's articles of incorporation. Other workers are sole proprietors or partners who make their own rules and can change them at will. Yet we all stand under God's new arrangement, whether or not our missions align with it.

I belong to a family: a group of people founded on a set of vows. My father and mother made a promise, and my life was one of the results. My wife and I in turn made a promise, and our children's lives are among the results. Others live in families with different kinds of beginnings, but their arrangements are similar webs of covenants, obligations, and commitments. Any of us can maintain or shatter those arrangements through fidelity and infidelity to them. Nevertheless, they and we all stand under God's Kingdom arrangement, joined together in it and accountable to it.

There are no red phones in Washington, DC, Beijing, Brussels, Moscow, Wall Street, or even the Vatican on which Jesus Christ calls to speak to his deputies. His Kingdom is no layer of conventional human bureaucracy, not even the top one. In future chapters we will explore the implications of this new arrangement specifically for humanity as a race, for descendants of Jacob, for other nations' arrangements and cultures, and for individual persons. Here we can note two implications that apply to every structure in the newly ruled world.

First, Jesus has promised to return and judge all things, not by the standards of our consciences or our cultures, nor even the old covenant, and certainly not by our intuitions about how Jesus surely thinks and feels (cf. Matt. 25), but by his Father's perfect will (5:48; 7:21). Until then, humanity is on a long leash: "Let the evildoer still do evil, and the filthy still be filthy, and the righteous still do right, and the holy still be holy. Behold, I am coming soon, bringing my recompense, to repay every one for what he has done. I am the Alpha and the Omega" (Rev. 22:11–13).

Second, Jesus has promised to share his leading role. His Kingdom's faithful subjects will not be permanent underlings in some eternal trinitarian oligarchy; they will be sons of the Father (Matt. 5:45), *heirs* (Rom. 8:17) who sit with Christ on his throne (Rev. 3:21). The meek shall inherit the earth (Matt. 5:5) and receive the power that every rebel has longed for and grasped at in the wrong way for the wrong reasons.

These two aspects of being newly ruled are intimately related. The judgment suits both the circumstances that precede it and those that follow. Jesus has made available the necessary resources for human beings to prepare ourselves for sharing in his rule: the Holy Spirit above all; the perfect law of liberty (James 1:25); a fellowship of gifts, discipline, and virtues in which to mature; and a theater of spiritual war—the stubborn world that is being made new—in which to offer the Kingdom's grace and truth with hospitality and perseverance. We who respond trustfully and fruitfully to that lavish grace while we are on that long leash are acknowledging Christ's new and different rule freely and joyfully, by living in the ways that will last beyond judgment day when "Christ is all, and in all" (Col. 3:11). God's unholy earthly ambassadors have been replaced (Mark 12:9–11) with new earthly ones, though the new ambassadors haven't necessarily proved themselves worthy (13:35–36). We usually call them the church.

What happened to the world's ousted ruler? The devil didn't just vanish after Jesus's passion. He still hides and plots from within his former holdings, as if they still belonged to him (Rev. 13:24). "Your adversary the devil prowls around like a roaring lion, seeking someone to devour" (1 Pet. 5:8). Think of ruined Saruman dwelling in Frodo's home and tyrannizing the Shire. Revelation 2:9 speaks of a community of Jews who slander Christians as a "synagogue of Satan." The vocabulary is significant. Anti-Judaism is not its point.[21] Rather, it alerts us that, underneath that group's persecution, the world's deposed ruler is up to his old tricks, still operating through the same spiritual channels as before. So de-spiritualizing the devil's insurgency will blind us to its character. In describing the beast, Revelation 13–20 emphasizes spiritual practices: worship, signs and wonders, idolatry, persecutions of the saints, and blasphemies specifically against God. Likewise, to identify the antichrist we usually look to politicians, but Paul anticipated a human outlaw who exalts himself against every god and idol, enthroning himself *in God's temple* as God himself (2 Thess. 2:4). No wonder the Reformers figured the antichrist would come from the clergy. After all, to seize Jesus, Satan had entered not into a king or governor but into an apostle.[22] The beast refers to an empire, but churches are logical environments in which to glimpse this displaced lion on the prowl as well as his prey.

## World Remaking

Back to John, and back to the eyewitnesses who have seen the Kingdom's new advent. Through these perceivers, the world can come to see truly (John 17:20–26). The world is now something we earthly ambassadors are more sent into than drawn from (vv. 13–18). We are, in Lesslie Newbigin's words, a "hermeneutic of the gospel,"[23] a bodily translation of the good news in the languages and lifestyles of the world's societies and even the dialects of its families.

*All* of these children of the Father belong to the Son (John 17:10) and share the Son as their heavenly representative. No world is an island. So the good news of his Kingdom, traveling through Christ's commissioned authorities, touches every world-circle it meets. His mission has to be bubble-crossing and bubble-bursting. Following the Son demands that we take on the adventures, discomforts, and exhilarations of his apostleship as our worlds meet their omega and alpha in his reign. As one who has enjoyed opportunities to do this on five continents, I recommend it.

---

21. They "say that they are Jews *and are not*" (Rev. 2:9 RSV).

22. I'm not saying that the pope is the antichrist, that the Vatican is Babylon, and so on. But in backing away from those old allegations, we shouldn't forget that they got some things right: The devil is God's rival, hungry for worship, and looking to reclaim lost territory. Spiritual institutions (now Christian as well as Jewish) have grown rather than diminished in importance since the days of the Gospels. And conventional political institutions are less sovereign and essential than they would like us to believe.

23. Lesslie Newbigin, *The Gospel in a Pluralist Society* (Grand Rapids: Eerdmans, 1989), chap. 17.

In *Invitation to Theology*, Michael Jinkins draws on Robert McAfee Brown's *Unexpected News: Reading the Bible with Third World Eyes* to describe the "hermeneutical circle" of disorientation and reorientation that happens when we venture beyond our bubbles.[24] Our action leads to a jarring experience. This pressures our world-circles and drives the need for new understanding. We turn back to the Scriptures and the rest of Christian tradition with our new questions, and we receive new answers that direct us to new actions and set the stage for another turn of the circle.

Such literal and figural travels are a kind of pilgrimage, not just to our faith's historical center but also to its eschatological frontier. They take us beyond the familiar to witness the Spirit's work, change us, and bring us back to a home that is now inevitably different. In *The Open Secret*, Lesslie Newbigin describes the crises and new creations that come from and lead to cross-cultural contact as a three-way exchange between the acculturated missionary, the cultural mission field, and Scripture, with Jesus at its center. We are all susceptible to being transformed in the course of our conversations as the Spirit guides the Son's disciples into all truth, showing the church and ultimately the world that all that the Father has also belongs to the Son (John 16:12–15).[25] Traveling these hermeneutical circles punctures our social bubbles and world-circles. It disorients as it reorients. It converts both the traveler and the locals to bigger and better perceptions of the world and its God.

This is not the ordinary flux and paradigm-shifting of traditions adapting to ever-changing circumstances and new information,[26] because what is converting our worlds is no internal phenomenon but the coming Kingdom of God. Jesus's omega and alpha might manifest themselves only over a long time, shaping and training the enlarging consciousness of a child growing up in a Christian home. Or they might melt away the world of an adult and reforge it in a matter of a few unforgettable minutes. Either way, they are still its definitive stone of stumbling and its new cornerstone, its omega and alpha.[27]

24. Michael Jinkins, *Invitation to Theology: A Guide to Study, Conversation and Practice* (Downers Grove, IL: InterVarsity, 2001), 64–65, drawing on Robert McAfee Brown's *Unexpected News: Reading the Bible with Third World Eyes* (Louisville: Westminster John Knox, 1984).

25. Lesslie Newbigin, *The Open Secret: An Introduction to the Theology of Mission* (Grand Rapids: Eerdmans, 1995), 147, 187.

26. These are variously described by scientists and philosophers such as Michael Polanyi, Thomas Kuhn, and Alasdair MacIntyre.

27. I find a reassuring instance of conversion in the story of Jonah—not just because Jonah is converted along with the king of Nineveh but also because Jonah's tale shows that the process works even when the traveler is unhappy or unwilling. Along with reluctant Jonahs, in my time as an ambassador of the Kingdom, I have come to know enigmatic Abrahams, shrewd Jacobs, fiery Moseses, cooperative Rahabs, insistent Ruths, hospitable Naomis, weeping Jeremiahs, insecure Isaiahs, daring Nehemiahs, quiet Marys, dispirited sons of Zebedee, grateful Magdalenes,

## Creation Waits

Throughout this chapter's treatment of the cosmos, humanity has taken center stage. The Bible supplies abundant reasons for this. After all, "you have given [human beings] dominion over the works of your hands; / you have put all things under their feet" (Ps. 8:6 NRSV). Yet the rest of creation will all undergo the renewal. In fact, Paul envisions the universe crying out in the pain of the final stages of its delivery (Rom. 8:22). His apocalyptic vision seems hard to square with appearances, since nothing that happened in Jerusalem two thousand years ago affected wider creation in any perceptible way. The sun, moon, and stars all still shine as before. But Paul knew this too. It was obvious. So it is probably not coincidental that his imagery can take it into account. After all, a mother's labor pains and symptoms are not distributed through her whole body. If the world is one world, then the universe is truly involved in its own Maker's strange arrival from within, whose locus is more or less confined to the affairs of one species at a single time and locale on the earth's surface.

Today we might add that the earth is one galaxy's marginal solar system's marginal planet. But what does that change? All that the past few centuries of astronomy have done is add zeroes to the scale of a problem that wasn't quantitative in the first place. Incarnation has to take place somewhere and not somewhere else. The ancients already knew a world of many species, even spiritual ones. Some were relatively intelligent; angelic creatures were understood to be more intelligent than humans (Matt. 24:36). Christ's new reality was an alpha for all of these orders of creation (Heb. 2:5–9). Not much needs to change to adapt these convictions to contemporary cosmology.

Jesus was made an ephemeral organism and became one of sin's victims. But he didn't suffer as just another of sin's victims, let alone just another ephemeral organism. By suffering the cosmos's omega as its redeemer and by rising as the cosmos's firstborn of many (Rom. 8:29), he broke creation's old bondage. The world was not *his* omega; rather, he was *its* omega. So Paul envisions all those orders of creation waiting and waiting, as if in line, for God's heirs to be revealed so that they can get in on the heirs' freedom from decay. The only begotten Son is the alpha for human creation first, and then, at his appearing, for all the rest.[28] So Paul can move beyond the terrible truths

---

suspicious Thomases, blinded Sauls, suffering Pauls, generous Lydias, mystical Johns, dazzled Corneliuses, and baffled Peters. Or, rather, we have come to know each other. Best of all, we have experienced the promise that the Spirit is already on the other side of the barriers we are afraid to cross, leading us into God's future rather than simply pushing us out of our present.

28. So "ecotheology" worthy of the label "Christian" must end and begin with Christology and eschatology, though it shouldn't reduce itself to them.

of the world's suffering and decay—not just a human plight, but the plight of all temporal existence—with the same realism and hope as the Father: "Won't the one who didn't spare his own Son, but handed him over for us all, grant us all things along with him?" (Rom. 8:32, my translation).

Since the cosmos is waiting in line behind the humanity to which Jesus and his missionaries have been sent, let's narrow our focus to the end and beginning of humanity as such.

# FOUR

# Jesus—the End and the Beginning of Humanity

You know the message he sent to the people of Israel, preaching peace by Jesus Christ—he is Lord of all. . . . *They put him to death* by hanging him on a tree; but *God raised him* on the third day. . . . He commanded us to preach to the people and to testify that he is the one ordained by God as *judge of the living and the dead*. All the prophets testify about him that everyone who believes in him receives *forgiveness of sins through his name*.

Acts 10:36–43 NRSV

We saw how Paul characterized the plight of the created universe as it awaits its omega: *Subjection to transience. Bondage to decay.* That same bondage, minus the note of hope, weighs down Ecclesiastes's weary observations on the specifically human condition. The Preacher ("Qoheleth") has done us all the favor of trying everything under the sun in search of an escape from the purposelessness of human life, and has come up empty. We all end up in the same graveyard whether we're wise or foolish, prosperous or poor, dutifully observant or sacrilegious, righteous or wicked, the helpers or those they help. The Preacher concludes that a person should "enjoy life with the wife whom you love, all the days of your vain life that are given you under the sun, because that is your portion in life and in your toil at which you toil under the sun. Whatever your hand finds to do, do with your might; for there is no work or thought or knowledge or wisdom in Sheol, to which you are going" (Eccles. 9:9–10 NRSV).

We might as well make the most of what little we have for the short time we have it, but we shouldn't fool ourselves into thinking that there is more than that. But why *not* fool ourselves? Ignorance is bliss. Empiricists as courageous as Qoheleth are rare. Whether we absorb his wisdom by reading, replicate his results the hard way by traveling the same roads, or daydream our way through life and learn nothing, we return to dust soon enough anyway. It is better to accept our lot (Eccles. 5:19), but only marginally so.[1] This is natural humanity's predicament. Life under the sun comes to an endless end. That pitiless banner hangs over all our toils, from personal development to career achievements to public service to childrearing.

The one ray of nondespair (it is too weak to deserve the word *hope*) in Ecclesiastes comes in its qualifier, which the author probably did not even intend as one: "under the sun."[2] Life *under the sun* leads to Sheol. It sounds as if neither love, nor faith, nor righteousness, nor powers, nor keeping the commandments, nor anything else in all creation can separate us from the despair of Sheol. But what if *under the sun* is not an image of limitlessness but a boundary? What if there is human existence that isn't under the sun? That would limit the scope of the Preacher's empirical observations, wouldn't it? Life *might* conceivably be different.

Through the prophets, God graciously unveiled promises of new heavens and a new earth, and a new human situation that lay beyond the Preacher's empiricism. That kindled Israel's hope for a truly meaningful future and fostered courage to order its present life in anticipation of it.

But what would it be like? What would it mean to be human then? Humans, shaped by life under the sun, lacked any capacity to imagine more than extensions of that life's best aspects and restrictions on its worst: longer life spans, plentiful food, harmless beasts, secure property, and thriving children (Isa. 65:17–25). They dreamed essentially of a world like what modern human ingenuity has given us an increasing share of. (We are now so dependent on it that many regard its benefits as human rights.) So Israel's hopeful were still in for a surprise. They had to be.

---

1. This bleak picture is merciful compared to the visions of Hinduism and Buddhism, which cry out against the injustice of life's vanity by positing a law of karma by which the universe's moral agents are reincarnated to reap what they sow. For Buddhists, we must struggle to gain the detachment and altruism necessary to reach the nirvana that Ecclesiastes promises everyone. For Hindus, life's long and tortuous road offers no such shortcuts. These too are vanity, chasing after wind.

2. I do not think the epitaph in Eccles. 12:13–14 delivers the book from its hopelessness. It merely underlines the observation already made in 8:12–13 that life's vanity doesn't warrant immorality among the living. One can read God's coming judgment in 12:14 as an unintended qualifier like "under the sun," which points out a limit line of the author's world without revealing anything about whatever lies beyond it.

Jesus's reign comes from "over the sun," from God's dwelling place.[3] His humble entry into the world, his exalted exit to the Father's right hand, and his gift of the Holy Spirit had to mean the end of our old arrangements' absolutism—our world's powers and principalities, thrones, nations, states, businesses, cultures, technologies, and religions, all toiling under the sun and its vain glare. Our old human institutions—even the Law, the Prophets, and the Writings—no longer have the last word, and those that resist Christ's reign cannot last.

Those structures are the warp and woof of humanity. So Jesus is the omega of humanity. Sooner or later, his coming is the end of what we were, or would have been, and the beginning of what we will be.

## New Tricks, Old Man

Jesus announced this coming upheaval early in his ministry, in an exchange with the disciples of John the Baptist. The Gospels portray John as an early supporter of Jesus and his movement who soon found him puzzling and frustrating. So John's disciples came to Jesus and asked why Jesus's disciples weren't fasting like they and the Pharisees did. *We thought you were with us! Aren't you?* Jesus's response was shocking: My coming, he says—my newness—can't conform to the old ways any more than a piece of fresh, unshrunk cloth can patch a hole in an old weathered cloak. The old order can't accommodate me any more than already stretched wineskins can accommodate still-fermenting new wine (Matt. 9:16–17). The old ways don't have any stretch left in them; their adaptation to prior conditions has made them rigid and brittle. You sclerotic disciples of the old just fast and mourn; but my disciples know that it's time to celebrate now that I'm here (9:15). My disciples' new ways flex and change with the fluid conditions of the moment. You and your ways can't do that.

I'm trained against seeing how extreme Jesus's response was. If these Pharisees or John's disciples had come to me with their question, I probably would have politely invited them to open their Jewish subcultures to the good news and adjust. It's never too late! But Jesus says, *Yes it is*. It's too late for used

---

3. "The most ineradicable reason Solomon gives for vanity is the very nature of time itself as cyclic. And the four great divine deeds revealed in the Bible all break the cycle and introduce something radically new, something from without, outside time itself, something from eternity rather than from the past, therefore something radically new: Creation, Incarnation, Resurrection, and Last Judgment. Here IS something new under the sun because it comes from beyond the sun. Here are meaning and hope, though terror too. Here is true transcendence." Peter Kreeft, *Three Philosophies of Life: Ecclesiastes, Job, Song of Songs* (San Francisco: Ignatius, 1989), 56.

wineskins and old cloaks, and that's what your ways are to me. If that's who you are, if they are your identity, then it's too late for you too.

When the new approaches, old-timers face four options: first, to *leave* the old and embrace the new, as Jesus's disciples had done; second, to *deny* or refuse the new and stick with the old, as the Pharisees were doing; third, to use the new like a piece of cloth, to *patch* or repair the old; and fourth, to use the old like a wineskin to support or *contain* the new.

John's disciples were waiting for God to restore Israel to its old covenantal faith. Jesus's baptism was such a promising moment, but afterward his tactics seemed inconsistent, even impious. Jesus's response to their query suggests that they were inclined to the third or fourth options. Historically, they're in good company. Christian history is shot through with attempts to patch worn-out garments with the gospel or store it in used wineskins, and Christian theology is shot through with rationalizations for doing so. After all, the old—my culture, my country, my religion, my way of life—is too good to throw out! God made them, and they have been a blessing (Luke 5:39).

And these old blessings *have* been blessings. Even allowing for the ways sin compromises them, they *are* good. We are right to take healthy pride in them. That old cloak served me well. Giving it away feels ungrateful and disloyal. Besides, isn't bringing new life to old things what redemption is all about? How could we abandon these?

The irony is that what John's disciples were clinging to is *fasting*. They didn't want to let go of waiting—waiting for the restoration that they wanted. They *wanted* salvation to be just a patch, or more of the same aged wine. They were trying to plow while looking back (Luke 9:62).

Our patching and containing fail because the old and the new are incompatible. We can't have it both ways. We cannot patch our old lives with the Kingdom of God or contain the Kingdom of God within our old lives. Jesus's response carried a note of impatience and judgment. You already know not to patch old clothes with new cloth, he said. You already know not to pour new wine into old wineskins. These are rookie mistakes. Why are you even asking me this question? You must not understand the Kingdom. You must not realize that this alpha entails an omega.

Jesus's exchange with John's disciples was interrupted by a father who wanted him to raise his dead daughter (Matt. 9:18). Qoheleth would have countered that the day of death is better than the day of birth, that a house of mourning is better than a house of feasting (Eccles. 7:1–4). But Jesus knew a new sun had dawned, a sun of righteousness (Mal. 4:1–3). Life and even death under *that* sun would no longer be condemned to vanity. While we had once busied ourselves chasing after the wind, God's wind would now be chasing after us. So Jesus cut off their discussion and left. This was not out of urgency, as he entertained another interruption along the way (Matt. 9:20–22). He left because John's disciples knew all they needed to know.

Does it seem unfair to read all these intentions and desires into an innocent question from John's perplexed disciples? Yet that is what Jesus did. Maybe you had to be there. Or maybe it's not so innocent a question after all. Clutching the old at the expense of the new is unbelief, whether it arises from loyalty or fear. At any rate, Jesus closed the door here on the third and fourth options. That left two: embrace the new or refuse it.

John's disciples apparently chose the second. None followed him out the door. John was the greatest of his age (Matt. 11:11), but in that age he stayed. Refusing the new only postpones the inevitable conflict. The end of all things remains near. The Kingdom still approaches, always beckoning, willing to be rejected and even persecuted for the time being, but never surrendering. Taking the first option, letting go of the old and vain and embracing the Kingdom, welcomes that conflict right into one's heart and life. The ensuing engagement plays out in and around every disciple, in every place and every generation that hears the good news.

Let's choose one such disciple through whose life we can see humanity ending and beginning. Decades before John's disciples learned that their ways were stretched-out wineskins, Jesus's coming had already put a premature end to several unfolding lives and ushered in new, totally different ones. The first one was Mary's.

## Humanity Ended: Mary

The Bible says precious little about Mary. But no other human being—maybe including Jesus himself—has fascinated Christian imaginations more. Who is she? How was she chosen? What was it like to mother her own Creator? What was it like to see him scorned and executed? And then raised and ascended? What became of her? Who is she to God? Who is she to us if her son accepts us as brothers and sisters?

Orthodox, Catholic, Protestant, and Pentecostal Christians have come to strikingly different, seemingly incompatible answers. Yet they all depend on Mary's relationship to Jesus, the one whose coming so disrupted her life, and that makes them relevant to our topic. So I think it's worth the struggle to understand one another's versions of Mary. We won't convince one another, but we can honor the different visions enough to suspend our disbelief temporarily, the way one might with a good fantasy novel or film. We will find some common ground, from which our traditions soon depart into contested territory. Both the common ground and the contested territory are fruitful areas for exploring what it meant to be human and what it means now that Jesus has come.

All agree that the old Mary was a faithful Jew. Certainly her reflexive response of trust in God's surprise announcement suggests a faithful disposition. At the same time, her surprise displays an expectation that she was on her way to leading an ordinary Jewish woman's life under the sun.

Young Mary was already betrothed to a man of a similarly honorable disposition. If God had left them alone, they would probably have settled down in an unremarkable place and lived worthy but unremarkable lives. They would have struggled to make ends meet. They would have had a family. Joseph and Mary would have accommodated the Roman Empire through its unsympathetic tax collectors and soldiers and through the vassals of their puppet king, Herod. They would have depended on their eccentric and frustrating (whose isn't?) extended family, and they'd have been dependable in return. They would have kept the festivals and the other covenantal rules of their society, as interpreted by its religious authorities. They would have spent most of their strength and attention on life's daily details, social matters, and material necessities. Like many other faithful Jews, and especially others who bore David's faint royal line, they would have set their hopes on some kind of Maccabean-style messianic deliverer sent by heaven to make things right again for their people. They would have had their hearts and bodies broken by the world's cruel realities, which were far crueler in their day than ours. Mary's last years would likely have been lived as a widow, in poverty, though supported by the tenuous social security system of a modest-of-means Jewish family, until her rendezvous with destiny in a grave.

Not a bad life, especially by the standards of the day. Not easy, but something to look back on with satisfaction and even gratitude. There is no hint of the human drama that perks up our ears—no foreshadowing of scandal, marital discord, a dysfunctional family, high-maintenance friends. While no one escapes these kinds of things entirely, the biblical texts give us no reason to anticipate them as we do with some biblical characters. By all indications, Mary was headed for a good life.

But an unremarkable and a conventional one, and an old cloak compared to what Jesus's coming would bring.

Could such a significant woman have had such modest origins? Many have doubted it. A long Christian tradition glorifies Mary's beginnings instead. The (probably second-century) Protevangelium of James supplies traditions about her wealthy yet willingly ascetic father, Joachim, and her intense yet steadfast mother, Anne. We learn that their lives paralleled those of Samuel's parents, Elkanah and Hannah. We read about Mary's first birthday being celebrated throughout Jerusalem, and about her childhood serving in the temple and being fed by angels. We find that an angel arranged her marriage. This life was already quite remarkable indeed. In fact, her story is too remarkable to harmonize completely with the canonical Gospels. Nevertheless, despite early doubts about this apocryphal text's authenticity, it became influential in both the Christian East and West. When you look at a Renaissance painting of the annunciation or the nativity, you are probably seeing details from the Protevangelium.

Do you believe these legends? Frankly, they bring out the Protestant in me. However, the apocryphal depictions of Mary that seem so different from the canonical ones are still helpful for my purposes. Mary's canonical and apocryphal versions span the spectrum of faithfulness that runs from the low and obscure ends of her society to its highest and most glamorous and beyond. In Matthew, Mary is a meek and silent young woman dutifully coping with life's exigencies in a world of male protectors and persecutors. In Luke, she is an advocate for her people, curious and a little edgy, not unlike Moses. In the Protevangelium, she ranks up there with Rachel, Hannah, Samuel, and Elijah, managing to echo all of them by the time she became a teenager. Yet even such an elevated childhood didn't burst the engorged wineskins of Jewish antiquity. Apocryphal Mary's character fits comfortably within the categories of Hellenized Second Temple Judaism. To be sure, she was a sparkling jewel of her people's social and religious elite rather than a virtuous but invisible commoner. But even apocryphal Mary still lived an old-fashioned, old-style life under the sun.

Jesus's arrival means a departure from Mary's old humanity that is as radical for the apocryphal version as the canonical one. However extraordinary her childhood *might* have been, her perplexity at Gabriel's words in Luke 1 was still genuine, and the Holy Spirit's work still profoundly mysterious. However carefully and thoroughly her purity *might* have been protected (the Protevangelium claims, and Catholic and Orthodox traditions maintain, that she retained virginity and a virgin's physiology despite delivering Jesus and marrying Joseph), she still faced an unprecedented life as a wife and mother.

Whether Mary's beginnings under the sun were plain and unnoticed or miraculous and dazzling, her vocation as the mother of God left them far behind for new human cloth and wine.

But when did Mary's life begin to follow that new trajectory? Christmastime can bring on the impression that the incarnation of the Word *in itself* transformed everything. Icons portray the Christ child securely in the arms of regal and serene Mary.[4] As we will see, the reality depicted in the Gospels is more complicated. The Gospels suggest that while the Lord's conception and birth *ground* his new alpha for humanity, they do not by themselves *constitute* it, even for Mary.

## Family, Old and New

The time from the prophets until John the Baptist was for preparing and waiting for that promised new heavens and earth (Matt. 11:7–19). This usually meant settling down: building houses, planting fields, having families, and nurturing communities.[5] It meant continuing the long covenantal line of Abraham (1:1–17). It meant raising new generations—one of the pervasive human concerns that crosses eras and cultures.

Raising posterity involves much more than just acquiring the bare necessities; in our competitive world it calls for striving to improve one's family position. It means all the conscious and unconscious calculus involved in finding a livelihood, winning an advantageous mate for oneself and improving the children's prospects, struggling to move up the social ladder, cultivating a family ethos, and securing a durable legacy.

Conventional long-term thinking takes a temporary back seat for interruptions, when what Greeks called a *kairos* moment arrives. A *kairos* suspends *chronos*'s steady flow. We pause or even end the normal course of our lives to cope with a crisis or seize an extraordinary opportunity. These can be little emergencies that override life's ordinary priorities ("If any of you has a sheep and it falls into a pit on the Sabbath, will you not take hold of it and lift it out?" Matt. 12:11 NIV) or they can be historical cataclysms that change our lives forever and reverberate for millennia ("Flee for your lives! Don't look back, and don't stop anywhere in the plain!" Gen. 19:17 NIV).

However, these interruptions aren't alphas. After the moment has passed, life goes back to normal. Life after Sodom was like life before Sodom, just not in Sodom itself. The same was true of life on both sides of Noah's flood and both sides of Babel's fall. Luke makes this point by tracing Jesus's genealogy back all the way to Adam (Luke 3:23–38). For every *kairos* that came and went, what really changed? Afterward, people's ordinary priorities always returned to establishing their livelihoods, marrying and giving in marriage,

4. Protestants should be aware that icons portray the theological significance with embellishments of historical scenes. This iconographic convention does not automatically satisfy the objection that this makes them inaccurate.

5. E.g., Deut. 30:8–10; Prov. 24:27; Jer. 29:5–7; Mic. 2:2.

rooting themselves securely in communities, and leaving a significant legacy. Under the sun, nothing new.

Inside this old framework, once in a while a truly eternal *kairos* would beckon. God's first word to Abram commanded him to leave behind the legacy he built on and enter a new land and life where he would father a nation and bless all the families of the earth (Gen. 12:1–3). The childless seventy-five-year-old promptly set out. The *kairos* of Isaac's birth proved that an alpha was approaching. Yet it wasn't the alpha itself. Abraham settled down again, at the Lord's command (20:15; 21:34). Israel was leading to something new, but only leading. Abraham and many later generations of faithful ones "were all commended for their faith, yet none of them received what had been promised" (Heb. 11:39 NIV).

Luke 1–2 is electric with the expectation of the *kairos* of Israel's newborn king, and Matthew 2 is heavy with its turbulence and trauma. Humanity's alpha loomed just ahead, tantalizingly near. When Mary received the news, she knew without even being told that it was the omega of her people's generations of waiting. So, like Abram, she left for Judea to stay with Elizabeth (Luke 1:39–40, 56) and prepare to bring Israel's messiah into the world. She also returned home, as Abram had, after her few months with Elizabeth (1:56).

Then—and this is surprising—everyone drifted back to waiting. Mary's alpha remained a ways off. Thirty more years of life's same old *chronos* ticked away under the sun. Mary and Jesus would still be part of a family with a husband and other sons and daughters (of some sort, anyway). Moreover, Jesus's neighbors regarded his family as conventional (13:54–56). Did his own family members think so too? It seems so, at least to a point, because Jesus's later ministry made no sense to the brothers and sisters who had grown up with him. In fact, his mother went with them to confront him (Mark 3:20–21, 31–35). These odd scenes, and the tense exchange in John 2:1–4, are Mary's main appearances in the space between Jesus's baptism and his death. How is this? If Jesus's birth was humanity's alpha (Matt. 1:23; Rev. 12:5), how did she not know?

Mary must have known *that* it was, but apparently not *how* it was. Jesus surprised even her. The one reported exchange between Jesus's infancy and his baptism, when he was twelve (Luke 2:48–51), foreshadowed—but only foreshadowed—the shocks and personal transformations that started after Jesus was baptized. Jesus's baptism ripped through his old family like, well, fermenting wine exploding a stiff wineskin. The Father called him, at the age of thirty, to go south to seek John's symbol of renewal. Soon the Holy Spirit led him on a mission to ransom Israel's lost sheep. He returned to his home territory and went to work. A deliberate distance now opened up in his family relations. The glue that had always held together human communities was too fragile and feeble to accommodate humanity's future. Jesus announced that he had come to bring not peace among family members but a sword to make them enemies (Matt. 10:34–36).

Modernity has been disintegrating our family structures for centuries, and his words are still shockingly strong. Even in an American culture that treats family far more casually than Mary's did, we know that personal and societal flourishing depends on stable, healthy family relationships. Nonetheless—or therefore—families are among those old wineskins that the Kingdom's expansive energy will burst.

Family structures are human fundamentals. Modern and postmodern experiments in replacing family as the primary element of successful human nurture have repeatedly failed. Self, state, peers, affinity groups, careers, and so-called "communities" of identity are ever-popular substitutes, but in most of the world family still comes first and lasts the longest. When someone is in trouble, it's usually family that musters the courage to act and has the power to intervene, just as Jesus's family did when they thought he was out of his mind (Mark 3:21). People without those relationships are terribly disadvantaged.

Yet Jesus was right that family structures are old wineskins. Like Mary, I was raised in one family that the gospel sliced through. Like Mary, I have raised another that the gospel has cut apart just as acutely. Jesus rebuffed his family's rescuing efforts, informing the crowd that his true family consists of all who do God's will (Mark 3:32–35). Mary's life under the sun as a daughter, wife, and mother was swept away—not because she was unique, though she was, and certainly not because natural families are unnecessary or bad, but because humanity had now come to its omega for her too.

Addressing the topic of wealth elsewhere, Jesus listed family among essential resources such as homes and fields (Mark 10:29–30). We count on them to live under the sun. So they preoccupy our thoughts, fill our prayers, drive our relationships, and shape our hearts. However, God's providence voids the primordial human conviction that family and family resources *come first* (Luke 14:26). Our Father understands that we need food and shelter, Jesus assured his disciples (Matt. 6:32). So we can afford to strive first for what belongs to God. In fact, we can't afford not to. We intuitively sacrifice ordinary resources for still worthier things, like a shrewd merchant does who discovers treasure hidden in a field or an extraordinary pearl up for sale (13:44–46).

That priority is integral to Jesus's teaching, but it's not an alpha. There is nothing new about it in Israel's holy tradition. Those essentials ought *never* to have come first (Deut. 8).[6] Israel's history made it painfully clear that above all we must fear God and keep his commandments (Eccles. 12:13). And Jesus's arrival didn't end those human essentials or needs. There are still homes, fields, and families on both sides of Jesus's omega and alpha, even for Mary. Life's necessities still matter, and still only as means to a much greater end.

However, the Kingdom's approach *is* a new context in which these old verities take on radical new significance. It is a *kairos* of unique and unsurpassable value. If we recognize its opportunity, we'll let go of what doesn't last anyway (Matt. 6:19–21) and joyfully make every other necessary sacrifice to avail ourselves of it (19:29). When it is boarding time, travelers must mobilize (Luke 12:29–31; 13:24 // Matt. 6:32–33; 7:13). We have to hang up and log off and unplug, pick up what we are bringing with us, leave behind the rest, and go.

Even what we hold on to changes. Now that the Kingdom's *kairos* has arrived, these resources can no longer be for maintaining a status quo while we wait for the coming age. It is one thing to build a legacy under the old arrangement. It is something else to try to continue doing so under the new arrangement, because the new arrangement *is* the legacy.

Jesus told a striking story to get this point across. There was a manager who learned that his wealthy boss was going to charge him with financial irresponsibility. His place in that old arrangement would soon end, and in condemnation. It was an old, leaky wineskin, so to speak. So the manager used his remaining time and power to make friends so he would have a new place to land. You do the same, Jesus told his disciples. Your worldly resources will soon be worthless. Use your "unrighteous wealth" while you still can to obtain the only true legacy (Luke 16:1–9).

What is true of ordinary goods applies all the more to that more sacred and precious resource, human relationships. In biblical times, ancestral lineages, royal lines, tribal identities, and the like were particularly prized. Preoccupations with these must cease in light of Jesus, because the whole *point* of biological lineage ends with his coming.[7] As Matthew 1 puts it, from Abraham to David the king there were fourteen generations, from the king to the exile there were fourteen, and from the exile to the Christ there were fourteen. It is a mistake to try to go further down the line from there. He is the omega of the lineage.

6. Maslow's hallowed hierarchy of needs notwithstanding. See Abraham Maslow, *Motivation and Personality* (New York: Harper and Brothers, 1954).

7. They did not stop mattering because Jesus had no biological children. If he had, they would not have succeeded him as king, because his reign is eternal. Besides, royal lines just route around childless people to the closest heir, and he had those.

In the same Gospel, Jesus warns us to call no one "father," for we have one Father in heaven (Matt. 23:9). That's the genealogy that finally counts: the heavenly one that begins in the Father, ends in the Son, and is shared with us through the Holy Spirit. If we are co-heirs of the Father, who even cares about our earthly tribe? So Paul considers his fine breeding worthless compared to knowing Christ (Phil. 3:3–8), and he advises Timothy to pay no attention to people who occupy themselves with endless genealogies (1 Tim. 1:4). It is not that they waste time on trivial hobbies. The problem is that they profoundly misunderstand the times. Lineage found its omega. And its alpha, for its ending was also a beginning, a "genesis" (Matt. 1:1).[8] Jesus is now the firstborn of many brothers and sisters, Paul says in Romans 8:29. When we gain Christ, we gain a new family and a new lineage: sibling of Jesus, heir of the Father, enough said. To add anything to this is to take away everything, because it is to revert to the old and vain humanity.

Some Christians call Mary "mother." They are applying the Kingdom's logic to her natural family relations. The Kingdom's alpha for humanity concludes the old purposes of relationships of biological age, lineage, and other ordinary social structures, but it does not annihilate the relationships themselves. Joseph remained Mary's husband, Joachim and Anna her parents, Jesus her son, and so on. Luke notes that she and other natural family members were with the disciples gathering and praying. However, Luke lists them *last*, not first—after the apostles and the other disciples (Acts 1:14). Another family had come into view as Mary grasped the significance of her son Jesus. It was new humanity's supernatural family. The old blood relationship between Jesus and his biological kin persisted, but it no longer defined them. Mary's new family is founded on blood, but *shed* blood, which has joined her to all others whom Jesus has made his brothers and sisters in one new humanity (Eph. 2:15).

I have a biological family, and we members of that family are immensely significant to each other. Mary has one too. In the upper room in Jerusalem she is gathered with the apostles *and Jesus's brothers* (Acts 1:14). One of them is James. Like Mary, apparently James saw something new from a distance at some point in Jesus's ministry that he had missed back when they were growing up under the sun and under the same roof. Now he is "the Lord's brother" (Gal. 1:19) in more ways than one. His title in Galatians demonstrates that the old way persists. And according to the Gospel of John, Mary has gained a new son alongside those. "Woman, behold, your son," Jesus said to

---

8. Christopher J. H. Wright, *Knowing Jesus through the Old Testament*, 2nd ed. (Downers Grove, IL: IVP Academic, 2014), 7.

her from the cross; and, "Behold, your mother," he told his beloved disciple (John 19:26–27).

Traditional Catholics and Orthodox extend this logic to all of Jesus's disciples, seeing Mary as *our* Lady who mothers her Son's whole church. Conservative Protestants tend to restrict it to the one person whom she takes into her own home to support and be supported by. In their different ways, both groups understand that Mary has a new-human family, not just an old-human one. Jesus does not say, "Behold your brother, behold your sister." He doesn't need to; they already know. Within the Kingdom's new context, he is instituting a human relationship rooted in the old arrangement. His word of command joins Mary to a fellow disciple Jesus has taken on as a brother. After all, old people and young people still need another's care. Human dependencies obviously haven't come to an end.

The New Testament letters feature "household codes," rules and advice for how relationships like these can function fruitfully in the Kingdom's new context. They are forever being misunderstood by both Christians and skeptics who fail to appreciate the redefining role of that context. Children today still need parents to raise them—but not so they can cooperate to build a vain legacy that has already been superseded (Eph. 6:1–4; Col. 3:20–21; 1 Tim. 3:4–5). Husbands and wives need one another's love, respect, and faithfulness—but not so they can harness Darwinian biological forces to advantage their genes or even themselves (Eph. 5:22–33; Col. 3:18–19; 1 Tim. 3:2), or even just so they can just enjoy the pleasures of life's fleeting youth and help one another cope with the onset of old age (Eccles. 11:8–12:8). Christian families are still families, but they have been repurposed in far-reaching ways.

When we Christians appeal to one another as Christians—whether to fellow Christians within our families and local congregations, to "Mother Mary," or to heavenly patron saints—I suspect that often we're projecting old-human dynamics onto these relationships rather than truly perceiving their revolutionary new character. What *kind* of mother to us is Mary? Not the old kind. Old humanity is sustained and governed by relationships of reciprocal obligation toward fellow insiders that are not fully extended, and cannot be, toward all outsiders. Corruption is endemic because we exercise this double standard *sinfully*. We violate our obligations to outsiders for the sake of insiders. This abuses our reciprocal obligations to both sets of people.

It's tempting to respond by rejecting the double standard altogether. But we deny the essential distinctions between insiders and outsiders at our peril. It is wrong to neglect a widow, orphan, or impoverished stranger (James 1:27–2:9), but I cannot be the father to my children's peers that I am to my children, nor can I expect them to be children to me. I should move lovingly in that direction to some extent, especially as God directs, but even then I can move only so far before straining inherent limits and jeopardizing both people and relationships. The solution is to exercise these necessary double standards righteously.

Among Christians, corruption remains endemic. There seem to be two reasons for this scandalous situation. First, we continue to abuse old humanity's lingering necessary double standards rather than bringing Christ's righteousness to them. Second, we project old-human qualities onto new-human relationships. The result is syncretism rather than omega-alpha transformation.

People everywhere seek "blessing" through holy people, places, and practices. If I want some *berakah*, I visit a shrine, say a prayer to some powerful someone, sacrifice an animal, light a candle or burn a stick of incense, offer money or a promise, kiss an icon, spin a prayer wheel, buy a statue, receive a sacrament—whatever thickens the obligations of our insider relationship. You've got my back now, right? Surely you wouldn't let me down.

If I needed a favor from a relative, my actions wouldn't be that different. I might not burn incense, but I'd do something nice. This is more *mercy by works* than *justification by works*. You don't *owe* me exactly; I couldn't take you to court and collect. But in practice the distinction gets murky. After all, isn't a *quid* from you the right thing after that *quo* from me? In ordinary life it sure is, and people who don't sow under the sun end up regretting it when they can't reap.

Many Christians treat saints this way, including Mary. Why wouldn't they? It's what they know. When they pray "Hail Mary," they anticipate better lives under the sun rather than envisioning the dynamics of the Kingdom. They may not even be aware of the difference.

In the Christian world, corruption is by and large lower in historically Protestant countries, where invocation of the saints was discouraged.[9] I doubt that this is coincidental. Now there are many underlying factors to consider, and correlation doesn't mean causation, and Protestant Christianity is clearly neither a panacea nor an instant cure. (Newly Christian societies and church scandals in the global South demonstrate that evangelical faith doesn't quickly overturn cultural corruption. In fact, the prosperity gospel's worldwide popularity shows that restricting our insider-exchanges to Jesus alone doesn't extinguish the mindset.) Nevertheless, at the very least, the correlation demonstrates that our traditions of invoking other members of

9. See, for instance, Transparency International's "Corruption Perceptions Index 2017," https://www.transparency.org/news/feature/corruption_perceptions_index_2017.

Christ's supernatural new family haven't effectively restrained our abuse of old humanity's proper double standards. The opposite seems to have happened: these practices supply ways for us to hold on to our old mindset and extend its abuses *to* our supernatural family.

Jesus refused to play our *berakah* game. Obedience to his Father's will defines family (Matt. 12:49–50). And his Father wills sacrificial love even to enemies, not just to old or even new insiders (5:43–48, though new insiders are still a special focus in 25:40). Here reciprocity works differently: having received God's grace, we pass it on to any and all (6:12–15, though fellow servants are still a special focus in 18:32–33). God has our backs, so we have others'. Mary's motherhood has been repurposed and reframed under these new family rules. Christians who invoke her and other saints for the old reasons, or invoke Jesus for that matter (7:18–23), do so in vain. They put themselves as well as the church's credibility in grave danger.

Every fixture of human life under the sun is similarly repurposed for the Kingdom. Peter Kreeft, as we saw above in our discussion of Ecclesiastes, labels the Preacher's list as wisdom, pleasure, wealth, power, duty, altruism, social service, honor, piety, and religion.[10] Jesus is each one's omega and alpha. To treat each topic in turn would be repetitive and tedious; besides, family is a mighty nexus of most of them anyway. The mother of God exchanged her old wardrobe—whether it was humble or glorious doesn't matter that much—for the new cloak that lay beyond the Preacher's imagination.

Yet we shouldn't skate too quickly past that last item on Kreeft's list: religion. Religion is a persistent feature of human life under the sun, and not just the idolatrous variety, but also recognition of the true God (Eccles. 3:9–15). We saw its underappreciated importance to the world and its toppled ruler. A fuller treatment will have to wait until the chapters on Israel and the nations. But as we have Mary in our sights, it is instructive to see how Jesus has transformed her religion. The Gospels introduce Mary as a character whom John Howard Yoder characterizes as "a Maccabean."[11] She was so immersed in Jewish messianic expectation of "radical social change" that the vocabulary of Hannah, mother of Samuel the prophetic revolutionary, poured readily out of her mouth in the Magnificat (Luke 1:46–55). She was ready for a life that would no longer be vain and under the sun. However, Mary quieted down as Jesus's surprising ministry unfolded, as thoughtful people do when confronted by something genuinely new. We last see her after Jesus's resurrection praying

10. Kreeft, *Three Philosophies of Life*, 35, 37.
11. John Howard Yoder, *The Politics of Jesus*, rev. ed. (Grand Rapids: Eerdmans, 1994), 21–22.

with the other disciples (Acts 1:14): she remained faithful. But her community changed, and *was* changed, into something quite new. And over the course of Acts, it continued to develop into a far-flung multiethnic fellowship that far outgrew the expectations and horizons of Mary's youth. Whatever she became, she was no longer a conventional Maccabean, because that school of eschatology was an old wineskin too.

Orthodox and Catholic traditions portray Mary's religion with greater intensity, on both sides of the rupture. In her childhood she was a flower of a Judaism longing for deliverance; in eternity she is the mother of God, co-redemptrix, and queen of heaven. What on earth happened in between? "Deification," these Christians call it. Mary had exemplified the old human-ity at its faithful best, and now she exemplifies the new humanity that Jesus has pioneered and perfected (Heb. 12:1–2), a new humanity that has been invited into the holy triune fellowship that incarnation opened to creation.

These depictions seem like vastly different pictures. However, they share considerable common ground. In both the canonical and the traditional por-trayals, Mary is an early and honored beneficiary of humanity's ascension, through Jesus Christ, to life from beyond the sun. Either way, Mary is a leading indicator of humanity's new life as the Kingdom's beneficiaries.

### From Evolved Humanity to New Humanity

Mary is but one of the many glimpses God has given us of that new life. We still live under the sun, of course, but differently now, because these glimpses from beyond have birthed in us the new and living hope of that future (1 Pet. 1:1–5). Like children counting the days until Christmas morn-ing comes and we can finally open the boxes with our names on them, we await an imperishable inheritance that will someday be revealed to everyone. This so occupies our thoughts—or should, anyway—that we feel "exiled" in our old present circumstances. But this detachment doesn't paralyze us, at least not if we're thinking about it in the right way. Peter perceives that it frees us to sojourn through life under the sun with radically new thoughts and actions:

> For Christ also died for sins once for all, the righteous for the unrighteous, that he might bring us to God. . . . Jesus Christ . . . has gone into heaven and is at the right hand of God, with angels, authorities, and powers subject to him. . . . Arm yourselves with the same thought . . . so as to live for the rest of the time in the flesh no longer by human passions but by the will of God. . . . The end of all things is at hand; therefore keep sane and sober. (1 Pet. 3:18–4:7)

This is a pervasive theme in the New Testament, and we will return to it again and again. God calls us to leave behind human passions, *epithumiai*, and approach the Lord Jesus at God's right hand. We are to set aside the under-the-sun life we could never see beyond and take on something we could never have imagined until it came to be.

The Greco-Roman-Jewish world of Peter's day intuitively associated *epithumiai* with humanity's "lower" nature, and virtue and character with its "higher" nature. Modern thinkers from Hegel to Darwin to Freud have trained us to approach human desires differently. Nevertheless, Peter's advice remains sound. It grasps the existential import of humanity's omega and alpha.

I'm influenced by some of these modern thinkers, so I don't think the human traits that Peter calls *epithumiai* simply follow wholesale from our fall from grace. We perceive them already in life's distant past and in humanity as portrayed before our rebellion against God's mission (Gen. 2:23–25). Genesis 1–2, Psalm 104, and Proverbs 8 all regard this natural state as good, even though it features some of these traits that Peter wants us to leave behind. Scientifically speaking, evolutionary theory accounts rather thoroughly, and to me persuasively, for many if not all of them. Many of our longings carry considerable survival value. It is not hard to see how prehuman and prehistorical struggles under the sun should have encouraged and shaped our appetites and self-interest, our sense of justice and outrage at injury, our limited social loyalties and sympathies, and our longings and attractions. We perceive these in other animals inhabiting what we call "God's good creation," especially in the species that are humanity's closest relatives; and other species perceive them in us.

What should people do with these traits? Tame them with discipline? Remove them with logic? Spurn them with spiritualism? Embrace them with romanticism? Exploit them with pragmatism? The question splits us today like it split the ancient Greeks into rival philosophical schools. In learned circles today we tend to approach them as objects of neuropsychological, physiological, and social analysis and classify them with technical vocabularies. The results sound impressive and they make headlines, but it's not clear that these "discoveries" are yielding much insight beyond those of the ancient Greeks.[12]

12. Here is a recent example from my electronic bookshelf. For over a year Scott Adams analyzed the 2016 presidential race in terms of persuasion rather than policy. For example, his July 18, 2016, entry "How Persuaders See the World" (*Scott Adams's Blog*, http://blog.dilbert .com/2016/07/18/how-persuaders-see-the-world/) is an insightful "scientific" exposure of human irrationality. He describes the dynamics of human thinking and persuasion, and how these dynamics can be exploited. This is what the New Testament labels "darkness." It takes a kind of light to illuminate human behavior like that. Adams's is a rather *persuasive* combination of Enlightenment rationality and modern rhetorical technique. But it is more like a candle than

Of course, it is too simple to chalk everything up to evolution or primordial human physicality. Humanity's old nature can't be reduced to natural causes and forces. Genesis 1–2 artfully depicts humanity receiving a unique call and responsibility to image *God*, an uncreated being who neither evolved nor conformed to the conditions of material life under the sun. This suggests a standard for human behaviors and character that is not available in nature, as well as a supernatural source—relationship with God—of qualities that meet that standard. And Genesis 3 depicts humanity's subsequent and universal refusal to meet that standard in good faith, adding the further complicating factor of disordering sin on every aspect of fallen human life. The further covenantal arrangements under which human beings survived, adapted, and waited for better conditions, and our further betrayals, add more and more messiness. Human desires are involved in ordinary created life, God's "upward" call toward something new, and sin's "downward" pull away.

All these nuances still do not prevent Paul from characterizing every generation from Adam through Abraham and Moses to the present in blunt terms: we have lived in the flesh (e.g., Rom. 4:1; 7:5; 8:4), set our minds on the things of the flesh (8:5–7), and gratified its *epithumiai* (Gal. 5:16), with fatal consequences. Sin found opportunities to exploit *epithumiai* in every divine call, human rebellion, and covenantal provision (Rom. 7:11).[13]

And righteousness will find opportunities to restore and sanctify them. We see *epithumiai* righteously celebrated in the Psalms and Song of Songs, and present in Jesus and his holy ones (Luke 17:22; 22:15; Heb. 6:11). But I am getting ahead of myself again. Their omega comes first.

## Passions Remade

Peter reminds the exiles of the "futile ways" they inherited from their ancestors (1 Pet. 1:18). Whatever utility those ways might have under the sun is irrelevant to the Kingdom's new context. It is not enough just to remove sin's

---

sunlight. It doesn't penetrate the darkness but only exposes its vastness. Adams is a postmodern sophist. As the Enlightenment fails to accomplish its aims, it is mainly exposing its own limitations: *Human minds aren't that rational! Then how rational is our rationality? Education and technique and policy cannot counter the mass effects of human appetites and mental quirks.* The faint light of natural reason isn't enough to dispel the darkness. So the darkness *is* overcoming it, tempting us to despair as one does after lighting a candle in vast darkness.

Christ operating in the context of quirky *and* fallen human thinking is also light in darkness. But Jesus's coming is a different kind of light: full sunlight that radiates to our perceptual limits and beyond—light that humanity's darkness cannot overwhelm.

13. Paul testifies that he hadn't known covetousness (*epithumia*) until he learned that the law said "you shall not covet [*epithumēseis*]" (Deut. 5:21 LXX, quoted in Rom. 7:7).

stain when old deeds, habits, and instincts shaped to serve in those obsolete environments are out of place anyway. Those old wineskins will only burst if we try to adapt them.

Peter says Jesus bore those ways in his crucified body so that we would die to them too (1 Pet. 2:24). Not that *they* would die to *us*, but that we, much more radically, would die to them. Those passions are still around, still structuring the old world, but in death and rebirth we have passed beyond that world's grip.

Paul puts the great divide more baldly: Jesus is the omega of what Paul calls "the old human being with its practices" (Col. 3:9, my translation; cf. Rom. 6:6) and the alpha of the new one (Col. 3:10), renewed to walk in newness of life (Rom. 6:4). *We ourselves* are old cloaks and spent wineskins. You can't teach an old person new tricks, so to speak; that person must be born again to enter the Kingdom of God (John 3:5). God had to dispose of our old nature and start again. So he put Jesus forward as the necessary vessel for its disposal.

Disposal doesn't just happen by itself, though. The world's vices don't just fall away from humanity, and the Kingdom's virtues don't just shoot up. Human will plays a vital role in humanity's end and new beginning in Jesus Christ. Jesus *teaches* us to shed our old human being of disordered *epithumiai*, to be renewed in mind and spirit, and to put on the new Christlike human of genuine righteousness and holiness (Eph. 4:22–24). The old is still there, but Jesus has not simply confiscated it. The new is now here, but Jesus has not forced it on us. *We* walk by the Spirit by whom we live; *we* crucify our flesh with its *epithumiai* (Gal. 5:16–25).

Will manifests itself in concrete human lives and human communities, the topics of later chapters. For now it is enough to affirm that some proportion of people who encounter Jesus *do* will to walk by the Spirit and crucify the flesh. Whatever the reason, the gospel's course in the world produces a harvest of new humanity. This is still true whether that proportion is 9 in 10 or 1 in 10,000, and whether or not you or I are among them.

It is astonishing that the New Testament letters can already outline the shape of that new humanity after only a few decades of observing its beginnings. Apparently the results were already impressive. Here is just one juxtaposition:

| Ephesians 2 | Ephesians 3 |
| --- | --- |
| "dead through the trespasses and sins in which we once walked" (vv. 1–2) | "strengthened with might through his Spirit in the inner human being" (v. 16) |

| Ephesians 2 | Ephesians 3 |
| --- | --- |
| "following the course of this world" (v. 2) | "rooted and grounded in love" (v. 17) |
| "following the prince of the power of the air" (v. 2) | "filled with all the fulness of God" (v. 19) |
| "sons of disobedience" (v. 2) | "Christ [dwelling] in hearts through faith" (v. 17) |
| "we all once lived in the passions of our flesh, following the desires [*epithumiai*] of body and mind" (v. 3) | "power to comprehend with all the saints what is the breadth and length and height and depth" (v. 18) |
| "by nature children of wrath, like the rest" (v. 3) | "know[ing] the love of Christ which surpasses knowledge" (v. 19) |

Such dramatically different lives oriented toward drastically different ends! Ephesians 2's description calls to mind scraggly thornbushes and tumbleweeds, while Ephesians 3's evokes images of majestic cedars. The contrast begs an objection: If this is true, how come the world's supposedly "new" Christians often live such ugly lives, especially compared to the inspiring lives of some of the supposedly "old" non-Christians? It's a formidable objection.

In outward appearance, these two groups may not contrast all that starkly. For instance, there are all the people who take on the mantle of Christianity and say "Lord, Lord" but ignore—or never learn—the Father's will (Matt. 7:13–27). They claim a reorientation, but their fruits show them up as nothing but rehashed old humanity.[14] Jesus anticipated this objection right away, calling these people weeds growing among his wheat, and warning us that they will be denied the Kingdom's inheritance and thrown away. Paul delivered the same warning about people whose lives continue to be characterized by old-human practices that are inappropriate for Kingdom heirs (1 Cor. 6:9–11).

Old humanity is caught up in a struggle between the twin legacies of created human goodness and sinful depravity.[15] To empirically trained eyes, an

14. For instance, the Institute for Family Studies points out that in a recent study of correlations between faith and divorce rates, "communities with large concentrations of conservative Protestants actually produce higher divorce rates than others." However, the depth of faith commitment is all important as "active conservative Protestants are statistically no more likely to have divorced in the first few years of marriage than their active peers from other Christian denominations, and both groups who attend church frequently are significantly less likely to have divorced than their non-religious peers. The group that stands out . . . is the nominal conservative Protestants, the *most* likely group to have divorced." Charles E. Stokes, "Findings on Red and Blue Divorce Are Not Exactly Black and White," Institute for Family Studies, January 22, 2014, https://ifstudies.org/blog/findings-on-red-and-blue-divorce-are-not-exactly-black-and-white.

15. For a particularly insightful account of this, see Robert Barron, *And Now I See: A Theology of Transformation* (New York: Crossroad, 1998), part 1.

"Ephesians 2 life" can look pretty good. It is mature and well adapted to the harsh landscape of the old order, like a windswept and grizzled coastal tree perched on the precipice of an eroding cliff. And an "Ephesians 3 life" can look like a mess, since the old legacy's momentum resists the still emerging and contrary reorientation to the Kingdom's still-coming legacy. It is newly germinated and struggling to grow into surroundings that are themselves only partially realized, a verdant but fragile seedling springing up from the decomposing hulk of that fallen old giant. In fact, as long as the old setting persists, it may not ever match the first tree's conventional beauty.

None of these considerations contradict the descriptions in Ephesians, but they may help us not to read too much into them.

## Ultimate Humans

The qualities of that outwardly inconsequential little seedling hint at humanity's final mature shape. Christians love to talk about "new life in Christ." However, many have no idea of how truly new that new life really is. New humanity is newly ruled and no longer enslaved to our own *epithumiai*. As usual, Jesus presents a clear picture.

The opening chapters of Hebrews sample the Psalms in order to do something no Jew ever grew up expecting to do: glorify a human being. Why? Because this human being was faithful to the Lord, who appointed him over the house they had created together (Heb. 1:2; 3:5). As a result, he became as superior to angels as the name he received (1:4). This human was crowned with glory and honor and set above all things to control them (2:7–9). Through suffering he pioneered others' salvation and glorification, was perfected himself, and remains merciful even now (2:10–18). Jesus blazed the eternal human trail that we, through his grace, can follow. His suffering faithfulness, loving sympathy, honorable authority, and perfect glory are previews of humanity's new and eternal life (12:1–3).

It shocks my students sometimes when I say that to be holy is to become *more* human, not less. They say, "Wait! To err is human!" The second half of that line, "to forgive is divine," proves that the first half refers to *moral* error. Jesus's life revealed something else: we're just very poor at *being* human. It puts an end to what's wrong with humanity, not humanity as such. It's the omega of human sin and human death, and of the false impression that such things ever described what it means to be human. It's the beginning of righteousness and life—what it means to be truly and fully human. Sanctification (what some Christians call *theosis*) is humanity increasing and intensifying.

The saints are *more* human than I am. Sin, death, and the unholy ruler of this world stand in contrast. They face Christ's omega without living hope in his alpha. To try to add human nature to this refuse pile is a fundamental category mistake. Yet even Christians keep making it.

Where the human path finally ends is a topic of endless speculation in and out of Christian circles. Three related outcomes recur in biblical treatments: life, fruitfulness, and exaltation. Each is repeatedly contrasted with its opposite: death, disposal, and reclamation, respectively.

> For God so loved the world that he gave his only begotten Son, that whoever believes in him should not *perish* but have *eternal life*. (John 3:16)

> To every one who has will more be given, and he [or she] will have *abundance*; but from him who has not, even what he has will be taken away. And cast the *worthless* servant into the outer darkness; there men will weep and gnash their teeth. (Matt. 25:29–30)

> Your life is hid with Christ in God. When Christ who is our life appears, then you also will appear with him in *glory*. Put to death therefore what is earthly in you. . . . On account of these the *wrath* of God is coming. (Col. 3:3–6)

All of these are personal destinies. They describe what lies at the end of those wide and narrow roads. Jesus is the omega of what comes to be dead, worthless, and condemned and the alpha of what is alive, productive, and glorious.

A cluster of biblical images makes each pair vivid and compelling. The first pertains to humanity's intrinsic yet necessarily gifted quality of being alive. Sheol and Hades image the realm of death, whereas the river and tree of life in new Jerusalem image eternal life. The second pertains to humanity's capacity to beget, create, and nurture. Outer darkness and the incinerating fires of gehenna conjure up the discarding of useless things, whereas employment, the storehouse and treasury, and vineyard are centers of worth and fruitfulness. The third pertains to human belonging and loyalty. The lake of fire signifies *cherem* and *anathema*, God's wrathful foreclosure to repossess what is rightfully his,[16] whereas the Spirit's temple, bride and banquet, crown of righteousness, and shared throne of Jesus symbolize exaltation and glory.

---

16. *Anathema* is the Septuagint's translation of *cherem* in Josh. 6–7 and Zech. 14:11. It is applied to Israelite rivals such as the Amalekites in the Former Prophets but to wayward Israel in the Latter Prophets (Isa. 43:28). It is not a stretch to hear echoes in Paul. *Cherem*'s connotation moves the image beyond wrath as vengeful punishment out of emotion to an act of definitive and final reclamation of wayward possessions—which is still essentially different from both withdrawing life and discarding refuse.

Heaven captures the heart of all three positives, not as some final destination for disembodied human souls as so many suppose, but as the Lord's headquarters to and from which flow glory, service, and life. Hell comes to represent the Lord's place of banishment—or footstool of forcible subjection (Ps. 110:1)—of seizure and condemnation, futility and disposal, and death.

A headache for my field of theology is that these clusters do not necessarily cohere. Actually, that's only half true. The positive clusters do cohere. There is no tension in being abundantly alive, prodigiously fruitful, and gloriously exalted. Jesus is demonstrably all three. It is the negative clusters that don't hang together. How does eternal repossession square with disposal? How can burned-away chaff and lifeless bodies be punished everlastingly? This puzzle has frustrated systematicians who approach biblical portrayals of human futures literally and analytically. The negative symbols don't seem to converge in the way that the positive ones converge on the risen and ascended Jesus Christ.

Some would turn this puzzle into an invitation to favor some of these images over others or select which to take seriously: annihilation over torment, for instance, or vice versa. But the biblical witness is shot through with all three. In being selective, we would only trade the fullness of Jesus for a thinner abstraction that is more to our own particular liking. Others force them together anyway, while still others plead "metaphor" and "mystery" and back away. Instead, let's follow this wrinkled logic all the way to its clear implication.

God's creation doesn't feature two coherent centers, one good and the other evil. It can't. Such a universe would have two causes, or else "one" cause that would itself be incoherent. Humanity's two possible destinations are not symmetrical like that, because a life has one Creator. It comes from one God and through one Lord (1 Cor. 8:5–6). Jesus is creation's sole focal point. Every alternative is necessarily unfocused, off-center, and unstable—a *wide* way, not another narrow one.

What word should we use to describe it? If "Christ" sums up and focuses all things, including the personal lives of Mary and all the rest of us, then the only single word that could ever sum up all of its unfocused, unstable, eccentric alternatives would be *antichrist*. And despite its popular usage, that term does not refer to *one* thing but *many* (1 John 2:18): not an alternative order but chaos. The Bible's disintegrated images for them are the right way to represent that awful outcome of lives unraveled.

Christ's grace and truth don't just "save" human persons; they *humanize* and *personalize* those who are otherwise headed for dissolution. I don't mean to suggest that only saints are persons or human beings, but becoming a saint is the only alternative to the destruction we experience along the wide road.

It's the only way for us to *stay* persons and come into our own *as* persons. The rekindling, restoring, and consummation of our lives is the new life that is not just imaginable in metaphors but already concretely visible and describable in the risen Jesus and in the life of every saint who is growing up into him.

All this notwithstanding, human imaginations are captivated by a picture of the human spirit living on as a ghost after it escapes the body at death. It's amazing that so many Christians think of the church as headed not for bodily resurrection but for a permanently disembodied life in heaven—trying to sit on clouds when we have no backsides, wear robes when we have no shoulders, and play harps when we have no fingers. It is amazing because the whole New Testament teaches *and* demonstrates otherwise. Even if there *are* such things as ghosts and spirits (cf. Mark 6:49; Acts 12:15), Jesus expressed humanity's true embodied future. He was the first to inherit "new creation" as creation's Redeemer, and he rules over it as its Lord; and when we see him, we will be like him (1 John 3:2). Jesus's apostles taught that those who die in Christ receive the kind of bodies that Jesus enjoys in his resurrection. Nothing over the centuries has changed that.

Paul wants the Christians in Corinth to be sure of that trajectory too, so they don't get stuck in either Qoheleth's mortal-body-under-the-sun mindset or their traditional Greek disembodied-soul-over-the-sun mindset. So he reminds them that their bodies are of God's making: "The first human, Adam, became a living soul" (1 Cor. 15:45, my translation; quoting Gen. 2:7 LXX). Then Paul adds his own postscript to that verse from Genesis: "The *last* Adam became a life-giving spirit. . . . As was the human of dust, so are those who are of the dust. As is the human of heaven, so are those who are of heaven" (1 Cor. 15:45–48 RSV alt.). We are humans of dust, which in itself is a good thing, even if sin ruined it; but we are becoming humans of heaven, which is a much better thing. "Just as we have borne the image of the human of dust, we shall also bear the image of the human of heaven" (15:49 NRSV alt.).

The "first Adam" was the beginning of what we might call Humanity 1.0: old humanity. The first human came from the earth's dust, ushered in sin and death, and returned to dust. We share in that old humanity. But the "last Adam" is the beginning of Humanity 2.0: new humanity. He came from God's capital city, ushered in righteousness and life, and ascended to reign from there. And we share in that as well. Paul describes the risen Jesus as "the first fruits of those who have fallen asleep" (1 Cor. 15:20). A seed looks nothing like the tree that will grow from where it was planted. One kind of human body is buried—a mortal, "soulish" (*psychikos*) one—but a whole different, "spiritish" (*pneumatikos*), yet still human body is raised (15:44). So we don't leave bodily humanity behind, but live and die anticipating its perfection in us.

That is what Paul means when he tells the Colossians they can live differently, seeking Christ's ascended human life and crucifying their old earthly lives of *epithumiai* (Col. 3:1–10). Humanity 2.0 isn't *merely* our future. It is Jesus's present. Humanity 1.0 isn't *merely* our present. It is Jesus's terminated past. If we are "in Christ," then his present is ours now. If we and Jesus intersect, then his already-past oldness and present newness are syncing with our present oldness and still-future newness. As in a car's clutch, our relationship is catching us up to him. "Though our outer nature is wasting away, our inner nature is being renewed every day" (2 Cor. 4:16). As our head, Jesus is drawing us into his present. Paul and his churches are "always carrying in the body the death of Jesus, so that the life of Jesus may also be manifested in our bodies" (4:10).

In the Gospel of John, Jesus assured his worried disciples that he was going to the Father to prepare a place for them. We usually imagine great mansions in heaven that Jesus is building with his divine carpentry. However, "the Father's house with many rooms" is not some heavenly piece of real estate. It's Jesus himself. Earlier in John's Gospel, Jesus had spoken of the temple, "my Father's house," being destroyed and raised in three days. By this he meant his own body (John 2:16–22). *He* is his Father's house, heaven's embassy. Accordingly, he told his disciples that he would return "to take you to myself"—not to some other place but to himself—"that where I am you may be also" (14:1–3). Jesus is both the Father's home and ours.

Paul says very similar things. In Ephesians 2:19–20 Jesus is the cornerstone of the temple, and we are the temple built together with him. And in 2 Corinthians 5 we have an eternal building from God in the heavens, one not made with hands. (Not even Jesus's hands.) What is Paul referring to? Our bodies, both times. Our bodies are not just the tent that's destroyed; they are also our house in the heavens. Every time Paul speaks of a dwelling (*oikodomē*), it refers to Christ's body, and 2 Corinthians 5:1 is no exception. The building we have in the heavens is the risen bodily reality of Jesus himself, with which we will be further clothed when he returns to us at our personal resurrections. "While we are still in this tent, we sigh with anxiety; not that we would be unclothed"—that is, not that our souls would be separated forever from our fragile bodies, as so many Americans expect to happen when they die—"but that we would be further clothed" in that new eternal body (2 Cor. 5:4). The human future is not on some extraterrestrial or astral plane. It's Christ's new bodily humanity, which already shows up in the death-with-Christ and the life-with-Christ of the earthly sector of his church. That means the human *present* is capable of previewing that future. Having learned not to regard Jesus from a fleshly perspective, as he once had, Paul no longer regards anyone from that perspective (5:16). Jesus has supplied us with a kind of foreknowledge, now that his glorification has given away the ending of the human story.

The word *spirit* appears again and again in Paul's descriptions of new humanity. Humanity is newly spiritual. "The last Adam became a life-giving spirit"—not just someone God's breath blew life into, but a *source* of life for the dead. And since he is "spiritish" and life-giving, his body's brothers and sisters are too. This has to do with the renewal and fulfillment of the amazing human spirit that God created and destined to bear his image. It also has to do with something related but distinct: humanity's destiny as the Holy Spirit's temple. Both of these fulfill God's eternal purpose for humanity. We saw in chapter 2 that Jesus is the omega and alpha of the Holy Spirit. As the Father's heir, Jesus is the Spirit's destination, and in sharing the Spirit with the Father and with us as co-heirs, Jesus is the Spirit's origin. So new humanity lives "in the Holy Spirit."

Here are at least five ways how. (1) As the Spirit conceived the Son in the virgin Mary, so the Spirit generates believers' new beginnings.[17] (2) The Spirit is the agent of God's direct Kingdom rule, standing over Christian communities as well as private Christian consciences.[18] (3) The Spirit falls on the charismatic church to anoint its gifts, preaching, and tongues of praise.[19] (4) The Spirit in Christ's body provides its faculties of insight and discernment.[20] (5) And the living water of the Spirit flows into and through the church, bringing life to us and to the world through us.[21] The Spirit surges through the body's new-human lives of prayer, solitude, mission, sacred relationships, responses to persecution, and reconciliations. The essential contrast between old and new is so stark that to settle a theological question Paul could just ask the Galatian church an empirical one: When was it that you received the Holy Spirit? When did the evidence start piling up? Was it when you believed the good news, or was it when you started relying again on works of the Torah (Gal. 3:1–5)?

The rest of this book sketches ways that the life of Spirit-filled new humanity unfolds both under the sun and beyond. Let's close the present chapter by circling back to Mary, because we have left some significant things unsaid about her. Catholic readers may be waiting to hear them affirmed, and Protestant readers may be waiting to hear them repudiated.

---

17. John 3:8; Rom. 8:11.
18. Rom. 8:1–8; Gal. 5:16–26; Heb. 10:6–7.
19. Acts 2; Rom. 12; 1 Cor. 12–14; 2 Cor. 3:7–11.
20. John 14:15–17; 16:12–15; 1 Cor. 3:16–17; 2 Cor. 3:12–17.
21. Rom. 8:1–27; 1 Cor. 2; 2 Cor. 3:17–18; Gal. 4:6; Eph. 5:18; Rev. 22:17. We'll return to these five relationships in chap. 5.

## New Mary

Protestants treat Mary as an early recipient of the transforming grace of a personal relationship with Jesus. She looks a lot like the rest of us. She was a faithful Jew whose old life Jesus ended and began anew. She moves to the sidelines as Jesus's ministry unfolds, and we see his ministry begin to revolutionize her character and role. For whatever reason, the Bible doesn't show us much more than the early stages of that process. Accordingly, Protestants see the Mary of Orthodox and Catholic piety as overdeveloped and dangerously exaggerated, as "too much" compared to the real Mary.

Orthodox and Catholics tend to read rumblings of humanity's omega and alpha back into Mary's earlier life differently, treating her as an early recipient of sanctification and glorification in ways that sometimes wash over nearly every trace of her old humanity. For instance, Catholics teach that Mary was always free from both original and actual sin. (How else could she have been a suitable mother for her Lord?) And the third- or fourth-century *Book of Mary's Repose* depicts her earthly days as ending with the assumption of her mortal body into heaven. Catholics and Orthodox theorize that she either escaped bodily death or received an early resurrection and ascended to heaven, where she reigns and intercedes today as the queen figured in Revelation 12, and where these believers hail her in prayers from earth. The Protestant Mary seems in comparison a tragically stunted figure, "too little" compared to the real Mary.

What Orthodox and Catholics claim of Mary will eventually come true for all who are in Christ. She looks a lot like the rest of us will look after our human transformations. We will have crowns as she does. We will sit on Jesus's throne with him as she does. We will be with Jesus as she is. We will love each other powerfully and fruitfully as she does. When we see him, we will be like him. We will be sinless. We will be justified, sanctified, and glorified.

So the fundamental disagreement comes down to a question of timing. Was Mary's sinlessness an unmerited grace she enjoyed all along, or was it given to her through faith at some point in her earthly life and awaiting fulfillment on judgment day? Is she the "secondfruits" who confirms Jesus's promise to all his followers, or is she still groaning and waiting for adoption like the rest of us in Romans 8:23?

On the one hand, if Mary is placed on some different track of salvation than the rest of humanity, then something has gone badly wrong. Jesus would no longer be her omega and alpha. It might even turn both of them into gods in a nominally Christian pantheon of pagan-style gods. That happens when syncretism confuses the gospel with rival stories and co-opts it. Mary may even be at risk of being misunderstood as *Jesus's* alpha and omega—as if he needs her more than she needs him. The Qur'an disputes that kind of interpretation, implying that in Islam's early days there were people who held it. On the other hand, when Mariology over the centuries has seen her as ahead of us on the same track of salvation that runs through Jesus's life, death, and resurrection, it has been more benign and even illuminating. Dante gave her such a role in his *Purgatorio*, encouraging her children as they progress in holiness. Even if (from a Protestant perspective) this portrayal neglects her significance as a representative of *old* humanity, it does still preserve her biblical status as illustrative of all believers, indicative of our new humanity, and worth our reflection and respect.

In theological jargon, one view reflects a more futurist eschatology that sees the grand transformation coming to all of us later on, while the other reflects a more realized eschatology that envisions Mary's transformation coming earlier, beginning as early as her own conception.

The Protestant complaint, then, is not that Catholic Mary is too much but that she is too much too soon. Yes, Mary has a rich share in Christ's glory, power, and sinlessness. But did her gifts really arrive so early? Even now they may not have arrived fully. So she doesn't presently stand out from our cloud of witnesses as disproportionately as Catholics and Orthodox suppose. That is a smaller complaint.

Conversely, the Catholic and Orthodox complaint it not really that the Protestant Mary is too little but that she is too little too late. Yes, Mary is a mere human being who is no more worthy of worship than any creature. But hasn't her proximity to Jesus profoundly affected her from the beginning, with the rest of us benefiting handsomely? She's no longer back in the old life with the rest of us, if she ever was. So she does stand out from that cloud of fellow witnesses in unique and wonderful ways that Protestants haven't adequately appreciated. That's also a smaller complaint.

These are both still genuine complaints. It matters whether Mary is in a position to hear our requests and forward them to the Lord with her saintly authority, and it matters how much of our attention she rightly deserves. Seeing our contrasting Marys as mainly reflecting different eschatologies will not dissolve our differences. But it might make Mary less of a battleground and more of the blessing that God intends her to be.

Either way, it is worth keeping in mind that the Triune God is making this much of all of us . . . and in the future, far more than even that. Our inheritance is a Christmas gift to eclipse all others.

# FIVE

# Jesus—the End and the Beginning of Israel

He unrolled the scroll and found the place where it was written:

> "The Spirit of the Lord is upon me,
>     because he has anointed me
>         to bring good news to the poor.
> He has sent me to proclaim release to the captives
>     and recovery of sight to the blind,
>         to let the oppressed go free,
>     to proclaim the *year of the Lord's favor*."

And he rolled up the scroll, gave it back to the attendant, and sat down. . . . Then he began to say to them, "Today this scripture *has been fulfilled* in your hearing."

Luke 4:17–21 NRSV

From creation and then humanity, we zoom in further. We must. That's what God does, again and again. In a creation swarming with creatures, God focuses on one being and then a second (Gen. 2:5–25). In an earth filled with violence, God focuses on one favored family (6:5–13). In a world already filled with ever-branching family trees, God focuses on one elderly, childless couple (11:27–12:2). It's a scandal, "the scandal of particularity" we call it, to choose a few when so many others are there, but it's the Lord's style. And it yields one nation—alongside all the others, yet unique in having "the sonship, the glory, the covenants, the giving of the law, the worship, and the promises; to them belong the patriarchs, and of their race, according to the flesh, is the Christ" (Rom. 9:4–5). In grasping Jesus as universal omega and alpha, there's no getting around Israel and her[1] intimidating list of belongings. "You can't understand Jesus if you don't understand him as he understood himself," Lesslie Newbigin says. "He is the one in whom the whole story is fulfilled of the long, patient wrestling of God with his chosen people to make them the place where the holiness of God and the sinfulness of men would meet and the final victory would be won. What Jesus did was the decisive turning-point of the whole story of creation and of humanity, the point from which every human being must in the end take their bearings."[2]

The New Testament sees the Messiah's passion as a constellation of specifically Jewish events. Jesus's body was the destroyed and raised earthly temple and became the cornerstone of a vastly expanded new human dwelling for the Holy Spirit. His body was also the serpent lifted up in the wilderness that brought conviction and healing. His self-offering was a sin offering: found acceptable, he ascended to the presence of the Father and brought his own blood to heaven, the capital of God's Kingdom, to offer in the heavenly temple and intercede for us forever. His shed blood was also the protective sign of the Passover sparing his people from the coming judgment against God's enemies, as well as the sign ratifying God's new arrangement with his people. These are only a few of the relevant images.

So what? you might ask. Doesn't every ethnicity embody human universals such as love, mercy, and justice in particular cultural forms? Didn't these cultural events and images just happen to be the ones around Jesus? Siddhartha's were Indian, Socrates's were Greek, Muhammad's were Arab, and John Locke's were English. Jesus's had to be *something*. But his Jewish heritage wasn't just happenstance. No, God chose Jacob to *exist* and *receive* those cosmic blessings and promises, and God's further actions along the way shaped Jacob's descendants' national life for just this purpose. In all the groaning and struggling universe of old creation, Israel was the nexus, "the mountain," where all human suffering was swallowed up in victory (Isa. 25:6–8; 1 Cor. 15:54). So it's equally true that in grasping Israel there's no getting around Jesus, her omega and alpha. To construct some other end or some other basis

---

1. Please indulge me in this classic way of referring to a people. It's an elegant way to distinguish the man Jacob/Israel from his body of descendants—to whom, after all, God betroths himself. In other aspects of their relationship, Israel is God's "son," an heir; in those contexts I will refer to Israel as "he." Other times it is more precise to emphasize Israel's multiplicity, in which case the right pronoun is "they."

2. Lesslie Newbigin, "Face to Face with Ultimate Reality," *Third Way*, March 1998, 17.

for her legitimacy is to miss her point—as Paul tearfully taught in Romans 9–11, which he devoted to the question of Israel's continuing significance.[3]

What *did* it mean to be Israel? And what *will* it mean? In Simeon's expectant words to Mary, Jesus is the Lord's "salvation, prepared in the face of all the peoples, a light unto nations' revelation and your people Israel's glory. . . . This one is for the fall and rise [*anastasis*, "resurrection"] of many in Israel, and for a sign of opposition, and your heart will break; so that doubts from many hearts would be revealed" (Luke 2:30–35, my translation). Those ominous words suggest the arrival of Israel's moment to falter and then to shine anew as God's showcase to the world. One life is the omega of the Law and the Prophets that focused on Jacob's descendants (Matt. 5:17; Rom. 10:4), and the alpha and finisher of the trusting people who look to Jacob's faithful descendants for inspiration and strength to complete their own race (Heb. 12:1–2).

I'm jumping ahead again. To understand Jesus as Israel's end, we should slow down and investigate the "old Israel" that ends in him.

## Old Israel: Jacob

The picture of "old Israel" that emerges from the biblical accounts is remarkably consistent. Moreover, Jacob nicely personifies his namesake people. Genesis's account of his life is prescient, announcing beforehand the most important themes that develop more fully through the rest of the Old Testament.[4]

On the one hand, God was way out in front of Jacob, predicting and accomplishing his purposes. Jacob's very existence was God's answer to childless Isaac's prayer (Gen. 25:21). On the other hand, again and again Jacob barely avoided ruin from his own horizons, ambitions, and habits. He made his way in his treacherous ancient world in a manner that was as inconsistent as God's way for him was consistent. An immense gap yawned between God's place for Jacob and Jacob's own lived reality. It hardly narrowed as his life progressed. Sometimes his actions were impressively shrewd, other times startlingly foolish. Sometimes they were godly, other times Machiavellian. Sometimes we readers cheer for him; other times we shake our heads in disappointment. He is neither a figure to revile nor one to imitate. He simply

3. Christian history is littered with ethical failures that spring from misunderstandings of what being Israel means. And to act wrongly is, according to Jesus, to understand Jesus wrongly: "I never knew you; depart from me" (Matt. 7:23).

4. Treatments of "the theme of the Pentateuch" from scholars such as David J. A. Clines and John Walton tend to reflect the somewhat narrower scope of the rest of the Torah as a whole rather than the cosmic scope of these chapters in Genesis.

is what he is: interesting, even fascinating, yet morally uneven, and portrayed from a narrative distance that leaves him opaque not just to audiences but even (I suspect) to himself. Yet this ambiguous human being was and remains a pivotal figure in the realizing of God's cosmic will.

The youthful Jacob was disadvantaged by both his birth order and his father's favoritism for his older twin (Gen. 25:26–28). He used deceit rather than righteousness to overcome his unpromising circumstances and outwit his rivals (Gen. 27), gaining the kind of blessing from his hoodwinked father that today's prosperity gospel teaches and millions chase after. In blessing him, Isaac tried to impart on a son every parent's dream of a wildly successful life for his child and the generations of his descendants. For a while, that's what happened. In fact, under David and Solomon, God actually granted Isaac's wish in a form he would have recognized and applauded. Yet the nation's brief gilded age mainly reinforced her fallen and worldly ambitions, convinced her that these ambitions were God's deepest desires too, and set up her next round of failure.

At Bethel, God had pronounced a quite different blessing on Jacob: his descendants would spread out in every direction in the world and become a means of other nations' blessing (Gen. 28:13–15). That plan was advanced less in Israel's triumphant occupation of the promised land than in her miserable exile among those nations.

Jacob left Bethel sure that he had stumbled on a "sacred space," one to commemorate with a name and a memorial. He failed to realize that he himself was the true object of God's electing promise. It is a classic religious error of interpretation, imposing human sensibilities about holiness on a God who is holy in ways we cannot imagine. The so-called gate of heaven that God showed Jacob—the access point of a "ladder" of traffic to and from creation's capital city, so to speak—is not some sacred space on the earth's surface. It is his people's own sacrificial and missional service. The gap between God's intention and Jacob's apprehension had not been bridged. Israel would still serve that mysterious mission, but in ways inconceivable to Jacob.

The personal identity that emerges in these few chapters of Genesis is totally consistent with corporate Israel's later story. Jacob's life is a confluence of mysterious divine action and human conniving and struggle. Stephen's shocking sermon in Acts 7 characterizes old Israel aptly.

This doesn't make Israel inferior to her ethnic counterparts. Her fallen national character is typically "old human" (Rom. 1:18–2:11). In uniquely electing this one family tree, God accommodated her old-human concerns and faults in a way that neither glorified those traits nor annihilated them. Israel's divine calling and covenantal life did not automatically align her character with the Kingdom of God. However, God was working through Israel to accomplish his purposes—his *cross purposes*. Israel's burden has been to be carried where she has not wished to go (cf. John 21:18).

## Life Support: Moses's Covenant

The rest of the Pentateuch exhibits a deep, lasting, and downright painful disconnect between God's will and vision for Israel and Israel's own character and self-understanding. It is a wonder that Jews can bear to cycle through it every year in the synagogue.[5] Like pilgrims (or tourists, if you want to be cynical), Christian readers mainly visit the inspiring parts such as the exodus and Sinai, whereas Jews dwell in Israel's sobering first years under the further covenant of Moses. Scripture's account of that era gets underway with two alternating narrative perspectives that continue from the middle of Exodus right through the rest of the Pentateuch and beyond. God issued list after list of directions for how Israel was to behave, in general (so the Ten Commandments) and in particular (so the hundreds of directives that involve relations with one another and carefully delineated religious observance). Meanwhile, episode after episode of Israel's actions revealed a completely different heart, no different from the world's other nations: curved in on itself and bent on mistrust, despair, surrender, rebellion, bravado, and misunderstanding. Jacob is "a stiff-necked people," YHWH said. "If I were to go with you even for a moment, I might destroy you" (Exod. 33:5 NIV).

The most vivid juxtaposition of the two comes early in this section of Scripture, as a harbinger. While God was first detailing his covenant arrangement with Moses and the elders, Israel was running wild under Aaron and worshiping the golden calf he had made. In those two scenes we glimpse a dynamic that hardly budged over the centuries of biblical history: a patient, firm, determined divine disciplinarian laying out a structure for fruitful living, and a stubborn and equally determined rebel who took the comforts of living under his father's roof without its (to him) senseless responsibilities. The covenant's laws make contemporary readers uncomfortable because the laws are so accommodated to Israel's brute existence in the ancient Near East. Even so, they were still miles ahead of Israel's own heart. (Jesus had his

---

5. It is an impressive testimony to the Holy Spirit's work in their midst that God brought this people to such an acute recognition of their past flaws without driving them to desperation. People do not naturally come to such profound self-awareness. Scripture's painful realism is one of the more subtle and powerful signs of its inspiration, and Jews' love of it displays a holy character.

followers observe them, but in a way that reflected his Father's heart rather than Israel's internal and external conditions.)

The narrative cuts from one perspective to the other and back: additional commandments repeating and intensifying Israel's liturgical and cultural distinctiveness (for instance, Exod. 34) to resist assimilation to its neighbors; then a story almost always of Israel faltering; then more commandments; then further failure and hard lessons; and on and on. Paul aptly summarizes: the law "was added because of transgressions" (Gal. 3:19) . . . and added, and added, to little avail.

Genesis through 2 Kings depicts a stubborn people who nevertheless did not frustrate God's superintending purpose. Wave after wave of repeated and new rules and regulations pointed a way forward. They seemed to do no good at all, yet they kept coming. And the unruly people they governed kept manifesting signs of their gifts and call alongside their failures. While they improved slightly over the generations, they never showed themselves ready to be more than unworthy and probably doomed beneficiaries of the promises and covenant. Occasionally they did the right thing out of fear, but they displayed precious little trust. Old Israel led a tough, messy covenantal life under its legal disciplinarian. Jacob's posterity, though an heir of glory, was an heir whose freedom was no better than a slave's (cf. Gal. 4:1–2).

It's hard being an oldest child with no example to follow. It's hard being in a strange family. It's hard being singled out. It's hard being called to a legacy that neither you nor any other is ready for. Israel deserves our admiration and empathy for bearing the extraordinary burden she was born into.

This is not to say that the narrative is uniformly bleak. Far from it. Deuteronomy's more optimistic rhetoric is surprising and welcome after the depressing span between the morning after the exodus and the end of Numbers. Joshua's hopefulness was a similarly necessary and powerful encouragement for the task ahead. "Be strong and courageous" (Josh. 1:6–7 NRSV) is a call to righteousness through faith, and despite some serious and debilitating failures, there were many moments under Joshua's leadership where Israel *was* faithful (so 24:31–32). Nevertheless, Joshua warned Israel that Jacob's old character had not been erased by either time or success: "You cannot serve YHWH; for he is a holy God; he is a jealous God; he will not forgive your transgressions or your sins. If you forsake YHWH and serve foreign gods, then he will turn and do you harm, and consume you, after having done you good" (24:19–20 alt.). The book of Judges chronicles how soon and how inexorably this decline set in.

That is the long historical perspective. What about the everyday cultural picture? We should not overlook the backdrop of ordinary covenantal rule-following that was going on as Israel's headline-making failures and successes unfolded: Sabbaths kept, ordinances implemented and followed, penalties meted out, customs observed. The two pictures together allow us to make a series of observations.

First, perhaps it is easy to let the disasters make us too pessimistic about Israel's old character, given all the obedience that goes unmentioned. A newspaper doesn't give us the whole life of a people.

Second, just how effective was all that daily obedience? It was barely moving Israel's needle faith-wise. Years passed, then centuries, and all that daily rule-following—much of it motivated by fear and enforced by civil power, by the way—barely changed Israel's heart.

Third, that doesn't mean their humdrum obedience was unimportant. As Israel ceased to obey those rules, she fell apart in division, defeat, disaster, and exile. Covenantal observance was a lifesaver, or at least a life-prolonger, even if the life it was maintaining wasn't too impressive. The covenantal life was and is necessary for old Israel's survival, but plainly insufficient for her flourishing and especially her transformation.

Fourth, a far more significant factor over these centuries was faithful and anointed leadership. The right person—a Moses, Joshua, Gideon, Samuel, David, or Elijah—could lead God's people into extraordinary achievements and eras. These did not automatically replenish themselves; sometimes God provided them, and other times Israel went without.

Fifth, even those leaders that God sent proved unable to transform her. When they passed from the scene, mediocrity returned.

In sum, Israel's old arrangement was a life-support system maintained by a series of temporary interventions, not the lifesaving procedure she really needed (Exod. 20).

### Three Gifts: The Point of Old Israel

What was God expecting Israel to be over these centuries? What was old Israel for?

Israel was a people, obviously, living in others' midst in a territory in which they could not help but interact. Her life was structured in a way for those others to see her peculiarity, and to see uniquely in her life three gifts from God. The gifts provided means for satisfying God's call to Jacob. Blind Isaac's blessing of the one he thought was Esau (Gen. 27) foreshadowed them. God's words to Jacob at Bethel (28:10–22) ratified them, even if the forms they took came as a surprise to future generations. These gifts made Jacob the bottom of a heavenly ladder, as it were, reaching to and from heaven.[6]

First, Jacob's tribes and God *belonged to each other.* "My son . . . YHWH has blessed" (Gen. 27:27–28, my translation). Their relationship has persisted throughout Israel's history, for better or worse, for richer or poorer, in sickness and in health. This was so from before the covenant of Moses: "I have seen the affliction of my people who are in Egypt" (Exod. 3:7). "Israel is my firstborn son. . . . Let my son go that he may serve me" (4:22–23). This is a public relationship, not a secret marriage, so outsiders could glimpse God's identity and character through Israel's relationship to him (32:11). Even when God's chosen people rejected God (1 Sam. 8:7; Hos. 1:6–9), God did not cut her off, and to this day both parties are still known in terms of each other (Hos. 1:7; 1:10–2:1). These two entities, YHWH and Israel, are each relational: essentially (God is relationship, and Israel is relationship; the terms *YHWH*, *elohim*, and *Israel* all express relationality), mutually (God is the God of Israel, and Israel is the Israel of God), and permanently.

Second, Israel was given visible *power and prominence.* Isaac declared to Jacob, "Let peoples serve you, and nations bow down to you" (Gen. 27:29). Not in the usual ways, though. The power God bestowed was of a kind that distinguished her from her conventionally stronger and more famous neighbors. Israel's power did not take the form of vast armies, full treasuries, ever-expanding territory, or subjected peoples. The Bible's apocalyptic prophecies depict these ephemeral wonders as wild beasts, who rise to terrifying heights one after another, only to fall in succession before God's judgment (Dan. 7:1–8). That was not God's desire for Jacob, though Israel could degenerate into a conventional nation anyway. In the brief season that she did enjoy these trappings of worldly power, her internal fault lines caused her to crumble just like one of those fragile beasts.

Nor did Israel's power take the form of uncanny invulnerability. Otto von Bismarck is alleged to have said, "God has a special providence for fools, drunks, and the United States of America." The same could not be said for Israel. The nation was humiliated in battle right after an astonishingly successful campaign in Canaan. She was erratically led throughout the periods of the judges and then the kings, to say nothing of the foreign emperors that subdued them. She was harassed by Canaanites and Philistines in her political

---

6. Theologians sometimes ask whether the incarnation of the Word in a human being would still have happened if the fall had not. We can ask a similar question about Israel and answer it with some confidence. Israel's purposes so grandly exceed mere deliverance from sin that it seems safe to conjecture that a human history spared the fall would still have featured a chosen people from which new creation and new humanity would spring in the midst of the old.

youth and adolescence, harassed and subjugated by regional empires in middle age, and internationally subjugated and harassed ever since.

Nor did Israel's power or prominence take the form of a covenantal claim on earthly territory. Deuteronomy describes Israel's Abrahamic rivals as having similar entitlements to neighboring territories (for instance, Deut. 2:4–5, 9, 18–19) and describes other nations as having forfeited similar divine rights because of their wickedness (2:10–12, 20–23; 9:1–5). Israel was not so special among Abraham's clans in this respect. Even if her license to her promised land was everlasting, unlike these other nations', for twenty-five hundred years the status of that claim has been obscured or completely contradicted by historical events. "Jews" are named "Judeans" after their lasting connection with Judea, but their relationship with the land has been more of a complication for old Israel's visible relationship with God than a clear display or confirmation of it, a question mark rather than an explanation point, and certainly not the manifestation of quasi-imperial power and prominence that Isaac seemed to expect. Israel's old dream of being king of the hill, ruling a world of servant-nations offering perpetual obeisance and tribute and adulation, never came to pass during the biblical era and has never come to pass since.

How then can it be said that peoples served her and nations bowed down to her? Were these empty promises? Did God abandon his elect, as the Qur'an claims (2:134, 140–41; 3:187; 5:12), or has their status as God's chosen people been superseded, as some Christians have claimed? Or were these promises just another prosperity gospel dreamt up out of old humanity's fleshly ambitions and projected onto God?

Here's how: the Old Testament's histories depict other nations as serving God's providential purposes *for* Israel. They did this whether, like Balaam, they acknowledged and respected Israel's mysterious power (Num. 22–24) or, like the Amorites, they acted unwittingly as God's appointed agents to discipline Israel as a father disciplines his son (Num. 14:40–45; Deut. 1:43–46; cf. Deut. 8:5–6; Prov. 3:11–12, quoted in Heb. 12:3–13). God preserved his opponent Pharaoh so that God's name may be proclaimed throughout the earth (Exod. 9:16). God reached the queen of Sheba through Solomon's splendor (1 Kings 10). God made uncomprehending Assyrians his mouthpiece of judgment on Israel (Isa. 10:5–12; 28:11–13). No other nation received the kind of attention and "service"—horrific as it sometimes was—that God's chosen people did in the days Scripture chronicles.

As agents of blessing on Israel, these foreign servants shared in God's blessings; as agents of cursing, they shared in his curses (Isa. 10:1–19). These nations may not have *known* whom they were serving and bowing down to. But that is what they were doing. And the world has eventually come to realize this, especially by its exposure to the biblical narratives that provide the Lord's interpretation of the nations' intertwined histories.

A third gift that followed from the others was *wisdom*. Isaac declared to Jacob, "Cursed be every one who curses you, and blessed be every one who blesses you!" (Gen. 27:29). "The fear of YHWH," something Jacob learned literally firsthand, "is the beginning of wisdom" (Ps. 111:10; Prov. 9:10 RSV alt.). Israel displayed wisdom—alien wisdom, akin to Luther's alien righteousness—in several distinct and remarkable ways. First, wisdom *before* her, creating her from sheer promise and renewing her providentially. Second, wisdom *over* her, structuring her culture and regulating it in better ways than her people could have developed themselves. Third, wisdom *on* her, driving and moving her actions in directions these other nations would not otherwise expect. Fourth, wisdom *in* her, yielding perception not just of her invisible God but of her people's own mysterious selves. And fifth, wisdom flowing *into and through* her, setting Israel apart from her neighbors despite her own predilections, cleansing her from the accumulating impurities surrounding and especially within her, and yet spreading outward to reach those contaminating neighbors.

Wisdom here entails light, foresight, cardinal virtues (patience, fortitude, justice) and theological virtues (faithfulness, hopefulness, love), mentorship, and above all the powerful presence of what Christians come to call the Holy Spirit. Israel's distinctiveness is pneumatic. The Spirit's creating and providential power was signified in the circumcision of its young males as a sign that every new generation was a fulfillment of the original promises that brought Isaac, Jacob, and his tribes into being in the first place. His ruling power over Israel was headed by the commandments written by "the finger of God" on Sinai and amplified and extended in the hundreds of specifications that followed. His anointing power was displayed in the prophets who, like Joshua, called Israel to decisive actions that overrode her usually sluggish heart, and who, like Samuel, told the truth to Israel especially when she was unwilling to hear it and kindled memories and dreams of a different and better alternative to her sorry disposition. His indwelling power illuminated her dreamers, craftsmen, and sages to see the deep structures of the world's being and to understand her words and visions from God. His sanctifying power streamed right into and through this unclean people through her priest-led worship, and out to needy and powerless beneficiaries—strangers, foreign workers, even the people and cattle of Nineveh—through works of mercy.

Bear in mind that we are still describing *old* Israel during her centuries on the Torah's life support. Rival people after rival people disappeared or assimilated into others—as the next chapter shows, that is what ordinary nations do—while Israel as such remained distinct. However, none of these three gifts per se (visible relationship, displayed wisdom, and manifest power and prestige) perfected her (Heb. 7:11; 11:40). The covenant of Moses "finished nothing" (7:19, my translation). Simeon, whose prophecy to Mary touches on all three, waited all his life for Israel's appeal (Luke 2:25). Even today, when we read in Genesis about the misadventures of the patriarchs and their dysfunctional families, we do not breathe a sigh of relief and thanksgiving that our human communities transcended their foibles or escaped their destinies of election and servitude centuries ago. Instead we cringe, because we see the worst sides of our own selves (James 1:23–24) under Genesis's bright and unflattering light.[7]

Moses had set before Israel life and death, blessing and curse (Deut. 30:19), and old Israel has never escaped either one. Their life is both a sign and counter-sign. God's blessed people were and are still a mess, a witness to human sinfulness and limitation against which God's deeds all stand as a countersign (Josh. 24:26–28). As Isaiah put it, Israel's failure fueled gentile confusion and disrespect for God—the very opposite outcome from what God had foretold to Jacob (Isa. 52:5; Paul reiterates this in Rom. 2:17–24). At the same time, all this failure notwithstanding, God's cursed elect have still carried on. They remain a people of invaluable gifts and achievements whom we can still identify in the twenty-first century and who stand as a sign of their God (so Isa. 52:6–10), even while many have ceased to be observant of him.

Ethnic Israel's existence, then, has displayed her election in her failures just as clearly as her triumphs. She is the kind of people we all are; and yet she is a peculiar variety that *also*—uniquely—displays the kind of Creator, Sustainer, Savior, and Perfecter that we all have. That makes old Israel a particularly active theater of the flesh's war with the Spirit: the world's war against its eternal King, and that King's unremitting campaign to reclaim his world.

Paul was perceptive in seeing Christian debates over circumcision against these backdrops (Gal. 4:21–6:10). He looked back on God's protracted and unsuccessful campaign in the Old Testament and called the covenant of Moses "the dispensation of death" and "of condemnation" (2 Cor. 3:7, 9). Peter called it a yoke that "neither our fathers nor we have been able to bear" (Acts 15:10). Later Jews have regarded these men's descriptions as betrayals of their

---

7. We need this mirror to counter our age-old human tendency to puff ourselves up by putting down others. We see the usual dynamic in, for instance, snobby gentile takes on the Bible's criticisms of Jews, modern treatments of both the so-called Dark Ages and "savage" cultures, postmodern elitists' scorn of the supposedly uneducated and unsophisticated, mid-twentieth-century science fiction with its evolutionary visions of human character in a future whose historians would regard us as primitives, and political partisans' unfairness toward rivals.

Jewish tradition, but empirically the apostles' assessments are accurate. Lofty Jewish aspirations about the restoration of Israel and the fulfillment of the prophets' promises—of the kind we hear from a faithful and hopeful remnant in Luke 1, and hear to this day in Jewish liturgy—looked far away even then. They look even further away now, despite over a century of surprisingly successful Zionism. By contrast, Jewish sufferings have remained painfully near.

Comparing his present day to the old days, Paul admitted that "what once had splendor has come to have no splendor at all" (2 Cor. 3:10). In Isaiah 58–59 (quoted in Rom. 3:15–16) Paul read God's blunt verdict that the house of Jacob, to the last man, was so cut off from God by sin that there was no one among God's people through whom deliverance could come (Isa. 58:1; 59:2, 4, 16). Seeing his kin reject the one great exception God had provided brought Paul nothing but anguish, because his kin "are Israelites, and to them belong the sonship, the glory, the covenants, the giving of the law, the worship, and the promises" (Rom. 9:4).

Yet it also didn't extinguish Paul's hope for his people. In Romans 3:15–16 he acknowledged and even intensified Isaiah 59:2–15's wholesale condemnation of Israel, but reasoned the problem all the way through to affirming in Romans 11:26–27 in equally certain terms Isaiah 59:20–21's wholesale expression of hope for her. The sign and countersign would not be forever perpetuated in human history. Nor would God forsake old Israel and bestow his gifts and call on some other community with more potential (cf. Rom. 11:29). After all, the whole point of choosing such unpromising people was to demonstrate that God is the source of all such potential. How would abandoning her make God known? "You are always with me, and all that is mine is yours," the prodigal father told his petulant obedient son (Luke 15:31).[8]

Paul concluded that this paradoxical, dialectical, terribly frustrating situation *was* somehow what old Israel was for (Rom. 9–11). She was stuck there so that something new could arrive in, through, and for her (Rom. 11:28).[9] For that to happen, a lot had to end, and a lot more had to begin. Jesus indicated this himself when he quoted Isaiah after overturning the moneychangers' tables:

> The foreigners who join themselves to the LORD . . .
> I will bring to my holy mountain,
>     and make them joyful in my house of prayer;

8. For a brilliant treatment of the parable of the prodigal son, see Timothy Keller, *The Prodigal God: Recovering the Heart of the Christian Faith* (New York: Penguin, 2011).

9. Rev. 12 concurs: Israel's role in salvation is to bring forth the Son whose word and witness alone can conquer her enemy.

their burnt offerings and their sacrifices
  will be accepted on my altar;
for *my house shall be called a house of prayer*
  *for all peoples.*
Thus says the Lord GOD,
  who gathers the outcasts of Israel,
I will gather yet others to him
  besides those already gathered.

(Isa. 56:6–8; cf. Mark 11:17)

People conventionally interpret Jesus's action as a critique of greed. That barely scratches the surface of what Jesus was saying. He continued by quoting Jeremiah in order to foretell the temple's destruction. This would retire the system by which Israel thought herself obedient and justified in God's sight:

Hear the word of the LORD, all you men of Judah who enter these gates to worship. . . . Will you steal, murder, commit adultery, swear falsely, burn incense to Baal, and go after other gods that you have not known, and then come and stand before me in this house, which is called by my name, and say, "We are delivered!"—only to go on doing all these abominations? Has this house, which is called by my name, become *a den of robbers* in your eyes? . . . Therefore I will do to the house . . . as I did to Shiloh. And I will cast you out of my sight. (Jer. 7:2, 9–11, 14–15; cf. Mark 11:17)

The temple would never fulfill its purpose of focusing both Israel's and the nations' visions on God's wise and prominent people and gathering them to him. It was a failure, and it was time for it to go, along with the whole order it served.

John's Gospel adds the further clarifying detail that Jesus alluded to his death and resurrection as the *true* temple's *true* destruction and remaking— that is, the temple of his body (John 2:19–22), with which the Lord chose to tabernacle among his people (1:14). This new arrangement would work as the old system never had and never could have. It meant a decisive end for Israel's old life and an even more decisive beginning.

## Paul and Israel's Omega

In the previous chapter, Mary displayed humanity's omega and alpha in an exemplary and illuminating way. The New Testament suggests a different person through whom to see the old Israel ending and a new one beginning. The process unfolds in unparalleled intimacy and detail in the apostle Paul.

Orthodox, Catholics, Protestants, and Pentecostals alike are drawn to Paul as a visionary, example, and mentor of lived-out Christianity. What is it about him? I think it is the way Paul's *life, vision (confession), mission,* and *legacy* all cohere so powerfully. Such personal coherence had once eluded him (Rom. 7:5–13). Even if he remained a work in progress throughout his life (7:14–25), its new pattern demonstrated an inner integrity. Paul's personal integrity as a follower of Christ, a member of his body, a believer in him, an ambassador of his Kingdom, and a witness to his work holds out the prospect that the rest of us can gain a measure of such integrity in our fragmented lives too.

Paul was and remained a creative, apocalyptic, messianic rabbi. Jesus transformed his life, purpose, perspective, and character. Paul went from being a passionate persecutor of the church, a spiritual leader who personified "this world" and its prowling ruler, to becoming a passionate vehicle for "the good news of God" not just in his own people's world of synagogues, Scriptures, and rabbis but in the Greco-Roman world as well. Paul was a brilliant missionary strategist in a treacherous multicultural context. He was a tenacious pastor and mentor. He loved sacrificially and suffered for it, traveling a "way of the cross" both in his vexing congregations and from Jerusalem to Rome: "always carrying in the body the death of Jesus, so that the life of Jesus may also be manifested in our bodies" (2 Cor. 4:10). Paul owed his biographical integrity entirely to Jesus, his omega and alpha as well as Israel's. In his old life, new life, and death, he is the gospel literally fleshed out.

Paul was born of prestigious Jewish ancestry, was trained as a rabbi, and became a Pharisee under Gamaliel. We often say that Paul started off his life as "Saul," with a Hebrew-Jewish name, and traded that name for a new one when he became a Christian. Churches will keep repeating this mistake until the end of the age, but it tells the wrong story of both his omega and alpha and Israel's. Luke says that Saul the Pharisee was "also called Paul" (Acts 13:9), his Roman name. Luke does not say that he was "then" or "later" called Paul. The man was bicultural, a Jew from Tarsus, capital of the Roman province of Cilicia in what is now south-central Turkey. I have students from Asia and Africa who adopt biblical and Western names for convenience and hospitality, and I have colleagues from America who teach in Asia and Africa and adopt local names for the same reasons (my name among Chinese students became Wang). So Paul had a name from his own *ethnos* or people and also had a name from his surrounding local culture. He was always *Paulus* (Paul), even before his conversion, and he was always *Shaul* (Saul). This is significant. His omega was not the end of his ethnic Judaism, and his alpha was not the beginning of some new postethnic or nonethnic identity. Paul the Christian *still* had these Jewish traits (Phil. 3:4); he lost only his old misunderstanding of their significance (3:8).

Yet this is too simple a way to put it. Christ's invasion into Paul's life introduced a distance between him and his kin. Paul called them "children of the flesh," "the present Jerusalem . . . in slavery with her children"—labels that would have been unthinkable before—while he counted himself among "the children of the promise," "the Jerusalem above" that is "free, and she is our mother" (Rom. 9:8; Gal. 4:25–26).[10]

If someone today were to talk like that about his or her ethnicity, we would view it as betrayal, false consciousness, and self-hatred. Our contemporary tribalism turns "solidarity" into a virtue and a mandate. We even project it on Jesus, who is said to have shown "solidarity" with some or other subset of human beings (the poor, the oppressed, etc.) merely on account of their condition. I disagree. The only unconditional solidarity Jesus shows is with his Father. His mission is *to* the poor, the outcast, the sick, blind, and condemned; but he is not *on their side*, not their "ally" (cf. Josh. 5:13–14). The ways our culture trains us to see "solidarity" mistake distance, including Paul's new distance from his kin, for rejection. This son of Jacob parted ways with his extended family as Joseph parted ways with Jacob and his brothers (Gen. 37–45): because of forces out of his control, for a redemption greater than their present estrangement, never forgetting them, and always ready for whatever reunion God might engineer.

Paul was an exemplary Jew, "a Hebrew born of Hebrews" (Phil. 3:5). Fundamentally, that distance that has opened up is not between Israel and something else but between old and new Israel. Christ's work is that shift's whole basis and its content.

Donald Hagner identifies tension already in the Old Testament prophets between two goals.[11] The first is the political fulfillment of Israel's ordinary national longings. People wanted the Torah and the rest of their old institutions to perform to their full potential—wanted Israel to get off life support and return to health. These kinds of expectations about Israel's messiah were common in Jesus's day. Both his opponents and his would-be supporters were constantly reading his actions against that background, looking for signs that he was about to "restore the kingdom to Israel" (Acts 1:6) in solidarity with his people. Jesus frustrated supporters and enemies alike, and they abandoned and condemned him to die as a failed insurgent. The second messianic goal

10. Does Paul's surprising treatment of Sarah and Hagar, where Hagar mothers Israel but Sarah mothers the church, misread or distort Scripture? Stay tuned.

11. "How New Is the New Testament?," lecture series delivered at Asia-Pacific Theological Seminary, Baguio, Philippines, January 19–22, 2016.

involves apocalyptic prophecy's much grander fulfillment of a transcendent hope, a fulfillment that depends on God's unique and decisive action. Here the solution to Israel's failing old institutions wasn't just greater faithfulness or performance but a whole new arrangement without the old one's vulnerabilities. This envisioned course of history involves a far clearer omega and alpha for Israel. It exceeds the combined glories of the exodus, conquest, return from exile, and regained Davidic and Solomonic glory.

Yet the shift from old to new is not merely from that second goal to its fulfillment. As Paul puzzled over the astonishing course of events in Jesus's ministry and then in his own, he realized that the shift is also from *incorrect expectations of both goals* to *surprising fulfillments and corrected expectations* (Rom. 10:2–4). He came to perceive "the mystery" of God's eternal plan through Israel that now lay disclosed in Jesus (16:25–26).

God left hints in Israel's Scriptures, and Paul followed up on them once God showed him the interpretive key of Christ's crucifixion. There is too much material to review here. For economy, we will center (though not exclusively) on Isaiah's relevance to Paul and his theology.


### Jesus, Israel's Death and Resurrection

In Romans 9:27–33, Paul quotes four passages from Isaiah 1–39 that display an awakening and deliverance among a small number of Israelites in the midst of massive confusion and destruction. Then in Romans 10:15 he jumps to the joyful Isaiah 52. The good news there concerns Isaiah's famous "suffering servant." Paul describes it as "the preaching of Christ" (Rom. 10:17).

When the servant is first mentioned, it refers to Israel as a whole (Isa. 20:3; 41:8–9; 42:18–20; 44:1–3; 49:3), whom Isaiah foresaw as suffering rejection. But the servant also picks up an individual personal character: "I will put my Spirit upon him, he will bring forth justice to the nations" (42:1) and "raise up the tribes of Jacob . . . as a light to the nations" (49:6). This *one* servant of God who suffers is Israel, and yet he is also Israel summed up in one life. That ambiguity in Isaiah is pivotal to solving the puzzle of how a chronically unworthy Israel could fulfill hopes that go so far beyond the conditions it was always mired in. While "no one was worthy," in fact one Jewish figure—a lion of Judah, no less—was worthy after all (Rev. 5:2–5; cf. Isa. 29:9–14, quoted in Rom. 11:7–11).

In Acts 8, an Ethiopian eunuch was reading a passage from Isaiah—a particularly evocative passage in his Greek translation—and couldn't understand what it meant:

As a sheep led to the slaughter
  or a lamb before its shearer is dumb,
  so he opens not his mouth.

In his humiliation justice was denied him.
  Who can describe his generation?
  For his life is taken up from the earth.
  (Isa. 53:7–8 LXX, quoted in Acts 8:32–33)

*Led to the slaughter! Then taken up from the earth!* Was Isaiah speaking these mysterious words about himself? the eunuch asked. Or some other person—and if so, whom? Philip's answer was the good news that Jesus is that servant. The lion that people were expecting was quite unexpectedly an offered and acceptable lamb, slaughtered and now taken up into God's presence to accomplish all things.

Philip knew that in Isaiah's context of worthless and helpless Israel, the servant suffers providentially, inheriting the covenant's curses on its transgressors. Paul came to a similar conclusion and put it more memorably: Jesus became sin for us (2 Cor. 5:21) and a curse (Gal. 3:13). So Jesus is the omega of those curses and the sins they address. He is also the destination of the covenant's blessings and the righteousness they glorify, the very personification of Israel's three gifts of belonging, global prominence, and wisdom: "The root of Jesse shall come, he who rises to rule the Gentiles" (Rom. 15:12, quoting Isa. 11:10). He is the target of the covenant.

How can he be both cursed and blessed?

If we read Deuteronomy casually, we will conclude that there are two paths—obedience that leads to life, and disobedience that leads to death—and we must choose. There are broadly two kinds of people: righteous ones and unrighteous ones. Psalm 1 says this. Ecclesiastes notices it. Proverbs follows it. People sort themselves into these two groups by which path they take. Moses challenged his people to choose the right one. There is the remnant that believes and the rest who do not.

Well, it turns out that there aren't really two varieties of Israel, one righteous and one wicked. There isn't even a spectrum between the two ideal types. At least that's not the way God sees it. After Moses delivered that exhortation, God told him that his people made their choice long ago. They wouldn't be choosing life. They had already chosen death and were well along their road to destruction. So, God told Moses, go and teach them a song that will still be with them to remind them after they have fallen away, forgotten the covenant, and been destroyed.

Moses was shown long in advance what Isaiah announced much later: Israel was not going to experience one path or the other. Instead, she would travel one path and *then* the other. So when Moses wrote the song that appears near the end of Deuteronomy, he included an extra stanza at the end about how God would restore Israel and atone for her sins after the disaster of God's judgment on her (Deut. 32:43). The covenant has one target after all. Israel would receive its curses and then its blessings. That is what Isaiah foresaw: "I have been found by those who did not seek me. . . . I have spread out my hands all the day to a stubborn and rebellious people" (Isa. 65:1–2 LXX). Paul quoted these verses to the gentile and Jewish church in Rome to help them understand how Jesus's coming had precipitated Israel's falling and rising (Rom. 10:20–21).

But a serious wrinkle had appeared. While in Isaiah both of those verses refer to Israel, Paul used the first one to refer to believers who were mainly gentiles and the second to refer to Jews who rejected Jesus as Israel's messiah. The line of Abraham "according to the flesh," as Paul called his fellow Jews, had become for the time being a "barren one who does not bear," more like Hagar's fruitless line of descendants; whereas the "children of promise" were demonstrating that they were Abraham's truly fruitful line through Sarah. To prove it, Paul drew on a line from Isaiah 54 meant to reassure Israel of God's will to restore it: "the children of the desolate one are many more" (Gal. 4:27, quoting Isa. 54:1).

Wait. Isn't that a return to the supposedly discredited schema where some choose life and others death?

Not really. Sure, for now there was a remnant (Isa. 10:22, quoted in Rom. 9:27; cf. Isa. 65:8–10; Rom. 11:5). But Paul still saw Israel on the whole *someday* completing her path of righteousness and life, not just her path of condemnation and death (Rom. 11:11–16).[12] Israel's cold and uncomprehending reception of her messiah was not an insuperable obstacle to fulfilling its role any more than Israel's other failings were (Isa. 29:9–14, quoted in Rom. 11:7–10, 25). Rather, it was an extension of her exile. And in that otherwise hopeless situation, God would take away Jacob's sin (Isa. 27:9 LXX, quoted in Rom. 11:27), in order that "Jacob's children will sprout, Israel will bloom, and the world will be engorged with its fruit" (Isa. 27:6 LXX).[13] Israel was still experiencing her unhappy, uncomprehending, and barren season of God's

12. Israel on the whole, "all Israel" (Rom. 11:26), does not mean every last Israelite, as Paul makes clear again and again throughout his letters.

13. So Paul's "allegory" in Gal. 4 is doing justice to Isaiah, and in the process it is doing justice to Isaiah's vision of the fulfillment of God's promises to Abraham in Genesis. Christ crucified, the embodiment of barrenness, is actually far more fruitful in producing emancipated

severity; but God had found a way to make even her exile productive, and God's kindness was still on its way (Rom. 11:22–31). Her gifts—belonging, prominence, wisdom, and all others (9:4–5)—as well as her call are permanent (v. 29).

So Simeon's predicted fall-and-rise of many in Israel was arriving after all. (It was not the fall of many and the rise of just a few, though in Paul's day they *were* few.) The germ was the righteous servant's suffering and vindication. His righteousness was now cascading through humanity, one relationship at a time (Rom. 5:12–19). It was in Messiah Jesus that Isaac's unseen heir most fully received the covenant's curses and its blessings. But Paul grasped that, in a wider sense, Jesus took on far more than just the arrangement at Sinai. He took on Jacob's primordial aspirations, wretchedness, and glory.[14] Jesus is the omega of Israel, on whom the promises landed in all their force. The prophets had all spoken truly: Christ's sufferings and glorification were necessary (Luke 24:25–26). He, the beginning of her true end, became the end of her beginning and her stuck and frustrating middle. And many others, including Paul himself, were being swept along.

### Israel's New Beginning

Isaiah speaks not only of the suffering servant who shall live to see the fruit of his suffering and be satisfied (Isa. 53:11) but also of the anointed one, gifted with the Spirit of the Lord to preach good news, healing, deliverance, sight, and liberty (61:1). In his hometown synagogue, Jesus announced to his stunned neighbors that he was the one of whom this passage had most fully spoken (Luke 4:16–21). The Spirit was upon *him* to do those things like they had never been done before: to release stuck and stymied Israel, to stop the suffering, and to unlock the goodness of the covenant and Jacob's bright destiny.

Jeremiah 31:31–34 speaks of a new covenant that is not like the old one. What's different about it? Jeremiah answers that now it is written on hearts and empowered by the Holy Spirit. The old written code that was Israel's life-support system keeps killing—it killed Israel again and again, and was even used to kill Jesus—but the Spirit through this new covenant gives life (Jer. 31:31, quoted in 2 Cor. 3:5–6). The distinction drawn here with old Israel's arrangement is, more than anything, between impotence and power. The difference is the Holy Spirit. "God has done what the law, weakened by

---

descendants for Jacob than biological Israel's covenant. This irony does not bring Paul joy, but it does honor Isaiah's insight into the suffering servant's legacy (Isa. 53:10).

14. Adam's too, but that was the topic of the previous chapter.

the flesh, could not do . . . in order that the just requirement of the law might be fulfilled in us, who walk not according to the flesh but according to the Spirit" (Rom. 8:3–4).

The first sentence of Romans puts Israel's omega and alpha crisply: the Son "was descended from David according to the flesh and designated Son of God in power according to the Spirit of holiness by his resurrection from the dead, Jesus Christ our Lord" (Rom. 1:3–4). Anointing or "christening" Jesus with the Spirit and raising him by the Spirit has transformed the reign of David's earthly heir. What Israel's royalty could never do before, Jesus has done enduringly.

All the generations of Levites and their sacrifices couldn't take away Israel's sin but only issue endless reminders of it (Heb. 10:3–4); but the risen Jesus can save forever (7:23–25; 10:11–14). What Israel's priests could never do before, Jesus "through the eternal Spirit" (9:14) has done eternally.

All of Israel's prophets spoke for God (Heb. 1:1). But not until the coming of Jesus did Israel receive her promised prophet like Moses (Deut. 18:9–19; 34:10–12), whose word actually gave Israel her needed new start (Acts 3:19–26). What the prophets could never do before, the Spirit-gifted Jesus (2:33) has done everlastingly. New Israel's Spirit makes the difference. From him spring the fruit of faith, peace, access to grace, joy, endurance, hope, and love (Rom. 5:1–5), and all their blessings, all thanks to the crucified and living Son of God (5:6–11).

The Spirit's fruit has even brought power to the law. Moses had promised near the end of Deuteronomy that if Israel kept God's Torah—*and it's not too hard to do that*, he assured her—then she would be blessed: "The word is very near you; it is in your mouth and in your heart, so that you can do it" (Deut. 30:14). This text seems to contradict Paul's conclusion that the law was impotent, but Paul went right to it for his proof. He asked, What word is it that is so near? Surely not the old written code that Moses had repeated and enlarged after every failure, because Deuteronomy 31:21, Jeremiah 31, and those many other examples demonstrated that it *wasn't* in Israel's heart. No, the word that is truly on the lips and in the heart is "the word *of faith* which *we* preach" (Rom. 10:8). God's real word to Israel is not false optimism that Israel can keep the covenant through her own righteousness—even Moses knew she couldn't—but the good news of God's righteousness, which now the apostles preach in the gospel of Jesus Christ. "Jesus is Lord!" "God raised him from the dead!"[15] These Spirit-fueled testimonies to God's righteousness

15. Some interpret these verses to deny that other actions, such as baptism, have any role in salvation. However, Paul was not compiling a list of actions that do or do not lead to salvation;

indicate what will justify and save us (Rom. 10:9–10). They are not the old works of our own weakened and weakening flesh (cf. Rom. 4:1–14) but the new deeds of God in which we put our trust.

Paul's reasoning is sound and totally consistent with the thrust of the whole Old Testament. After all, Israel began to be rescued from exile not when she finally started executing the Torah to perfection (much of what the Torah requires, such as holy sacrifices and civil procedures, was beyond exiled Israel's power to keep anyway) but when God initiated her restoration through actions beyond her control. Nevertheless, what Paul did with Deuteronomy 30 is impressive. He took one of the texts that seemed most clearly to threaten his interpretation and, by specifying Jesus as its content, turned it around to support it. It's a rabbinical version of piracy or capture the flag. And Paul was not misusing Scripture to do it. He perceived that Moses's claim could not have been wrong. And yet the Torah *proved* undoable, at least apart from Jesus. So what was the *doable* part of the covenant? Confession of faith. And the Spirit is the one who has made that doable. More than doable, actually—compelling. The story of Jesus *compels* the apostles joyfully to confess the justifying power of God's grace. So Jesus is the one who proves Moses right, by giving the covenant its new start.

In Acts Stephen concurred. The punch line of his sermon about God's frustrating relationship with stubborn Israel was already the punch line of Isaiah 66: God doesn't want stone temples and hypocritical worshipers any more than he wants exiled idolaters. For his temple he wants a man who is humble and contrite, and trembles at his word (Isa. 66:1–2). That's Jesus, and it's Stephen too. Both are filled with the Spirit (Luke 4:1; Acts 7:55). They are the Spirit's acceptable temple, the Israel of God (1 Cor. 6:19).

When Stephen's audience reacted with rage, he saw Jesus with royal authority not just sitting at God's right hand but standing to receive him. This rejected one of Israel is now in power and taking initiative. Stephen knelt down and cried, "Do not hold this sin against them," exemplifying God's desired Israelite in Isaiah 66:2, and fell asleep (Acts 7:60). This is a new kind of reign where subjects forgive their persecutors just as their King does.

Paul started out as Stephen's and Jesus's mortal enemy but ended up serving right alongside them. He counted himself in Israel's present remnant chosen by grace (Rom. 11:1–5). And in his case that meant a special commission. "The Lord called me from the womb," he said in Galatians 1:15 (my translation),

---

he was working with the language of Deut. 30 to demonstrate his point that God's righteousness, not Israel's, is at work in salvation. Whether God's righteousness is conferred to God's people through confession, baptism, inward belief, or some other vehicle is not in view here.

appropriating Isaiah 49:1 as if *he* were now the suffering servant. And he was, because now he had become a target of old Israel's persecution for serving the suffering servant's mission as a Jew to show the Lord to all nations (Isa. 49:6; Isa. 52:15, quoted in Rom. 15:18–22). So Paul could rightfully claim the suffering servant's words for himself: "Who has believed what he has heard *from us*?" (Rom. 10:16, quoting Isa. 53:1).

This now-multinational, global reign that transcends all oppressing powers, survives their interference, and even commissions its enemies is still Israel. More Israel than ever, in fact: "the Israel of God" (Gal. 6:16). Ethnic Israel's rejection of its reigning Messiah together with the suffering Messiah's gift of the Spirit who raised him means the exodus of an old way of being Israel and the genesis of a new one.

## Three Gifts Refreshed

What has changed, and what hasn't? Let's look at those three gifts to Jacob: belonging, prominence, and wisdom. Christ remakes all of them.

### Belonging

"I am with you," God told Jacob (Gen. 28:15). If Jacob's children belong to God in a new way, a lot of them haven't seen it. Many Jews to this day regard themselves as God's same possession that they always have been, and deny that Jesus belonged to God in the unique way his supporters have claimed. Israel's earlier character and its situation (and God's, and the world's, and humanity's) seem to persist, neither new nor old but continuous.

The people who have insisted on Israel's continuity for two thousand years now are not stupid. They have been thoughtful, knowledgeable, prayerful, and worshipful people. Whatever did change, it seems not to have affected either the perspectives or the lives of "Israelites according to the flesh," except to bring a new source of trouble in the form of Christian anti-Judaism. The situation baffled Paul. To discourage Christians from drawing the wrong conclusions and becoming conceited about themselves or condescending toward his kin, Paul advised the Roman church that this rejection reflected a mysterious "hardening" for God's providential and gracious purposes (Rom. 11:25–26).

Jesus's disciples, on the other hand, experienced fundamental changes in the *quality* of their belonging. Jesus did belong to God in a unique way, and he achieved an unprecedented reconciliation with God (Col. 1:19–20). Moreover, he did it with a righteous life and death that, while the Law and

Prophets testified to it and shaped it, operated above and beyond them (Rom. 3:21–26). Belonging to God now means something new. God had always treated Israel as a son (Deut. 8:4; Isa. 1:2; 43:6; Jer. 3:18–19; Hos. 11:1). But in Jesus, Israel now really *was* a Son (Ps. 2:7, quoted in Luke 3:22; John 1:18), and all who belonged to him were sons as well (Gal. 3:26–4:7; Hos. 1:10). The Spirit's baptism, indwelling fellowship, and disciplining lordship proved it (Rom. 8:15–17; Gal. 3:1–5).

To Paul, God's full presence in Jesus (Col. 2:9; cf. Rom. 7:4; 2 Cor. 4:4–6) suggested a series of analogies between God's former fellowship and his far more powerful and lasting new fellowship (Col. 2:10–19; cf. Rom. 7:1–6; 2 Cor. 3:7–18). "We are the true circumcision, who worship God in spirit, and glory in Christ Jesus, and put no confidence in the flesh" (Phil. 3:3). The gift of right relationship in Christ brings a new life pursuing the faithfulness and fruitfulness that *follow* reconciliation. Israel's new standing means that justification per se is not something for the church to pursue anymore, in either the old ways or new ones (Gal. 2:14–16).

Being God's elect is still hard. Belonging to the Lord who suffered and was glorified doesn't end our sorrows. However, they no longer need to dominate us (Rom. 8:16–17). Belonging to him delivers sufferers from bondage to the fear of death (Heb. 2:14–15) and frees mourners to grieve in hope rather than despair (1 Thess. 4:13).

One surprising sign of belonging is the constant war between our old rebellious selves ("the flesh") and the Spirit who continues to claim us (Gal. 5:16–17). As Israel's old struggles and even sufferings demonstrated that they belonged to a jealous God (Exod. 34:14), so Christian struggles to walk to the Spirit's beat demonstrate that they live to the Spirit (Gal. 5:25). Whether we suffer for doing wrong (1 Pet. 4:15; Rom. 13:5) or for doing right (1 Pet. 4:13–14; Rom. 12:14), we can gain from God's discipline (Heb. 12:3–13), since judgment begins in God's household and works outward from there (1 Pet. 4:17–19). Christians remorseful about our failures and those of our predecessors, possessed of divided consciences and incoherent lives, and who stand under judgment for our unthinkable actions are signs, even in our present sorry states, that we are not our own, nor the Torah's, but were the Son's expensive purchase to become the Father-given Spirit's temple (1 Cor. 6:19–20) and his own someday-spotless bride (Eph. 5:26–27; Rev. 21:9–11).

These characterizations transcend old Israel's. Christ has moved Paul from one law to another (Rom. 8:2). But Paul, who was once "*under* the law" of Moses, is not *under* but "*in* the law of Christ" (*ennomos Christou*, 1 Cor. 9:20–21). He belongs in a very different way: directly, vitally, joyfully, intimately, eschatologically. These qualities come across throughout his writings (and the rest of the New Testament as well). And that new way means he cannot belong in all the same old ways. In new Israel's nature there is no capacity for "Greek and Jew, circumcised and uncircumcised" (Col. 3:11).

A Jew has to stop being a Jew to belong to Israel? It's an incendiary claim, all the more after being so brutally abused for so long. Christian supersessionism hangs over the label "new Israel" like a thundercloud, giving it baggage I do not intend. Here's what I think Paul meant. Jesus's coming had aroused a maelstrom of domestic opposition to Israel's emerging newness. Mary typifies one response to God's call to belong to Israel in a new way; let's call it "apostolic." John the Baptist typifies the more usual reaction: despite God using him to usher in Israel's new way of being, his movement's own ethnic oldness left them trailing behind as the apostolic way moved on in the face of gathering opposition. The authorities that John's Gospel refers to as "the Jews" displayed the same sort of ethnic oldness. Paul did too, before his conversion to the apostolic way. Jesus's call to take up our crosses is a mortal threat to Israel's old ethnic character, which thus defends itself. In the next chapter, we will see the same for gentiles. But how could Israel, *or anything*, truly live and last that way? After conspiring to defeat Jesus on the cross, the oldness of Israelite nationhood and its practices has been cast off along with the old nature and the sin that they were caught up in. And with the new nature has come a new (in fact, new Jewish) way of belonging that Paul calls "the circumcision of Christ" (Col. 2:11). It features no capacity for ethnic oldness—Israel's or any other (3:9–11). The Israel of God is beyond both circumcision *and* uncircumcision (Gal. 6:15). It has moved on.

Israel's old ways of belonging to God have been retooled for a mission of obedience to the Messiah and for a harvest of cosmic praise, glory, and honor at his return (1 Pet. 1:2–7). In Peter's words, Israel is newly born for the end of the ages as a chosen race, a holy nation, a royal priesthood, and God's own (2:9–11; cf. Hos. 2:23). This new quality of belonging that Jesus brought to his people is on display in the church's life, evangelism, and even penitence, so it's visible to outsiders (1 Pet. 1:20; 2:9, 12; 3:16). Peter therefore described new Israel's unbelieving neighbors as the "Gentiles" (2:12) among whom they are exiled, even though his audience broadly shares their old ethnicity. Jesus has become the new principle through whom each group is identified and identifiable.

This means Jesus is also *the nations'* omega and alpha. Recalling Isaac's old blessing, they are cursed in cursing *him* and blessed in blessing *him*. The next chapter explores that topic.

### Power and Prominence

What has become of God's second promised gift to Jacob? On the one hand, a number of those outside observers have perceived a risen and ascended Jesus through the flawed people who belong to him, and that vision has changed their lives. Some were Jews who already had a robust appreciation of God's past and future exaltation. On the other hand, many have not come to share that life-changing perception—even after searching diligently and even after joining that royal priesthood for a while or being brought up by parents who belong to it. Where and what is this gift now?

Recall that the New Testament is consistently apocalyptic in outlook. Much of the *substance* of Israel's old hopes of apocalyptic cosmic prominence crossed over from old to new. But their *focus* came to center on Jesus. The apostles perceived and consistently proclaimed his new and unprecedented prominence as the crucified, risen, and ascended Son of God (Rom. 1:1–3). In him, Israel now had power and exaltation above all other nations, authorities, and powers in heaven, on earth, and under the earth (Phil. 2:11).

Whatever changed between old Israel's and new Israel's prominence, it has been subtle enough to leave plenty of room for doubt. It didn't take long for Jesus's critics to decide that "all things have continued as they were from the beginning of creation" (2 Pet. 3:4). Have they?

Jesus's life, death, and resurrection are obvious milestones in Israel's newfound prominence. Another is the Holy Spirit's Pentecostal empowering of the then entirely Jewish church. Less widely appreciated is the pivotal event of Jesus's ascension. Along with other New Testament writings, the Letter to the Hebrews treats it as a milestone, if not *the* milestone, in Israel's new exaltation. God has spoken to Israelites in a Son appointed heir of all things (Heb. 1:1–4).

The Kingdom's capital city is "the heavenly Jerusalem," filled with festal angels rather than Sinai's wilderness gloom (Heb. 12:22–24). But because Israel belongs to God differently, it is represented in the capital not by an ascended Aaron but by an ascended Melchizedek (Heb. 5:5–10). This fulfills that promise of a new arrangement with the houses of Israel and Judah (Jer. 31:31, quoted in Heb. 8:8 and 10:16). Revelation sees the Lord's capital city following him to earth at his return (Rev. 21:2–3), as it followed him to heaven at his ascension.

The structure of new Israel's life has changed since Jesus has assumed the roles of old Israel and finished what they could only start.[16] The prophetic,

---

16. For instance, it polluted the temple to be only one wall away from the Judean throne's idolized power (Ezek. 43:6–9). This provoked the prophet's word of judgment on both. Whereas

royal, priestly Son's more effective prophesying, reigning, and interceding are something his subjects can take heart in, benefit from, and participate in. In Christ the goal is attained and held in trust for trustworthy heirs to receive someday, with the Spirit shared as the symbol of his enduring commitment. The ends of the earth are his possession. God has given Jacob's heir the bounty of heaven and earth far beyond Isaac's imaginings (Gen. 27:28). Israel's holy goals are now in sight in a radical new way. That inheritance, present and future, is an appropriate focus of life in new Israel.

This explains why Christian worship in the New Testament carries such a pronounced and *sustained* tone of joyful exultation.[17] The church maintained that tone as the Israel of God waited longer and longer to receive it in full. Some were soon wondering whether Jesus would return at all (2 Pet. 3:8–9), while others jumped on rumors that Jesus's coming had already happened, even in the absence of signs they had been forewarned about (2 Thess. 2:1–10). These confusions notwithstanding, Jesus's waiting subjects continue to focus worshipfully on the glory and service of the Messiah, on the One who sent him, and on the One he received and poured out. That's another promise fulfilled: "Let peoples serve you, and nations bow down to you" (Gen. 27:29).

God has handed an Israelite "all rule and authority" (Col. 2:9–10). The Son is not only prominently but preeminently powerful (1:18–19). Christians demonstrate this by following him, *really* following him, as the Lord. No intermediating power—a state, a culture, a family, a party, an ideology, even old Israel's customs and regulations—can sustain its habitual claims of absolute authority or should expect to succeed in bullying believers. Even when Christians *obey* these earthly authorities, as Paul calls us to do as we can (3:22–4:1), we do it out of obedience to our heavenly authority, whom they too serve. Christian obedience is a sign of Christ's preeminence over powers whose authority would otherwise go unquestioned. "Set your minds on things that are above, not on things that are on earth," Paul told the church (3:2).

The trusting and obedient believers who do this take on Christ's authority. Jesus ascended to reign in the capital, and his reign extends through his ambassadors in the territories and on the frontier. They are joined together as a head and a body across that infinite distance (Col. 2:18–19). Israel is no

---

these three manifestations of God's power conflict over much of Israel's history, they converge perfectly in Christ's transformed threefold office of prophet, priest, and king.

17. The prophets can only exult like this in anticipation. Moments of victory such as those in Ezra, Nehemiah, and even Esther can't match new Israel's celebrating. And though the songs of Moses and Miriam in Exod. 15 do, Israel's gaiety vanishes within days.

longer at the bottom of Jacob's ladder; Israel *is* Jacob's ladder, top to bottom. And the Lord is no longer standing above it, but has taken it to himself in the Son, bottom to top. "Therefore let no one pass judgment on you. . . . Let no one disqualify you . . . [who is] not holding fast to the Head" (Col. 2:16, 18–19). Even slaves in the ancient world enjoyed a measure of their masters' social prestige, and Jesus's servants are *heirs* (Rom. 8:15–17). So Christ's church is submissive not like a pagan god's suppliants but like apprentices, ambassadors, and deputies. We are sent along on his apostolic mission to display the Kingdom's otherwise hidden glory, power, and prominence (3:2–4).

The apostolic church knew that prominence is a mixed blessing. Jesus warned his followers that the opposition he faced would be directed at them (John 15:18–25), and it was. New Israel *suffers* Jesus's glory (Col. 1:24–29). This is why Paul can be afflicted, perplexed, persecuted, struck down, and constantly bearing his mortality—a heavy omega for him personally and ethnically—and never crushed, desperate, forsaken, or destroyed but rather showing Jesus's life, a far more glorious alpha (2 Cor. 4:8–12). The character of new Israel's power and prominence is summed up in their source, Jesus himself. To paraphrase 1 Peter and echo Athanasius, Jesus became a substitute for us so that we could become substitutes for him, following in the steps of our worthy servant-shepherd who suffered for us unworthy sheep (1 Pet. 2:21–25, quoting Isa. 53).

### Wisdom

Clearly Paul's "Israel of God" still faces a lot of the problems of "Israel according to the flesh." Her third gift of wisdom demonstrates the same kind of ambiguous transformation as the other two. The New Testament church was soon struggling with, well, you name it: apostasy, misunderstanding and even heresy, conflict and even schism, hypocrisy and even corruption, idolatry, violence, old varieties of sexual immorality, complacency, snobbery, selfishness, passivity, and misuse of the Spirit's gifts and call. *Where's the wisdom?* Christians wince at Paul's churches just as we wince at the patriarchs, because we see ourselves so clearly in them. And Paul and the other New Testament writers regularly draw on Old Testament disasters as warnings and use Old Testament rules as guidance. *What exactly changed?* Whatever it was, it wasn't personal character—at least not by as much as one might expect. And whatever new gifts God's people received (whether you want to emphasize sacraments, manifestations of the Spirit, or sound doctrines), their use has not prevented or cured these persistent failures.

Paul must have realized this as painfully as anyone, because he worked so hard for so long to improve his churches. If he didn't see a lot of new wisdom in his churches, where did he see it?

Isaiah 29 had advised Israel not to look for wisdom in her own midst. Israel's storehouses of wisdom, and even her Torah, hadn't prevented her from stumbling repeatedly into disaster. Paul paid attention to that. To his deeply flawed but highly self-esteemed Corinthian congregation, he quoted a passage:

> Because this people draw near with their mouths
>> and honor me with their lips,
>> while their hearts are far from me,
> and their worship of me is a human commandment learned by rote;
> so I will again do
>> amazing things with this people,
>> shocking and amazing.
> *The wisdom of their wise shall perish*,
>> and the discernment of the discerning shall be hidden.
>
> (Isa. 29:13–14 NRSV)

Because the wisdom supposedly in Israel's midst was so external to its people— on their lips and in their books but not in their hearts—God told Isaiah he would do something surprising that confounded its so-called sages. God would extinguish their false "wisdom" and confound the judgment that *was* in those hearts. To Paul, that explained it. The good news of Jesus Christ is that genuine wisdom, preached without the trappings of worldly wisdom or even the trappings of the Torah that it had put to shame anyway (1 Cor. 1:17–21). God had made *Jesus Christ* "our wisdom, our righteousness and sanctification and redemption" so that, just as God had prophesied, we could boast in no other (1 Cor. 1:26–31; Jer. 9:24).

Isaiah later foresaw a restoration in which "all your sons will be taught by YHWH, and great shall be their *shalom*" (Isa. 54:13, my translation). That's how Jesus described the event of his own teaching in John's Gospel (John 6:45). The disciples being drawn to him were not just learning wisdom from an exceptional rabbi; they were the foundation of Israel's renewal.

New Israel's wisdom has a paradoxical quality. It necessarily remains beyond itself, in Jesus alone. Yet if it were *merely* beyond itself, nothing would have changed from the old days when Israel was stumbling in the dark. The good news *of* Jesus is on lips *and* in hearts (Rom. 10:9). It is not a commandment of fear learned by rote like the Torah had been in Isaiah's age. *This* word, this *new* word, "the word of Christ we preach," is near us in a new way. "I know that God is here," Jacob had said at Bethel. We can say the same in much greater depth and confidence.

This sets up a thorny question. If our awareness that "Jesus is wisdom" resides internally, but the wisdom itself remains external, should we be content to point to it while we go on being foolish? Paul anticipated the same kind of question regarding righteousness. If the righteousness is God's, not ours, shall we just go on sinning? Of course not (Rom. 6:1–2). Because the Spirit of life was *behind* the Torah and operated through it, the Spirit's freedom from Torah is not license to sin but direct and powerful freedom *for* righteousness. Likewise, knowing that our old wisdom is dead and buried, how could we keep trying to depend on it? The cross that put it to death has freed us to cling to the true source of our life. Many Christians *do* continue living foolishly (that is, relying on the world's received wisdom) just as they continue walking in wickedness. Christian moral failure and bad judgment do not themselves discredit the source of true wisdom and life. However, they do prolong Christian immaturity, which is certain to pass away one way or another along with the old age and its discredited rulers (1 Cor. 2:6–9). Something utterly different is replacing it: a wise mind, Christ's mind (1 Cor. 2:16, quoting Isa. 40:13). Through the Spirit, God has made it available to the spiritual (1 Cor. 2:10–15). It *does* internalize and mature, though not among those who continue walking in the flesh's old foolishness (3:1–3).

Old Testament Wisdom literature categorized humanity into two groups: the wise and the foolish. Ecclesiastes delivered the devastating insight that old-school wisdom wasn't that much of an advantage over old-school folly. The learned reaction to Jesus Christ proved that in spades. Paul was one of Jesus's learned opponents, and he never forgot how the Lord humbled him. For him it was the beginning of genuine wisdom. So 1 Corinthians' treatment of wisdom seems to feature two nuanced categories: the newly spiritual but immature, and the mature. Wisdom's role in new Israel is moving God's people into newness and toward maturity.

Before Christ's advent, this had remained out of reach, but it had long been God's stated intent. In the passage Paul quoted, Isaiah went on to describe the result of God's new direction. "The wise" imagine they can plot and act apart from God, but they are as deluded as a pot that denies that a potter made it for a purpose (Isa. 29:16, quoted in Rom. 9:19–20). But when Lebanon becomes lush and fruitful and when Jacob sees his children, they will understand. The ignorant will come to a new appreciation of both themselves and the Lord, and the obstinate will become teachable (Isa. 29:17–24). God will have moved them into newness and toward maturity. Echoing the verses in Isaiah that follow the one he quoted, Paul insisted that God has wisely (Rom.

11:33) placed hardened Jews and softened gentiles into their respective roles in bringing mercy and richness to the whole world just as Isaiah had prophesied (9:21–26; 11:17). He likened ethnic Israel's present and future to death and resurrection (11:15). Paul saw Jewish believers as a holy firstfruits of the fullness that is to come (11:16). God was shaping the pots of the nations through the pot of Israel, and vice versa. They both remained unfinished in Paul's day (11:12, 17–20) and in ours.

Like the prophets, Paul did not see this as some arbitrary act showcasing God's infinite power. Sure, it displayed divine sovereignty. But Job already learned that through his suffering (Job 42:1–6), and many others do too. If Jesus's coming were just piling on additional evidence of God's sovereignty, how could Paul regard the gospel as a mystery hidden for ages? To treat God's strategy for the nations as the arbitrary unconditional election of a sovereign and hidden God (Luther's term was *deus absconditus*) stops way too soon. Besides, demonstrations of raw, inscrutable power don't make people teachable, because they offer nothing to learn besides submission. No, God's way in Isaiah that Paul traces in Romans is *itself* wisdom (Rom. 16:27). The olive tree is growing wiser (11:24–25; 16:17–20), not just larger. So Paul concludes his whole extended exercise in Romans 9–11 of exploring the mystery of God's present actions with a call for transformation and perfection (12:1–2). The lessons of Christ crucified go beyond the humility of knowing that only God is God. They train new Israel away from even the world's very best old ways and toward new self-understanding; sacrificial regard for others (especially the weak); dedication to serving; generous love toward friends, strangers, and enemies alike; respect for authorities; and readiness for the end. All of these emphases in Romans 12–15 are what Paul in 1 Corinthians 1 calls the wisdom of the cross, which we grasp with the mind of Christ and exercise through the Holy Spirit's leadership and fellowship. They are Israel's omega and alpha extended into lives and across generations.

There is no incongruity in Paul drawing on Old Testament texts to contrast its era with ours. Old Israel's Scriptures have not lost their usefulness. On the contrary, they record the wisdom Israel gained in its "school of hard knocks," which was written down for us so that we can learn its lessons the easy way (1 Cor. 10:11). New Israel is like a younger child who has the advantage of an older sibling's experience and example to follow. And God is like a parent who, having once set a harsh example with the oldest child, can now rely on reminders instead.

Paul's guidance is not the New Testament's last word on Old Testament Scripture's usefulness. Jesus in Matthew illustrates its richness as a treasury out of which stewards can bring new things and old (Matt. 13:52). Mentioning the new things first honors the way that the Kingdom's coming has unlocked new meanings of Scripture that overshadow but do not displace the old ones. And 2 Peter urges Christians to pay attention to the prophets, not just because God spoke through them, but especially because they have been confirmed so abundantly by the living Christ (2 Pet. 1:16–21; 3:2). Old Israel's light and wisdom are even richer light and wisdom for new Israel (2 Pet. 2).

Old Israel displayed (and still displays) God's wisdom before it, over it, on it, in it, and into and through it. With the Father's gift of the Holy Spirit, each of these relationships has come into its own. The culmination of each way of encountering God's wisdom turns out to be a personal relationship that the Holy Spirit *himself* has forged with new Israel. The Spirit comes *in advance of* her as Creator, baptizing us into a sensible and sound life. The Spirit reigns *over* her as Lord, leader, commander, and guide, offering structures for an orderly life together and words of knowledge and rebuke that we could not have developed on our own. The Spirit comes *upon* her as anointing, empowering us to go into an uncertain world, deliver its captives, and proclaim his Kingdom's riches. The Spirit dwells *in* her as sanctifier, building up his temple as Christ's someday flawless body, intimately aware of the Lord and of our own selves, and truly at home with both. And the Spirit flows *into and through* her as living and life-giving water, replenishing not just our own selves but also the Lord's wisdom-parched world. All this amounts to a new instruction—a kind of Torah, but one suited to new Israel's life and to the coming city (Heb. 13:14).

If Israel takes advantage of her incredible new access to wisdom, she may forsake many of her legitimate but old and now obsolete concerns. Regaining or holding land in Canaan and meticulous observance of covenantal ritual were not Jesus's focus either before or after his crucifixion, so they are not his servants' proper focus either. As Paul put it, new Israel's focus has been (or should have been) shifted off of "earthly things"—that is, matters at the periphery and consigned to the past—and onto "heavenly things," matters in the Kingdom's capital, where Christ reigns and from where the future is arriving (Col. 2:16–3:4).

In old Israel's best moments, the Torah looked incomparably beautiful, wise, and just, despite lacking the power to deliver what it promised. Psalm 119's lavish praise of the Torah contrasts with the New Testament's more measured yet still appreciative appraisals, for instance in Romans 7:12. This is instructive. If we share Jesus's intentions (1 Pet. 3:18–4:7), followers cannot hold on to our old allegiances. Not in the same way, anyway. Jews' tutelage under Moses's old arrangement has come to its intended end, replaced by faith through the Spirit and inheritance *of* the Spirit (Gal. 3:23–26). Jacob's relationship with divine wisdom has changed forever. "The law of the Spirit of life in Christ Jesus has set me free from the law of sin and death . . . in order that the just requirement of the law might be fulfilled in us, who walk . . . according to the Spirit" (Rom. 8:2–4).

Many don't walk with the Spirit, at least not according to the New Testament's descriptions of what that looks like. They are missing out. They risk missing out on much more. But those who do walk with the Spirit are on the way to inheriting God's promises to Jacob with a fullness that even they cannot imagine, let alone Jacob.

### New Israel's Leaders

Paul spent his life in both old and new Israel and lived their distinct ways of life: first "Judaism" and then "the *ekklesia* of God" (Gal. 1:13, my translation). He knew them both well. He saw plenty of flesh acting badly in the latter and plenty of Spirit in the former. An ethical contrast isn't finally what distinguishes them. It's leadership.

The Old Testament chronicles God's construction of a people called and gifted to become something that they still couldn't. Not just because of sin, but because "flesh and blood cannot inherit the kingdom of God" (1 Cor. 15:50). Old Israel is a necessary beachhead from which God advanced something necessarily new (Jer. 31, quoted in 2 Cor. 3:1–18) and a pointer that foreshadows that coming fulfillment (Heb. 8:13; 10:1). The New Testament chronicles God's reconstruction of a people redeemed—not only from sin, but from servitude to the powers of the old order—who could begin living into Israel's lasting identity. God's people can finally be free to grow into who they are, by internalizing the loving substance of the old covenant, accomplishing God's missional purposes, and inheriting the new creation they themselves anticipate with lives of faith, hope, and love.

Of course, that's easier said than done. The Torah's vision, realistic and accommodative as it was, remained far above old Israel's reality. Jesus remains far ahead of his own people too, in the very qualities that have always distinguished Israel: belonging, prominence, and wisdom. Yet when we fail, our leader stands in glorious contrast, "for he cannot deny himself" (2 Tim. 2:13); and when we succeed, he stands in glorious likeness in our midst, for "if we have died with him, we shall also live with him . . . [and] reign with him" (2:11–12). As ethnic Israel displayed its election as both a sign and a countersign, so the church signals its ascended Lord in its defeats as well as its triumphs. New Israel is the Messiah's body: still a mess, but on its way to flawlessness on the day of its union, with infinite room to grow to the fullness of Messiah's stature.

So new Israel is different not because Christians are superior to fellow Jews or gentiles but because Jesus is their leader in their midst until the end of the age (Matt. 28:20). He established a hope for new Israel beyond the possibilities of old Israel's hopes. New Israel is higher because Jesus sits far above every authority, closer to God because in Jesus the fullness of God dwells bodily, more expansive because Jesus reigns in the heavens and on and under the earth, and eternal because his Kingdom shall have no end. And Jesus's people, who are themselves none of these things, benefit.

Capable leadership was essential to old Israel's success. God's people suffered terribly under corrupt high priests, grasping kings, and leadership vacuums. A worthy leader was never enough to solve all of her problems; even the best leadership could not eliminate Israel's character flaws or defuse external threats—but a worthy leader could compensate enough for these weaknesses that Israel could survive and even improve.

New Israel's situation is both alike and unalike. On the one hand, poor church leadership has still been a grave problem. Church leaders have been corrupt, ambitious, ignorant of the gospel and their own role in God's mission, heretical, complacent, schismatic, and unaware of mortal threats to the church's well-being. These shortcomings have drastically weakened Christ's churches. Jesus asked, "When the Son of man comes, will he find faith on earth?" (Luke 18:8). Was it a rhetorical question? Even if it was, it spoke to a besetting condition in his communities of so-called disciples.

On the other hand, *messiah* was the leader Israel hoped for, so Israel has the leader it needs. If Jesus is the priest for Israel that Melchizedek was for Abraham, then new Israel and God truly belong to each other through thick and thin. If he is David's royal heir, then new Israel's leader is preeminent in all things and *better* than world-class. If Jesus is Israel's long-awaited prophet like Moses, then new Israel has been supplied that source of wisdom from above without reserve. If Christ remains ascended and exalted in these offices forever, then no incompetent earthly representative can undo it.

In the fourth century, Donatists drew the opposite conclusion and claimed that immoral earthly leaders effectively annulled the church. Augustine helped convince the church that earthly priests shared the authority of Jesus's priesthood regardless of their personal morality. Jesus's leadership was decisive for the validity of the church's life and sacraments. Christian history confirms that the Donatists were wrong. Centuries of poor leadership have not prevented the Spirit from working salvation, giving gifts, and growing fruit. New Israel is indeed in a less precarious position than old Israel.

Yet Christian history also suggests that Augustinians were too sanguine about the state of a church beset with inadequate earthly leadership. The church turned into a kind of grace-dispensing machine whose own worthiness had little to do with its function. No matter how corrupt Catholic and Orthodox leadership became, God's grace just kept flowing, like crude oil from a decadent dictatorial regime. Protestant reformations in Europe generally debated the nature and means of the grace that was dispensed (imputed or imparted? through the biblical Word or through two or seven sacraments?), without adequately questioning whether the model of a grace dispensary really honored the role of new Israel's leaders. The New Testament writings show far higher concern for the personal integrity of leaders. Why is this, and why has poor earthly leadership been so destructive, if Jesus's heavenly leadership is decisive?

The answer is found between the lines of the many admonitions Paul and his fellow leaders issue to their churches, and especially their churches' leaders: "The aim of our charge is love that issues from a pure heart and a good conscience and sincere faith. Certain persons by swerving from these have wandered away" (1 Tim. 1:5–6). "Aim at righteousness, godliness, faith, love, steadfastness, gentleness. Fight the good fight of the faith; take hold of the eternal life to which you were called" (6:11–12). "Rekindle the gift of God that is within you" (2 Tim. 1:6). These longed-for leadership qualities are what Paul elsewhere calls "the fruit of the Spirit" that opposes "the works of the flesh" (Gal. 5:13–26). The decisive factor is the church's responsive relationship with the Holy Spirit.

Even with Christ's headship—*especially* with Christ's headship—the church must be extraordinarily receptive to the Holy Spirit's indwelling (belonging), lordship (prominence), and power (wisdom) in order to do more than just hold together.[18] New Israel is no longer under a custodian, with the limited capacities and responsibilities of a minor. New Israel has reached the age of majority. We are called to lives of walking with our resident Holy Spirit in freedom.

Now that Israel has come of age, the stakes of both success and failure are higher. Now that Israel has received the *arrabōn*, or down payment, of its inheritance, it matters all the more how we behave with that inheritance. Our failures to walk with the Spirit will not dethrone our Lord Jesus, nor

18. Old Israel's canonical history demonstrates that Christ's headship matters far more than the kinds of political considerations we dwell on nowadays in our civics and ecclesiologies: whether God's people are politically decentralized or centralized, hierarchical or (relatively) egalitarian, tribal or monarchical, and the like. Structures of flesh and blood matter, but they can neither compensate for the flesh nor substitute for the Spirit.

even sever the body from its head. But unfaithfulness can downgrade our fruitfulness, and ultimately it can sever us from the body and disqualify us from sharing the Spirit's blessings when the Son returns (1 Cor. 9:23–27). God is not held in contempt: walking with the Spirit means much more than just taking Communion, reading the Bible, or going to church regularly while otherwise gratifying our old selves. Whoever "sows to his own flesh will from the flesh reap corruption; but he who sows to the Spirit will from the Spirit reap eternal life" (Gal. 6:8).

Paul's new life, in its powerful integrity, respects all of this. Being joined to Jesus Christ and walking with the indwelling Spirit did not make him fruitful or perfect right away. However, it did open up his life to new possibilities of remarkable fruitfulness in his earthly ministry, and ultimate perfection for the age to come. Through Paul, *Saint Paul*, Jesus developed his Israel in ways that could never have come to pass when she was "confined under the law" (Gal. 3:23).

### Newer Israel?

Will there come an even newer Israel? There's no shortage of candidates. Muhammad's *umma* restored a community of pure faith after the corruptions of Jews and Christians. The modern Enlightenment established a new order of reason and progress following the ignorance and stagnation of what moderns derisively called the Dark Ages. The Church of Jesus Christ of Latter-Day Saints restored Christianity under a revitalized apostolic office. Christian Science unlocked Scripture's previously hidden meaning. Zionism ushered in a new season of Jewish initiative after waiting and waiting for a messiah left Jews victimized for centuries. And so on. According to all of these schemas, the coming of Jesus Christ in the first century was not Israel's omega and alpha. Something else was, or will be; or else nothing is, and everything simply goes on as before.

Let one contrary image refute all this: the scroll of Revelation 5. It contains all that must happen following the present church age (Rev. 4:1). Its words are both unknown and unfulfilled. Only opening it accomplishes them. They are like Daniel's sealed book of unknowns (Dan. 12:4), not Isaiah's already disseminated words that the supposedly wise and discerning cannot understand (Isa. 29:11–14), nor Ezekiel's scroll that can already be read, digested, and delivered (Ezek. 2:9–3:5), nor even Jeremiah's clear but buried deed to the promised land (Jer. 32:6–15). Revelation's scroll is a mystery disclosed only during the New Testament era. It shows that old Israel's full purpose could not have been revealed, let alone realized, until the one worthy to open them came and conquered.

John perceives that new Israel's formation as Israel restored (Rev. 7:4–8) and the nations' ingathering (7:9–17) are parts of that fulfillment, but only parts. These things happen only on the breaking of the *sixth* seal. There is still a seventh. This indicates that Israel's renewal, and even the nations' inclusion, is not itself the full and final goal.

Even before the first seal is broken, the heavenly chorus glorifies the Lamb for having ransomed God's people from every nation and having made them a kingdom and priests (Rev. 5:9–10). Those accomplishments are *not* the contents of the scroll; John does not envision old or new Israel fulfilling its purpose merely by existing. They are merely a basis for its unfurling. Here we can agree with all those heretical movements that see God's purposes as lying beyond the church: new Israel per se is not the whole fulfillment of God's intentions.

Yet no later figure or turn of events opens that seventh seal. The Lamb does (Rev. 8:1), not Muhammad nor Descartes nor Hume nor Joseph Smith. God's will for the whole world, which Israel was tasked with accomplishing, lies solely in Jesus's hands. He has died and lived; he has risen and ascended; he is the alpha and omega and the One Who Is (1:10–20). And because of his efforts for new Israel and through it, his new priestly kingdom "shall reign on earth" (5:10)[19] at the time that the nations rage, God's wrath arrives, the dead are judged, God's servants are rewarded, and the destroyers are destroyed (11:18).

Time to talk about those nations.

---

19. Revelation casts new Israel's prominence ominously as two witnesses in the likeness of Moses and Elijah: messengers God sent to free, teach, and convict a stubborn and resistant old Israel. Their unstoppable power and testimony would frustrate the world, their murder would cause God's enemies to gape and rejoice, and their vindicating ascension would terrify people into glorifying God (Rev. 11:1–14). Who are these mysterious figures? They seem to be Christ's church.

The two witnesses are the lampstands and olive trees of Zech. 4. In Rev. 1:20 lampstands refer to Christ's churches, so the clearest reference is to the church. The olive trees are more obscure, referencing two figures in Zech. 4:11–14 who are commissioned by being anointed (with olive oil, thus the imagery). God's point in Zech. 4:5 seems to be what the image alludes to: "Not by might, nor by power, but by my Spirit" (4:6). Zion's temple is sure to be restored, and every other competitor will be leveled (4:7; 8:3; 14:10).

# SIX

# Jesus—the End and the Beginning of the Nations

Through him both of us have access in one Spirit to the Father. So then *you are no longer strangers and aliens*, but *you are citizens* with the saints and also members of the household of God.

Ephesians 2:18–19 NRSV

Each chapter's scope seemed to narrow from its predecessor. Why now expand from one nation to all? Because the sequence has been following something deeper and more important than scope: *structure*.

The fundamental structure of being is grounded in God's triune nature; thus chapter 2. The fundamental structure of God's free creation is "the world" whose agents interact with God and one another, so chapter 3; and God has gifted humanity with pride of place there, so chapter 4. Humanity is structured into persons and into tribes, with Israel—the man and the nation—taking priority in both categories, so chapter 5. Other nations and other human beings are brought into Israel: nations are grafted onto and persons are baptized into the Israel of God, so chapters 6 and 7, respectively. All of this is Christ; all of these are Christ; Christ is all in all. Our sequence is tracing the deep metaphysical structure in which all things have their life from the Father, their death in the Son, and their resurrection through the Holy Spirit.

This deep structure is not some serene metaphysic that exists timelessly like laws of philosophy or physics (if they actually do). Rather, it is grounded, to borrow words from Blaise Pascal, in the "God of Jacob, not of the philosophers and savants. . . . God of Jesus Christ. My God and your God."[1] Reality's structure is *timeful*: storied, apocalyptic, violent, cross- and resurrection-shaped. That is obviously the case with this chapter's topic. Probably the single most historically verifiable aspect of Jesus's life is that Roman officials killed him. What does that mean for the nations? We will examine nations' ambiguous origins and nature, their opposition to God's order, Jesus's apocalyptic conquest in the face of their threat, and the end and new beginning it poses for individual nations, their constituents, their governing powers, their international order, and nationhood itself.[2]

## Nations in Genesis

When we talked about the cosmos, it was helpful to clarify the term. What is a nation? Here we are less interested in contemporary debates among anthropologists than in understandings of nationhood in the Old and New Testament eras behind biblical claims about the nations.

The term *nation* is usually used in plural and generic senses in Scripture. The nations are a swarm of foreignness. They tend to be regarded as sources of little more than grief when things go wrong and tribute when they go right. The swarm includes both the nearby foreignness of "cousin" nations spawned from the likes of Ishmael, Lot, and Esau and who had relationships with God and claims to nearby territory, and the faraway foreignness of Canaanites, Hittites, and Egyptians, who had no such special status. Whether they are being differentiated or not, they are *the nations*: peoples who aren't Israel.

Genesis is not mainly about the beginnings of creation, humanity, the fall, or even the nations.[3] Genesis concerns the genesis of *Israel*. Chapters 12–50 are devoted to the topic. Yet Genesis's primordial narratives pay sustained attention to other nations' genealogies and practices. That's a clue that the nations are more than just a swarm of foreign threats. Those foreign peoples are significant as the background and context in which Israel came into being.

1. Blaise Pascal, "Memorial," http://www.users.csbsju.edu/~eknuth/pascal.html.
2. Beyond a few brief references, we will not be discussing the long debate between and within circles of Dispensational and Covenant theology, Zionism and contemporary Israel/Palestine, postcolonialism and globalization, racial and interracial dynamics in the United States, or other current particular topics. Those interested in any of these are invited to approach this chapter with them in mind.
3. Narrative theology is fond of treating "the biblical story" as a five- or six-act play, in which acts 1 and 2 are creation and fall. However, the attention to both of them is miniscule compared to the attention lavished on Israel. If the Bible is analogous to a theatrical production or symphony with movements, a different analysis of the drama seems called for.

Genesis's narrative account of "nationhood" goes deeper than the purely phenomenological markers that contemporary anthropologists rely on. It carefully distinguishes between features of human differentiation that are natural to us and features that run counter to God's vision for humanity.[4]

Peoples first emerge after humans are exiled from Eden (Gen. 4:16–24). However, nationhood is not just fallout from the fall. One little hint in Genesis 2 suggests that nationhood is a human structural feature rather than just an effect of our sinfulness: the observation that "a man *leaves his father and his mother* and cleaves to his wife, and they become one flesh" (2:24). Unfallen humans would not have multiplied in an ever-growing mass like a colony of mold. We are not diverse and distant only because of sin, confusion, or competition. Humans are made to divide as well as multiply; families are made to disintegrate as well as form. They are naturally ephemeral. Sin complicated this picture, as we see when one brother murdered another and experienced an additional, "internal" human exile (4:12–17). But it seems that humanity would have been complicated anyway.

While "nations" refers to ethnicities rather than the nation-states we typically think of, the nations are political entities that are ruled by powers and authorities, both official and unofficial. A key dynamic of leadership is the identification a people makes with an authority, usually a king, who comes to represent them.[5] So we can't draw too sharp a contrast between ethnic and political nationhood.

Genesis 10–11 sketches a table of nations that grows from the lines of Noah's sons. As in Genesis 4, they are geographically distinct and economically specialized. Sandwiched in the middle of that sprawling genealogy is the story of Babel, which explains how humanity lost its ability to understand and cooperate as one. After the nations conspired against the Lord, he turned nationhood into a providential dividing wall that partitions us from one another for our own good. Like spousal relationships (Gen. 3:16), "nationhood" is an originally good aspect of human relationship distorted into a means and product of human disintegration, a mixed blessing like all the rest.

Genesis 1–11 allows us to imagine a kind of holy nationhood that is unmarred by sin and sinful conspiracy against God. Tribes would still be differentiated from one another. They would multiply, specialize, live in different spaces, and lead different lives. Yet they would share a common language and communicate, trade, work together, and worship as one.

4. This is so whether Genesis's primordial narratives are using history as a literary device to examine these different aspects of nationhood or are teaching a literal sequence of events.

5. See Oliver O'Donovan, *The Ways of Judgment* (Grand Rapids: Eerdmans, 2005), chap. 9.

That sounds like Israel, doesn't it? In Jacob's family we begin to see what Genesis 1–11 already lets us imagine. God did not accede to a world of nations enslaved to their own dysfunction. Instead, from Genesis 12 onward God started something new with Abraham. But not something entirely new. God didn't just abolish human nationhood and construct a new kind of social organization. Nor did God just directly repair those broken nations. Instead, God made in their midst a new nation (really a family of several nations) pretty much from scratch.

The nations had plotted to make a name for themselves with the tower of Babel so that they would remain united (Gen. 11:4). The world tried to assert a center for itself and with itself—to construct its own identity, you might say—but God prevented that. God then acted to make a name for *Abraham* by choosing him (12:2) to make a true center for scattered humanity, a different kind of center. Each act yielded nations, but they were different *kinds* of nations, nonetheless made with each other in mind.[6]

Last chapter examined how Jesus remade Jacob's uniquely gifted line as the Israel of God. Because Israel is a different kind of nation from the rest, or becomes one anyway, drawing a straightforward analogy with other nations would mislead. First we need a clearer understanding of how gentiles are distinct from Israel, what the two kinds of nations have in common, and what nationhood amounts to.

## The (Other) Nations

Go to museums anywhere in the world and you will see whole floors full of artifacts from far "greater" civilizations and empires than Israel. Some have fallen into obscurity, while others' descendant-societies still dominate the world stage. As far as God's salvation of the world is concerned, they're practically interchangeable. Revelation makes the point by calling first-century Rome "Babylon" (Rev. 14:8). Daniel characterizes every rival empire as a beast of some sort. They are different from each other, but not *that* different (Dan. 7:3). Rather than four, there might as well have been three or five. And in fact there have been many more than that. If Daniel imaginatively invents some kings and transplants historical kings such as Darius from one nation to another, well, that just confirms the Jewish view of "the nations." Any given empire and any given nation is significant, but ultimately dispensable, even superfluous.

6. Cousin-nations like Edom might be seen to occupy a third category: nations through promise or loyalty but not through election. However, Israel's election cuts across that common ground so cleanly that in the long run those nations may as well be lumped in with the others.

This seems like a terribly insensitive thing to say. Perhaps unforgivably so in our multicultural twenty-first century. Yet it is the Bible's consistent perspective, as well as that of the early patristic era. Individual nations just aren't all that notable in their own right.

Even Israel isn't much of an exception to the rule. This people is God's chosen vessel, unique and central to human history. "Salvation is from the Jews" (John 4:22). However, God transcends Israel. Their relationship is a true bond, but of grace rather than necessity. She was founded on nothing but God's sheer will to promise and create and provide (Ezek. 5:5), so her unique significance is not her own. "God is able from these stones to raise up children to Abraham" (Luke 3:8).

The other nations are utterly contingent peoples too, but for the opposite reason. They sprang up from natural forces of flesh and blood.[7] These creatures of ordinary cause and effect, so important in our own eyes and so powerful in one another's, are in God's reckoning "like a drop from a bucket . . . accounted by him as less than nothing" (Isa. 40:15–17). Linger on that statement. Your people and mine aren't even worth drops of our own. In fact, in God's accounting, we aren't even *nothing*. Our peoples are liabilities, dead weight. We detract from the value of humanity, like money-losing divisions of a beleaguered company. According to Isaiah 40, the world would be better off without us.

That valuation contrasts absolutely with the world's current cultural conventions. In fact, skeptics associate it with a genocidal mindset they see in Scripture and its God, and reject both. That's too bad, because God's judgment of the nations is just what our violent and traumatized age needs. It skewers nationalism's cherished homogeneity and unity and self-evident impulse to grow and dominate, *and* imperialism's cherished self-assertion and cultural envy and dissemination, *and* liberationism's subversive self-assertion and table-turning, *and* multiculturalism's cherished diversity and reverse snobbery. These conventional attitudes are idolatries. They are among the traits that make us liabilities to humanity in the first place. And, as we shall see, we can be rid of them.

Israel could fall right into these idolatries too, and it did whenever it chose to be like those other nations. And vice versa. Each kind of nation is susceptible to imagining that it is the other kind. Israel can treat itself as a natural entity and turn into "Israel according to the flesh," pursuing the good life

---

7. And their constructed patron deities are as contingent as they are. Odin and Thor without Germania flatten into colorful mythology and comic-book fiction. The nations are these gods' alpha and omega, not the other way around.

through its own efforts. And some other nation can treat itself as a uniquely destined vessel of glory to the world, created by a "mandate from heaven" for providential purposes and indispensable to salvation.[8] There is enough commonality between these two kinds of nation to make this kind of confusion possible. Israel and the nations are all *nations*.

### What and Whither Is a Nation?

What is this thing—whose varieties we call clans, tribes, families, peoples, tongues, nations, cultures, and the like—that is "less than nothing" yet so basic to human existence? A *phylē* (Gen. 12:3 LXX; Rev. 5:9) is an ephemeral way that humanity is organized. It is a temporary arrangement that evolves as generations leave their parents and join one another to produce and raise the next round of human beings. It involves some degree of common descent; common leadership; common life; common obligations such as military, social, economic, and religious service; and family resemblance.

A *phylē* is a matter of longevity. A family lasts for a few generations at most. A tongue (language) is longer lasting; after all, it is one particular way of expressing a particular way of life. A tribe often lasts even longer; and a people's existence can straddle even a succession of these. Yet all of these change and finally pass away, just as individual persons change and pass away. Next year's family is different from this year's. A nation may pass into the legacies of successors, or simply go extinct.

A nation seems like such a given, such an eternal and unstoppable thing in the moment—such a *beast*—that we tend to forget it is always in flux. That's because it's human, and "all flesh is grass, and all its beauty is like the flower of the field" (Isa. 40:6). Even Israel's flesh.[9]

If all flesh is grass, then think of a *phylē* as a patch of grass. Grass grows more luxuriant in a tuft or a patch than it does individually. Its constituent members rise with the rains and wither in dry summer heat never to return, but the patch itself revives when the next rain comes. Its soil, gene pool, microclimate, environment, and nearby competitors are all factors that give it both a distinctive shape and continuity over time. The patch itself exerts similar force on its own shape and surroundings. It leaves a legacy; it is itself

---

8. For instance, Rome, Arabia, Britain, Russia, Germany, the United States, Ethiopia, or Korea (I lived in the latter two while on sabbatical). All of these peoples have entertained such thoughts.

9. Israel's culture, social structures, gene pool, and languages have changed, diversified, split, faded, and reemerged. What distinguishes it and gives it continuity over centuries is not its flesh but its theological character as God's people.

a legacy. Someday an invasive species may wipe it out, or encroaching woods may choke off its sunlight, or a farmer may buy it and plow it under. A *phylē* is thus more fragile than we tend to think. It depends for survival on both its environment and its constituents, past and future as well as present.

Furthermore, next year's patch will be a little different and leave a somewhat different legacy for whatever succeeds it. Nature is always on the move, from natural wonders such as the Yosemite Valley and Arches National Park to the scene outside your window. So is culture. America is full of migrant communities that have labored to preserve their old-world ways. When Swedes or Vietnamese visit Swedish-American and Vietnamese-American enclaves, they feel like time travelers. Their home countries have all moved on, while the expatriates have turned into pressed flowers. Both groups identify with a legacy, but in shockingly different ways.

God affirms a nation's created glory (Tyre in Ezek. 28, Egypt in Ezek. 31, etc.). To loyalists, a treasured *phylē* seems a sacred and irreplaceable dispensation of special providence worth holding onto forever. Nostalgia taps into this sense when we reflect on ages past and long for them. But if nations are this tenuous and transient, what does it really mean to be Swedish or Vietnamese? And what does it really matter? In the long view, it seems to be nothing but a fleeting epiphenomenon of human sociality, an accident of nature that happens to appeal to our aesthetics, with no broader significance beyond its own temporary relative utility. Grass.

Not so fast. After all, you can describe human beings in the same way. Who is a human being, that God might take any note at all (Ps. 8:4)? Like you readers, I was born "of the will of the flesh" (John 1:13) to be one roll of my parents' genetic dice. I was shaped this way and that by the forces around me and by fluke events. Is "the real me" the cheerful five-year-old, the lonely eleven-year-old, the arrogant fifteen-year-old, the restless twenty-three-year-old, the busy thirty-five-year-old, the haggard forty-five-year-old, the calmer fifty-year-old, some version yet to come, or none of these? Does it even matter?

Yet it does, doesn't it? My loved ones are *persons*, not just moments of flux. Christians are comfortable describing each person as a special gift from God, though we know full well how babies are made and reared. My parents didn't beget and love and know just an impermanent epiphenomenon. They shaped a *person*. Our faculties of perception and memory don't just "construct" us; they respect us, allowing *relationship* rather than just reactivity. To know a person[10] is to know someone with a deeper significance, indeed one of the

---

10. Or a pet, for that matter. Our dog, Violet (see chap. 3), was more than just a throw of the canine genetic dice. She *was* that, but she was also special: an irreplaceable part of our family,

crowning glories of the works of God's hands (Ps. 8:5–6) whom God even grants an eternal personal future. God addresses whole nations too, not just for the moment but as legacies to be realized, cut off, and renewed (Isa. 23; Luke 10:13–15).

Somehow the good news brings a new and immortal beginning to mortal flesh (Isa. 40:6–8, quoted in 1 Pet. 1:23–25).[11] Nations experience a different kind of flux, so they don't necessarily have the same hope. They may be more like Yosemite Valley than Telford Work. Persons have a life span that habitats, families, and nations do not. People individually are born, develop, die, and then rise on the last day to face their Maker (Heb. 9:27). It is not clear how that would work for a *phylē*. When is it conceived? What is its point of death? What would be raised?[12] It is worth entertaining the prospect of a nation's omega and alpha as long as we don't jump to conclusions about its character.

Despite this major difference, persons and nations are both subject to God's judgment. It's uncouth nowadays to mention God judging the nations—you'll be considered a fanatic or worse. Talk of "the wrath to come" (1 Thess. 1:10) confuses and embarrasses many, but it runs through both testaments and the writings of the early church, and rightly so. As we saw in chapter 3, nations are not *just* patches of grass that flourish and fade naturally. These embodiments of creation's glory are also God's chief rivals. Rulers might steer and lead their nations justly and effectively, but they are a lot more likely to overreach and even conspire, plotting to "free" themselves from the Lord and his Messiah (Ps. 2:1–2). In places where Christians are minority populations today, they are most persecuted, so it shouldn't seem too outlandish to consider whether there's some deeper reason why.

In Daniel and other Old Testament apocalyptic literature, the nations are hazy mixtures of ruler, regime, ideology, and culture. They are menacing not just because of the scale of their human numbers and resources but especially

---

even a gift from God. Not a person—I'm not *that* sentimental—but a member, who gained an additional human significance by her relationship with the humans in her "pack." If she were a wild dog or a stray with no human relationships, she would be different (she would not be Violet), but she'd still be a unique and irreplaceable member of "dogdom" rather than just an epiphenomenon of "dogness."

11. We trust that promise even without knowing resurrection's precise details. Medieval Christians concluded that human beings would be raised in a perfected state corresponding to their mortal "peak" age. This was most likely thirty. After all, Jesus's resurrection had set the precedent. Whether or not that's true, it illustrates the challenge of imagining how what is perishable puts on imperishability (1 Cor. 15:54).

12. Regimes (which are distinct from nations) do fall like trees and go down to Sheol (for instance, Assyria and Egypt in Ezek. 31), at least metaphorically. Does that make them eligible for resurrection? Not in Ezek. 31's context of everlasting judgment.

because they tap into the formidable supernatural powers of the cosmos and even those of its heavenly top tier (Ezek. 31).

Apocalyptic's fundamental outlook is that God's people are helpless in the face of such powerful oppression, and their hope depends absolutely on God's coming in an act of definitive cleansing. Noah and his family were saved that way. So were all the Hebrew slaves in Egypt. Jews looked back on these events for assurance that God would come again to deliver them from present and future evils, and that God's anointed would come in judgment someday soon to put away all such threats and bring about a just and lasting order—an everlasting Judean empire, by the way, rather than a multicultural United Nations. In fact, God would use failed and helpless Israel to bring all nations light and salvation (Isa. 49:1–7).

Along one dimension, Israel's apocalyptic encounters are between Jews and their captors' various cultures. Along another, they are one long encounter between the Kingdom of God, to which faithful Jews witness, and every new embodiment of the opposing order. Individual episodes do not line up along some grand arc of history but constitute myriad temporal installments of the Lord's grand judgment and release of the old cosmos and its shadowy ruler. The beasts rule territories not their own, so their dominions are taken away while their lives are preserved "for a season and a time" (Dan. 7:11–12). Then God will act once and for all to end the nations' self-determination and the evil it brings and to inaugurate their eternal service as vassals of God's purified and renewed people. This will finally realize the latent potential in Israel's unique relationship with God, its powerful prominence, and its heavenly wisdom.

## Jesus, King of Kings

In Psalm 2, that coronation song that rang out from heaven at Jesus's baptism, the Lord responds to the nations' provocations by declaring his anointed one Zion's king and grants his "begotten son" those very nations as a heritage and a possession. Jesus is not just the king of Israel proper; he's the king of all (*Pantocrator*) and the King of kings. His story is part of the nations' stories.

When Jesus referred to himself as the Son of Man coming on the clouds (Dan. 7:13–14, quoted in Mark 14:62), he endorsed Daniel's apocalyptic vision of the future and signaled that he was the one who would put a stop to the parade of oppression and establish the Lord's secure and everlasting dominion. He was God's appointed agent on that day when God's enemies would finally meet their doom. And because he appears in the middle of history, not just at the end, he is also the power behind those individual installments of justice when nations' dominions are confiscated but their lives are spared for the time being.

Jesus's resurrection and ascension vindicated the Father's claim and his own. They anchored New Testament apocalyptic's continuity with Old Testament apocalyptic. Those who take refuge in him will find blessing and a new start, but those who kindle his anger are finished (Ps. 2:6–12). "God deems it just to repay with affliction those who afflict you, and to grant rest with us to you who are afflicted, when the Lord Jesus is revealed from heaven with his mighty angels in flaming fire" (2 Thess. 1:6–7). He can break them like pottery with an iron rod (Ps. 2:9).

As they become aware of the situation, this news terrifies them (Ps. 2:4–5). At least the psalm says it does. In fact, no general reaction of terror, relief, or anything else seemed to ensue after Jesus's baptism (Mark 1:9–11) or his ascension in accordance with Psalm 110 (Acts 1:9–14), nor even when Paul first delivered the news to Festus and Agrippa (Acts 25–26). So what do we make of Psalm 2 when we have seen only some details play out rather than the whole scene? What does the risen and reigning Jesus have to do with all those still-conspiring nations?

In the fourth century, the answer suddenly looked obvious: *Christendom* was the nations' future. Jesus had proved to be the end of pagan Armenia, Ethiopia, and Rome, and their new beginning as Christian realms. All other peoples were due for similar revolutions as recognition of Christ's reign spread throughout the world. Athanasius observed that "while idolatry and everything else that opposes the faith of Christ is daily dwindling and weakening and falling, see, the Savior's teaching is increasing everywhere!"[13] Christians of that time, both Byzantine and Catholic, even gained the sense that the Roman Empire played an indispensable part in the history of salvation. God had providentially supplied its structures and resources for bringing the apostolic faith to its maturity as a Holy Tradition that would spread to the ends of the earth and stand until Christ returned.

That is how things looked in the fourth century, but it was not to be. The new regimes could be nearly as worldly as the old ones, as Athanasius himself experienced during his five exiles under unsupportive emperors. Newer movements from Islam to the Enlightenment would rise to dominate, subdue, and eventually empty out Christendom's own centers. In fact, at times the world's most powerful opposition to Christianity issued *from* some of those former centers. And cultures other than Rome could be just as resourceful to missions

13. Athanasius, *On the Incarnation of the Word* 8.55, http://www.ccel.org/ccel/athanasius /incarnation.ix.html.

and churches and leave equally resilient legacies that were incompatible with the old Roman ones. A pessimistic take on Christendom flatly contradicts Athanasius's optimistic interpretation. John Wesley saw the Constantinian shift from persecution to tolerance and then official embrace as "productive of more evil to the church than all the ten persecutions put together."[14] Classic Anabaptists and Dispensationalists see the church as inevitably opposed by the world until eschatological divine relief comes at the end of the age. The problem seems to lie in confusion between the two kinds of nations that God created back in Genesis. Gentile nations have supposed that embracing Christianity turns them into Israel's kind of nation, with a sonship and glory and promises of their own. In reality they are still fleshy grass patches, now with new delusions of grandeur.

Christendom doesn't look like such a compelling fulfillment of Psalm 2's promises. Yet Christendom *did* happen, many Christians (especially Eastern Orthodox) still affirm it, and even critics concede it had its benefits. The gospel did change the courses of civilizations and renew them, in sometimes glorious and long-lasting ways.[15] But the fact remains that the Messiah's first coming left the broad shape of apocalyptic eschatology intact. It had not extinguished the nations' opposition to his reign, or his opposition to theirs.

What then *had* his coming changed? Several things, which together revolutionized the Jewish apocalyptic framework. Jesus's coming demonstrated the surprising character of his reign. As Daniel 7:12 intimated, it introduced an interval of mercy to God's enemies, including gentile enemies. It inaugurated a lasting reconciliation between God and sinners. It neutralized the enemies' greatest weapons: sin, death, and fear. It launched a mission to Israel and the nations to bring the Messiah's achievements to the whole earth. Finally, it yielded the Holy Spirit as a gift to the Messiah's followers, as an assurance of Jesus's loyalty to them until the time of his final appearing on the clouds. In each of these ways, even as apocalyptic eschatology interpreted Christ's

---

14. Frank Baker, ed., *The Works of John Wesley* (Nashville: Abingdon, 1984), 3:450; quoted in Thomas Buchan, "John Wesley and the Constantinian Fall of the Church," in *The Pietist Impulse in Christianity*, ed. Christian T. Collins Winn et al. (Eugene, OR: Pickwick, 2011), 148.

15. At this juncture, many would turn to H. Richard Niebuhr's *Christ and Culture* (New York: Harper, 1975) for a schema of the gospel's possible impacts on cultures. Niebuhr's treatment is more useful than some weighty criticisms have concluded, but it suffers some major flaws. See especially John Howard Yoder, "How H. Richard Niebuhr Reasoned," in *Authentic Transformation: A New Vision of Christ and Culture*, ed. Glen Stassen et al. (Grand Rapids: Eerdmans, 1994), 31–90. For our purposes, several shortcomings really get in the way. It neglects both the continuing relationship between Israel and gentiles and the apocalyptic perspective that the whole New Testament exhibits and that appreciates Jesus Christ as the omega and alpha that he truly is.

revolution and supplied its meaning, Christ's work transformed conventional apocalyptic assumptions and applications. We might say that Jesus was apocalyptic's omega and alpha too.

The last item on that list of accomplishments sums up the rest, so let's cut to the gift of the Holy Spirit. Acts 10 captures the moment when the international significance of the Spirit's outpouring hit the apostles. When the Holy Spirit fell on Cornelius and his household in the middle of Peter's preaching that *everyone* who believes in Jesus receives his forgiveness, it became clear that a wall had fallen too. "The gift of the Holy Spirit had been poured out even on the Gentiles" (Acts 10:45).

God's coming final wrath on all those nations and their idols is still set to arrive as promised (Acts 17:31). But their subjects can get it over with *now*, and in a life-giving way (17:29–30). Receiving that Spirit also means crossing over to receiving the fullness of Israel's blessings that we already examined: intimate belonging to God, association with Jesus's unique power and prominence, and divine wisdom. Maybe this is what triggered the crowd's amazement when the Spirit fell on Cornelius's house. None of these blessings are Jacob's private property! Having received them as Israel's only worthy heir, Jesus has chosen to share them whether or not recipients stand in the covenant of Moses, share Jesus's ethnic identity, or have even undergone his baptism (though such baptism logically follows: Acts 10:47–48).

Jesus had already planted seeds of this revolution during his ministry. He had been unsparing in his call to radical discipleship, insisting that hating one's own life and family members was a prerequisite (Luke 14:26). Any other good thing can become an idol when it is treated as ultimate. Nations have insatiable appetites for our loyalties, and we desire to supply the allegiance they crave. Israel could elevate her fleshly nationhood and confuse it with her spiritual calling, falling into a kind of Constantinian confusion too, what Paul called "confidence in the flesh" (Phil. 3:3–7). Jesus required his disciples to deny all this, not just where our broader identities are concerned, but even at the most primal level of immediate family.

The Lord practiced what he preached. Instead of heading right for home after receiving the Spirit and prevailing in the wilderness, he taught in other Galilean synagogues. When he finally came to Nazareth, he knew his old neighbors would be jealous because he had not started his healing ministry with them (Luke 4:14–16, 23). They expected his "solidarity." Rather than defusing the situation gently or diplomatically, Jesus provoked them to the point of attempted murder by reminding them of other times when foreigners got ahead of locals in line for God's grace, and by announcing that his neighbors' expectations of family solidarity would cause them to reject him and miss out on the Spirit's blessings (4:24–29).[16]

Jesus was not renouncing just one nation's idols of family and ego and culture. By requiring *every* disciple to reject his or her family and self, he renounced them all. That kind of nationhood is ended wherever he has true disciples. The people who obeyed this command did not abandon their respective nations—Peter stayed Jewish and Cornelius stayed Roman—but they now belonged to their peoples in new ways. Jesus had pried apart nationhood and idolatry. The King of all other kings had proclaimed emancipation from slavery to our own nationhood, and his Spirit sealed our freedom.

The nations stand, for now. Jesus's disciples were and are surrounded by idolaters. Some of them are "Christians" who confuse the distinction by using his name while holding onto their old loyalties (Matt. 7:21; Luke 6:46). But true disciples demonstrate the nations have taken on a whole new meaning.

We will draw on a series of New Testament letters to explore this unfolding revolution. The book of Revelation depicts the destruction of old nationhood; 1 Peter and Galatians illuminate the process of transformation to new nationhood from a culture's inside; and Colossians and Ephesians stand on the shoulders of Galatians in order to peer beyond the fading present and into the dawning future in store for the world's peoples and their international relations.

## Nationhood beyond Idolatry

For more on Christianity's revolutionized apocalypticism, it's natural to look to the book of Revelation, "The Apocalypse of Jesus Christ." It features a number of references to Daniel and its succession of empires. Every next beast seems to get worse; none of them seems to learn the lesson. Then comes one last beast of unprecedented power and reach. It takes a final dose of healing justice to stop the succession of beasts. Revelation applies Daniel's sequence to its present day, demonstrating that Daniel's vision applies to every such beast from then until Jesus's final appearing. The earthly tribes who pierced him will wail at his coming. In the meantime, he has taken subjects from them and made a kingdom (Rev. 1:5–7). He is the nations' victim, and he is their only hope.

His passion and resurrection are the self-destructive omega of the nations' legitimacy. His reign as King of kings is also their alpha, their only basis of

16. As I have already suggested, liberationists who expect Jesus's solidarity with some sociological class or other are heading for similar disappointment and rejection.

legitimacy after being disgraced. Jesus has raided them and ransomed countless disciples for himself—a multitude from every nation (Rev. 7:9–12). To have
one's own people honoring and glorifying one's old enemy brings no comfort
to a ruler! It only hardens that ruler's heart and provokes further persecution
(John 15:18–20). Yet the ascended Jesus is out of reach, and even wiping out
his churches will not bring back the old order (Rev. 11:1–13). Jesus knows
the churches in John's day are suffering. He knows they are being persecuted
by the beast, by Rome. Suffering disciples need to know that they are known,
loved, and safe. But Jesus wants them to know something else: Rome, "Babylon the great," is sure to fall (Rev. 18:2).

Does he push Babylon over, or does it collapse on its own? Both, it seems
(Rev. 18:12–14 vs. 18:15–17); and this is important too.

As good as it may be, a nation's glory (Rev. 21:24)—wealth, power, allies,
achievements—will not only fail to deliver it but will also destroy it from
within. The forces of nature, culture, society, and personality that its rulers
try to control and possess will possess them instead and jostle against one
another in fatal conflict. "The ten horns . . . and the beast will hate the har-
lot . . . and devour her" (17:16). This is by design. It is the same providential
structural incoherence with which God frustrated the builders of the tower
of Babel and set them against themselves in rivalry and confusion (17:15–18).
Their own honor and glory must trip them up and fail them. Nations rise
because they are valuable to their own constituents and to the powers behind
them, but they decline because they lack staying power. To grass, a patch is an
advantageous arrangement, so it occurs naturally. But it is not almighty. The
forces that make it strong strengthen rival patches and strains too, and a thriving patch's success makes it attractive to parasites and predators. Nations are
fundamentally unstable entities, and they lack the means to save themselves.

What a disappointment this is to the world in every generation, not least ours.
How it offends these idols to point out their limits. What despair it produces in
the people who were counting on the government to solve the world's problems.
When a disciple of Jesus breaks a taboo and points out the obvious, how outrag-
ing it is to the hearts of the people who put stock in those powers—nationalists,
internationalists, socialists, imperialists, technocrats, activists, patriots, revolu-
tionaries, and utopians alike. And how revolting it is when Jesus's disciples aren't
equally disappointed. No wonder they're shamed and persecuted.

Nevertheless, Jesus wasn't just accelerating the doomed nations' demise
by catalyzing their own internal dynamics.[17] God had sent prophets in the

---

17. A Hegelian-Marxist version of this is "heightening the contradictions" already inherent
in an impermanent social system.

old days to remind both Israel and its enemies that they were headed for destruction *and* that he would act to bring it. Jesus *did* bring the end of that ancient city that was destined to fall anyway, and ended every other with it.[18] He acted decisively, if mysteriously (Rev. 19:1–2). Conspiring Rome was duped into taking part in Psalm 2's fulfillment—not just played by this world's ruler (see chap. 3), but used by its true source and provider (John 19:7–11). Jesus appropriated his people from Rome's many constituent peoples and shared his Spirit with us as assurance that we are truly his lampstands, his bride (Rev. 22:17). If we persevere, we will conquer as he did (Rev. 2–3). There is simply no lasting peace or victory for the nations outside of God's reign. All nations can learn from the example of the beast who holds their future disaster and deliverance in his hands. Nothing is going to dethrone the Lamb now, and nothing else is going to save them.

The fall of the beast and the world that followed it will not mean the annihilation of the nations or their kings. Their tainted honor and glory are due to return to the Lord as the true treasures they are (Rev. 21:22–27). They are no longer worth less than nothing! Revelation 21:24 draws on Isaiah 60 to picture the scene: The new Jerusalem's light is Jesus, by whom the nations will walk, and their kings will go there to offer their glory. These dethroned kings are now paying tribute to the Lamb, the Lion of Judah, the kings' King. And they are finding healing in their old enemy who rules with an iron rod (Ps. 2:9, quoted in Rev. 19:15). Jesus is the alpha of the defeated peoples who take refuge in him. The old object of their rulers' scorn has become the object of their eternal worship.

*All* the nations take part in this procession of fealty, not just the Roman beast's governors and emperors, not even Jesus's most active persecutors. Rome is not a radical exception to the political rule, just the biggest and worst of the lot. Wherever the contemporary United States of America falls along the spectrum of opposition to the Lamb—history suggests that we are somewhere in the middle—he is America's victim too, and America's only hope.

The shift from old nation to new involves a massive transformation that resembles Israel's. Peter's first epistle shows us the process from the inside. Israel rejected its own cornerstone, though a remnant found him precious (1 Pet. 2:4–8). Now the same thing is happening among gentiles. Christ's ransomed Romans live as expatriates of the Kingdom among an unsympathetic

---

18. Jesus is not *merely* a scapegoat, and his atonement does not consist only in exposing our impulse to turn him into one. René Girard's insight into scapegoating is illuminating but hardly comprehensive in its analysis of Christ's significance and atonement. See René Girard, *Things Hidden since the Foundation of the World* (Palo Alto, CA: Stanford University Press, 1987).

population of unbelievers (1 Pet. 2:11). They endure their neighbors' mistrust and misunderstanding like the observant Jewish exiles in the book of Daniel. They are there, like Daniel and his friends are there in Babylon, to declare their deliverer and to live as an example of his goodness in ways that make Christ's reality visible and persuasive (1 Pet. 2:9, 11–16).

That multitude of foreigners in Revelation 7, then, is a harbinger; they are firstfruits (Rev. 14:4). Those lampstands in Revelation 11 are built to embody new ways of being Roman or American or whatever, so that unconverted kin can see what Jesus's work means in their context. Their actions and words are shocking to idolaters. In fact, just by existing and minding their own business these sojourners disappoint and offend. They are nations newly reborn, living in the midst of their aging old selves. The sight of Jesus therein (1 Pet. 1:3) is also what sparks living hope in the old. Peter hopes that those old nations will perceive, and give glory to God on judgment day (2:12).

The text does not say whether they will do that repenting only at the end, or sooner. Nor does it say whether nations as a whole, or only individual members, will turn around and worship their new rival. We can try filling in some of those gaps with the biblical and apocalyptic images that proliferate in the New Testament. I believe they discredit some popular expectations.

Jesus's growing reputation will *not* replace the old apocalyptic framework with some other. That is the hypothesis of postmillennialism: as a little yeast works its way through a whole lump of dough (Matt. 13:33), so the gospel will leaven the whole world and leave no one in their old state, and Jesus will receive only the hero's welcome he deserves on his return. It's an inspiring notion, but the apostles do not foresee the world's old opposition fading away like that.

Believers will *not* just enter a "heavenly" afterlife away from earth, bodies, and politics. That is what most people seem to think Christianity teaches, and what many Christians themselves expect. An endemic, spiritualizing tendency in Christianity insists on omegas for material creation, human nature, ethnic Israel and other nations, and bodily human lives but expects no real alphas. I doubt that careful teaching will ever overturn the sense that we have a future only as disembodied souls in some kind of ethereal mode of existence called "heaven." It's just too intuitive to people. Teachers who know better will just have to keep insisting that Jesus's resurrection *is* the apocalyptic alpha of new creation that remakes not just souls and individual bodies but the nations, the rest of this book's topics, and more.

Jesus's enemies will *not* succeed in their conspiracy to silence his witnesses— though for a time they may appear to. The church has indeed seen severe and lasting setbacks. Traditional Muslims, secular progressives, and other post-

Christian visionaries foresee its permanent demise. A time may come that seems to vindicate them (Rev. 11:9–10). But the One dwelling in the heavens scoffs at such triumphalism (Ps. 2:4). No earthly setback will put Jesus back in the grave, and the One dwelling in his earthly temple will destroy any who seek to destroy it (1 Cor. 3:16–17; Paul should know).

Jesus's present reign will *not* extinguish those heavenly powers (*stoicheia*, which we will cover shortly) that stand mysteriously behind his earthly enemies and their idols. Many so-called gods of most cultures are things we human beings take for granted as part of life: the sun, water and air, earthly territories, flora and fauna, and natural human forces such as fertility and death, wealth and loss, social status, love, aggression, and fear. These persist in the face of the preached gospel, and that is a good thing, because they are what life is made of. Each has its time and season (Eccles. 3:1–8). Things will change at old creation's final transformation, but opening one's eyes and looking around is all it takes to prove that we aren't there yet (2 Pet. 3:4).

All these scenarios are inaccurate because in some way they violate the apocalyptic framework that Christ's work retained but revolutionized.

Nevertheless, Peter is right that things do not just keep going on as before. In those transient fields of grass under the sun where the gospel of Christ's Kingdom has been planted, some of those shafts that spring up will display a life that arises from above the patch itself—sowed from above, so to speak—and that points beyond it. Like a genetically modified and invasive strain, their presence changes the dynamics and growing conditions in the patch, and provokes a struggle between the old and the new.

## Nationhood in New Humanity

Paul offered an astounding analysis of the situation in his letter to the Galatians. There he drew an analogy between the powers that pagans worshiped and the Torah. The powers had tutored and prepared gentiles for their adult lives as Christ's heirs in the same temporary way that the Torah had tutored and prepared Israel (Gal. 3:23–24; 4:8). Both were varieties of the same kind of structuring principles (*stoicheia*, 4:3) that shaped life and cultures everywhere. Sure, the Torah was a far wiser custodian for God's showcase people than the "weak and beggarly elemental spirits" were for the rest (4:9). But had that really made so much of a difference?

The analogy puts a ceiling on how much national differences matter, since they are preliminary and the *stoicheia* operate through them all. It also limits the theological significance of technological and cultural change.

Globalization and technological innovation may feel disorienting, unpredictable, and eschatological to us—a "singularity" even[19]—but theologically such shifts pale in comparison to the impact of the gospel's omega and alpha of every culture.

Paul's argument also confirms that last chapter's treatment of fleshly Israel applies by analogy to the nations, if only weakly. Israel's three unique gifts have gentile analogues. These peoples belong to God too. He rules them indirectly through the elements of nature rather than through the gift of Jacob's unique blessing. Gentiles enjoy a measure of power and prominence too, imaging God as all humans do. And they bear and benefit from a wisdom from heaven that was available far beyond the communities that God's special revelation had reached. Greek wisdom had impressed Israel's wise men so thoroughly that some of them maintained that Moses's teachings had somehow found their way to the Greek sages. Jacob's tribes stand out from the crowd, but they belong to the crowd from which they stand out.

## Colossians: A New Relationship with the Powers of Nations

In previous chapters we explored Colossians' characterization of creation's principalities and powers. They are particularly relevant to nationhood. These powers subsist in places that are "in heaven," "on earth," and "under the earth" (Rev. 5:3), both near and far from God. Christ, the creating Word, is their source and their point. Their role in structuring gentile societies corresponds to the role of the covenant of Moses in bringing up Israel. Indeed, the Torah can be characterized as one of them. What are they?

To make this talk a little more sensible and concrete, consider the seasons. Every earthly culture owes some of its character to its local environment and climate. In the tropics, rainy season structures life in innumerable profound ways. In the north, life takes shape according to winter, spring, summer, and fall, and solstices and equinoxes take on powerful and even religious significance. The seasons are merely side effects of the earth's tilt, but they're formidable and inescapable forces around which life has adapted and evolved. They are good details in God's good creation. They are also the Lord's subordinates (Deut. 11:13–17).

Pagans treat these powers not as the Lord's servants, to be approached with trust and respect, but as dominating powers to be influenced. We make them gods to appease, exult in, exploit, and even manipulate. And worshipers

19. See Ray Kurzweil, *The Singularity Is Near: When Humans Transcend Biology* (New York: Viking, 2006), for such an interpretation of technological progress.

become enslaved to these gods, quite apart from whether the gods actually influence the weather in any way.

Gravity, that elusive property of mass, is a power. We depend on it, fight against it, and harness it all our lives. It is both natural and "heavenly" in that it manifests the wisdom with which all things were made (Prov. 8:22–36). Say a prayer of thanks tonight for gravity's role in the order of creation, even if you were recently one of its victims. But say it to the God of Israel, not Atlas.

Those forces of *human* nature are more malleable, but they are not categorically different. Love, fear, and the rest come from the Creator who is responsible for all things, and they structure our lives in similarly unavoidable and massive ways. Rooted in our physiology, they are as "heavenly" as gravity or environmental physics. They certainly are not *mere* social constructions. Human beings are not at liberty to abolish or control them (except in limited ways through the hard work of personal and cultural discipline—though we sure keep on trying). Apart from sin they are good; if nothing else, they served the purposes of old humanity. In Jesus's flesh-and-blood human life, they functioned as needed and as intended.

What about *supernatural* forces? Ancients were less rigorous in distinguishing natural from supernatural powers and principalities; their treatments featured both varieties. They focused more on what the two had in common than how they differed, while still seeing special significance in "signs and wonders" and in supernatural personal agents. From our very different perspectives, we need to appreciate both the commonalities and the differences, and we especially need to resist the reductionism that would collapse one variety into the other. A creation big enough for a risen Jesus is big enough for forces beyond nature, and a cosmology that isn't big enough for a risen Jesus isn't big enough.

The Scriptures are full of angels, demons, and the enemy. What are they? I don't know what else to call them that would bring greater clarity or precision. Like human powers, they have their roles to play in God's created order. Perhaps some of them originated from humanity in some way;[20] your guess is as good as mine. They are heavenly too, in that their authority emanates from the Lord's headquarters. The creation is charged with power from its

---

20. Satan, for instance. His origins are *not* described in Isa. 14 (v. 4 makes it clear that the one fallen from heaven is the king of Babylon, not some prehuman angel) or Rev. 12 (v. 11 makes it clear that his exile from heaven came after the deaths of Jesus and his witnesses, not before humans were created). Genesis 3 mentions a snake of God's making, lumping it in with every other wild beast, with no indication that it is anything else or anything more. My hunch is that Satan is some kind of spiritual product of fallen humanity, since human beings are sin's point of origin and held responsible for it. But I wouldn't be surprised if Satan turns out to be something or someone else. Reality is a strange place.

Maker, operating on his behalf, though sometimes working in opposition. They seem not to reduce to natural, biological, psychological, or sociological forces, though each domain of action affects the others. Some of these spirits obey their Lord, and some rebel. Some usurp their Creator's glory and take on the mantle of deity, or have deity foisted on them (cf. Rev. 19:9–10). Creation is therefore in a state of spiritual civil war.

Pagan mythologies anthropomorphize this sensibility, personifying these forces and narrating their often violent interactions in and around our lives, and striving to harness them or protect us. Secularism demythologizes it with a thin cosmology that still assumes the powers' "givenness." To a physicist like Stephen Hawking, powers are properties of the universe that manifest no wisdom, purpose, or necessary coherence, just bare existence. They cannot obey or disobey a nonexistent lord. They might as well be gods, but gods without faces. (This magnifies their potential to abuse, and to be abused by, those who *have* faces.) In contrast with both these perspectives, apocalyptic magnifies this sensibility, emphasizing our powerlessness, but adds the emphatic warning that things are about to change. God has shaken the earth's foundations with his apocalyptic judgment of every unrighteous servant in and over all nations (Ps. 82), "whether thrones or dominions or principalities or authorities" (Col. 1:16). Peace is coming.

At any rate, Paul informed the Colossians that these heavenly usurpers of God's authority were made a spectacle through the cross. Jesus stripped them of their power to intimidate his followers, and God is using his followers to advertise his glory wherever they are. Nevertheless, the powers have not lost their hold on Jesus's followers altogether. Old habits die hard. Christ's ambassadors are susceptible to reverting to obsolete loyalties and deferring to those disgraced old powers.

All of these aspects of our cosmic situation apply specifically to nationhood. Colossians says Jesus is the omega of the nations' bullying of their own peoples. Not the end of the bullying itself, which has obviously continued right through the New Testament era to this day. It is not even the end of the power of that bullying, only its irresistibility.

Revelation 13 and other texts encourage us to think of a nation's leaders as its main bullies and patriotism as idolatry's main form, but the priorities of Colossians lie elsewhere. Paul warned instead of the widely distributed cultural power that is channeled within a people from every direction, including within churches. "Let *no one* pass judgment on you in questions of food and drink or with regard to a festival or a new moon or a sabbath," he advised. "Let no one disqualify you, insisting on self-abasement and worship of angels, taking his stand on visions, puffed up without reason by his sensuous mind"

(Col. 2:16–18). Remember, we're talking about seasons, gravity, culture, the Torah, money, social justice, identity, rulers, constitutions—the whole pantheon. Christ is their goal, limit line, and conqueror all at once. He's the omega of the kind of communal identity that's built around humiliated *stoicheia*.

What has replaced it is a new irresistible thing: Jesus's resurrection and ascension to rule above them all. His revolution doesn't leave the world in anarchy, since Jesus reigns from creation's heavenly headquarters. And his reign does not leave his disciples stranded in the provinces, because they live secret lives with him in the capital while he waits to appear to everyone (Col. 3:3–4).

Jesus's reign has not relieved nations and other powers of their roles as authorities in the world (Rom. 13). Nor has the King of kings even necessarily notified the nations of the change, with one central exception: through the witness of those disciples. The nations' believers in Christ are living signs of the future that awaits. Doing justice to God our ruler demands that we embody that future with lives of gratitude and peacemaking and with compassion, kindness, humility, and other Christlike virtues, rather than vices unsuitable for his Kingdom (Col. 3:5–17). These holy lives expose nations for what we are, and show what we can be instead. Remember, God created two kinds of nations. Augustine reflected them in his terms "City of Man" and "City of God." In Christ people can be transferred to the second (1:13).[21] In Colossians, Christian ethics is Kingdom politics that brings the ways of God's capital city to the many ethnic provinces of earthly humanity so that all of Christ's subjects can enter the new arrangement on peaceable terms and thrive, learning in the process why they existed all along.

## Ephesians: International Relations

Ephesians paints a similar picture of Christ's conquest and supremacy over all powers in every age (Eph. 1:18–2:10) and then goes on to describe how Jesus's work is an omega and alpha for nations' relations with one another.

We saw that in the face of untrammeled human ambition, God turned national identity into a providential dividing wall that disintegrates humanity for our own good into a host of rival powers (Gen. 11:1–9). It wasn't just gentile strangers and wanderers who followed the course of the world and the prince of disobedience; "among these *we all* once lived" (Eph. 2:2–3). Israel's *stoicheia* did play their unique role forming Israel as a distinct people, to whom belong the promises and from whom salvation came. But those

21. Augustine, *The City of God against the Pagans* 18.31.

*stoicheia* got in the way of the very salvation and promises they supported. Every ethnic identity would.

From the beginning it was not so, and at the end it will no longer be. God resorted to disrupting the human order in the service of a distant goal for humanity: "to unite all things in him" (Eph. 1:10). The goal was met through Jesus's resurrection, ascension, and eternal reign. What is it that has been so important all this time? Paul's simple and stunning answer is "the church" (1:22). The church is *with* Jesus atop the hierarchy of creation's powers and priorities, with Israel and the other nations below in new roles.

The Father inevitably sacrificed Israel's national character when he gave his Son. God dismantled the wall separating Israel and gentiles *from Israel's side*, using Christ's flesh to dismiss the Torah (Eph. 2:14–15). Why not dismiss the other *stoicheia* instead? Why not dismiss the powers behind Rome, Greece, Syria, Egypt, and the earth's other unclean peoples? Because it wouldn't have addressed the situation. Gentiles as such weren't the problem. The *stoicheia* weren't either. The problems ran deeper and were common to all. Jacob's nation needed much more than emancipation, and so do the rest. We all need to be reconciled to God and receive the Holy Spirit (2:16–18). Humanity's alpha as *one* humanity in Jesus (2:15) addresses the deep problems in ways that render obsolete the old measures for accommodating them.

In Jesus, nationhood functions differently. Exclusion no longer serves to display God's distinctness over against all rivals (Eph. 2:19). Conflict doesn't have the place it had before (2:14). Now that the Spirit dwells in Christ's whole body, Zion is no longer useful as a symbol of God's earthly dwelling place (2:21–22). Citizenship in God's household is no longer a fleshly birthright but comes with spiritual new birth that is available in principle to anyone (2:19). Life in that household as fellow citizens rather than strangers is the proof of all of this. While Ephesians preaches Jewish-gentile unity, that entails gentile-gentile unity as well across all those old fractures and rivalries and animosities. "One instead of two" implies "one instead of many."

Ephesians didn't have to put this so radically. Christ could have been said to have made one new *nation* instead of two. That would have been accurate (cf. 1 Pet. 2:9). But Ephesians goes further: Christ made one new *human being* instead of two. Two what? Grammatically, two meanings are possible: two human beings or two groups. In the first case, Ephesians would be speaking of *phylai* as humanities in their own right, as varieties of grass rather than just patches, divided in their being rather than just their present condition.[22] Or

22. This conjures images of nineteenth-century racism, polygeny, and the like. Of course, Ephesians is claiming nothing of the sort. The boundaries here are covenantal and social, not

Ephesians might mean one new human instead of the two *groups*, implying that the "groupishness" of old humanity, its propensity not just to differentiate but to divide, has been abolished. Either way, one or more ways of being human were extinguished, and one new way of being human was kindled in which ethnicity no longer has its old place.

No wonder this chapter has not managed to sketch a death-and-resurrection of individual nations rooted in Christ's death and resurrection. Ephesians prevents it. Jesus's death and resurrection worked against any such outcome. Church father Aristides sought to honor this ontological change in human ethnicity by referring to the church as a "third race."[23] Old patches or even old varieties of grass (Jewish, Roman, Korean, and the like) have not been ended and raised in new and imperishable forms. Jesus has; and in him so are creation, humanity, Israel, and (as we shall see) individual followers. But not ethnicities—not even Israel as an ethnicity. Their days are numbered.

An ethnicity's ordinary renewal, revival, transformation, and even resuscitation are all easy to grasp. They happen all the time. But an ethnicity's resurrection is a category mistake. A nation lacks the integrity of an individual life. A people, whether one's own or one's enemy, can appear to be eternal and inevitable: "Who is like the beast, and who can fight against it?" (Rev. 13:4). But look ahead a few centuries or decades, and where is it? It has flowed into others. Echoes of its character, habits, and voices still reverberate in new successor peoples, but somehow it has dispersed. It didn't die. No grave holds its remains and dates; no body waits to rise. Whether or not it ever fell, it ran its course.

New humanity intermingles like this too—ideally, more profoundly than before—but not with the old stakes. Nationhood's old form simply has no place in it. Ephesians helps explain why ethnicities diffuse and wind down like families and tongues rather than dying and rising like individuals. Like marriages, which last only "until death do us part" (Rom. 7:1–6; Matt. 22:30) and are not pursued in eternity, national identities run their courses in old creation, confined to our old nature rather than crossing over into the new. As the memories and stories of the risen, certainly, and maybe more. But not as powers and principalities in their own right. Genealogies end with Jesus. These institutions, valued so profoundly that millions on millions have given their lives for them (and often for worthy and honorable reasons), have

---

genetic. First-century gentiles could join ethnic Israel at any time by taking the covenant on themselves.

23. For a sympathetic but critical treatment, see Miroslav Volf, *Exclusion and Embrace* (Nashville: Abingdon, 1996), 49.

themselves been sacrificed—offered up in the flesh of Jesus (Eph. 2:15) for the sake of the Kingdom.

We glimpse this in an astonishing twist in Paul's reading of Psalm 68 later in Ephesians. The psalm offers a conventional vision of triumph: God scattered the kings in his territories, ascended to Zion while the other mountains looked on in envy, took captives, and received gifts from the people (Ps. 68:18). Its celebration of divine national conquest is the kind of thing that today scandalizes even believers, let alone skeptics. With one crucial modification, Ephesians draws on it to celebrate God's work unifying the clans (*patria*, close to *phylē*) of the heavens and the earth (Eph. 3:15) into one body and dwelling place (4:4). According to Paul, in ascending to the heights, God took along many captives and *gave* gifts to human beings. Here the captives are *freed* captives, and the gifts are spiritual gifts *given* to equip these emancipated people for ministries that build up that dwelling place (4:7–16). Christ's ascension was the mother of all Marshall Plans. God's conquest of the nations took a very surprising turn. God *did* free his captured captives, and he *did* give gifts to them, and his dwelling place *was* his own people rather than an inanimate structure made with people's hands (cf. 2:11).

What did God *receive* from those conquered peoples? What did he *take*? The tribute paid by the peoples of the earth is something Paul already mentioned: their present and future recognition of their Lord Christ's unsearchable riches and his many-sided wisdom in bestowing his inheritance on beneficiaries from among all those peoples (Eph. 3:6–11), and their sacrificed old identities that had stood in the way (2:13–17). So God's giving in Ephesians 4 increases God's receiving in Psalm 68. The more God equips his freed captives, the richer the nations' tribute. The Lord is a wise investor.

All this implies that the old nationhood is a fully depreciated investment. This originally good arrangement for old humanity, pressed into service as a work-around to limit human ambition, had become part of the problem. It lent a foothold to deadly ways of life characterized by "the passions of our flesh" and "the desires of body and mind" (Eph. 2:1–3). In Romans, Paul saw that even the law could have that effect when under the power of sin. At any rate, these kinds of arrangements were inappropriate for new creation.

So in Ephesians' version of Psalm 68:19, our old identities are whole burnt offerings, so to speak. Better yet, they are *cherem*. God has reclaimed and abolished them by superseding their original rationale and freeing us from their bondage. We "captive" freemen can receive Christ's new humanity, and with it receive gifts appropriate to the new kind of human existence we are beginning to enjoy even while still living among the old sort (Eph. 4:18–20).

As Colossians puts it, "Here is no Greek and Jew, circumcised and uncircumcised, barbarian, Scythian, slave, free, but Christ is all, and in all" (Col. 3:11 RSV alt.).

This is how Christ went about the holy business of conquest. Tribes across the world that were in bondage to their own originating mythologies, ancestor worship, and familial and cultural obligation have been receiving the news of his apocalyptic victory over the nations as the emancipation it really is. He brought about the omega of these futile identities through his alpha as the head of a new kind of body through the cross (Eph. 2:16), created in him for good works (2:10).

Revelation communicates this by merging two images for "the servants of God": Israel's 144,000, an echo of wandering Israel mustering for conquest (Rev. 7:4–8), and that famous multinational multitude glorifying God and the Lamb (7:9–10). Israel was perfected not just by being enlarged or strengthened; "God had foreseen something better" (Heb. 11:39–40) than for Israel just to become the winner that takes all. It was better for fleshly Israel to become merely a *part* of a bigger picture, one party to an inheritance of far greater and unsearchable riches (Eph. 3:8). She could only become adequate for accomplishing a plan like that by becoming a different *kind* of Israel—an international, even postnational (!) Israel.

Ephesians' treatment of nationhood leads us further away than ever from the competing identity politics of founding national ideologies, heavenly mandates, nationalism, imperialism, postcolonialism, multiculturalism, and relativism that saturate our present moment. It is a breath of fresh air, a deliverance from powers and principalities that oppress under the guise of liberating. Like other biblical writings, Ephesians takes a low and generalized view of gentile morality. Like the others, it is disinterested in how the nations' cultures and characters might differ from one another. Its focus and passion is Christ's one new humanity, and its persistent interest is how we ought to live it out as fellow citizens in God's household (Eph. 2:19), how we "walk" in it (5:2, 15). True to form, Ephesians' last half outlines a Christian ethic of virtues, righteous power dynamics, and spiritual preparedness that believers from a wide range of cultural backgrounds can recognize. Certainly the details of these conditions differ: societies may feature polygamy, cultures of divorce and cohabitation, slavery, hierarchies of age or social class, patriarchalism or matriarchalism or egalitarianism, drug cultures (and alcohol qualifies), strict taboos, and the like. Yet at a more fundamental level, "the nations" are still practically interchangeable, and vastly different from Christ's one new human. God's postnational household is a commonweal of a whole different kind.

## Nationhood after Old Nationhood

So far the Scriptures have mainly spoken to nationhood's omega. Is there *any* alpha for nationhood and nations? Sure there is. Jesus is the sower of seed that produces fresh grass. (And, lest we forget, his enemy still sows too.) His work renews a share of a patch's present constituents. And that sets a nation on a new course. That course involves conflict. The values he subordinates to his Kingdom are beloved, even totemic. The walls he demolishes are built with sacrifice, often generations' worth. They're sacred. So his peace is like a sword to every old order. It divides even families. Jesus is the alpha of a kind of civil war within every nation his gospel reaches, analogous to the war of flesh and Spirit in every believer (Gal. 5:17). It is a strange kind of conflict, where his forces seek to obey and honor the forces opposed to them (1 Pet. 2:13–17). However, they obey for different reasons than their authorities want (Eph. 6:7; Titus 2:11–3:7), so their obedience is revolutionary and traumatizing.

The apocalyptic framework predicts that each civil war can end in only two ways: at the end when Jesus appears in glory and puts all enemies under his feet, or in the middle when a nation successfully expels the gospel from within it.[24] The Kingdom enjoys no permanent wholesale consolidation among a people. Joshua's generation conquered, but then another arose that did not know the Lord or his work for Israel (Judg. 2:10). That's just how it goes. After all, grass fades. New blades and generations of both grass and weeds are continually sprouting up. Church history confirms the apocalyptic vision: every revival in history has subsided, and every supposedly Christian nation has seen its church's dominance wax and wane. In the meantime, Christ's civil war goes on, passed on to successor generations and successor nations. Momentum may shift with renewals, apostasies, and unstable truces, but a lasting cessation of hostilities can arrive only at the very end of the age.

This sounds pretty bleak. Does this unending war have an upside? Of course. Those new blades of grass are rooted in Israel's source of power and wisdom. They are no longer disconnected from the only truly life-giving and life-saving Spirit (Ps. 104:27–30; Eph. 2:12). They are no longer hopelessly tangled up in the vices that afflict and weaken their people (Eph. 4:17–24). Not *hopelessly*; they *may* still tangle themselves up in those futile ways of life and return to condemnation and destruction, but that is no longer the only future open to them. They remain free to grow up into the fullness of

24. Even when a people silences the gospel, it is in a different condition than before: post-Christian. And the gospel's expulsion is only temporary, so the old order's victory is only provisional.

Christ their leader (4:12–16) and, in doing so, to point a way forward for their neighbors in the grass patch.

This is wonderful news for an old nation, if only it can see it for what it is. The gospel's arrival is the alpha of a nation's freedom from the unbearable burden of having to be its people's savior. And since a nation *can't* be its people's savior, the gospel's arrival is also the alpha of a nation's freedom from the unbearable dread of its inevitable demise.

As a conscientious parent, I know what it feels like to suffer that burden and that dread. We want to protect our children from all harm. And we play important roles in the nurture and protection of the tender little blades that depend on us. Yet we *can't* save them from every threat—not the external ones, and especially not the sins that are within us and within them. Our heartache as parents is the heartache of every responsible patron, pastor, principal, and president. What we want to do we cannot (Rom. 7:15). And what we want *not* to do we cannot help but do: to pass on our own failures and inadequacies and then have to watch our wretched dependents suffer consequences for which we bear some of the responsibility.

Who will save us from this body of death? Only Jesus Christ (Rom. 7:24–25). He reigns *far* above these powers (Eph. 1:21), not just a little. His coming is the alpha of leaders' and their nations' release from impossible responsibilities and inescapable liabilities, to modest and more effective service under his reign.

Nebuchadnezzar awakened to the joy of this alpha for himself and his people after God undid him and then restored him (Dan. 4). Darius's joy at being humbled was even greater (Dan. 6). Belshazzar missed his opportunity (Dan. 5). These figures are emblematic. A nation in chronic civil war with the Kingdom is a far richer and more fruitful place than it would ever be as a hermit kingdom cut off from the Kingdom's ambassadors.

An influx of new life can give a temporary lift to a people and a culture. The lift *is* temporary; legacies don't last forever; "the church is always one generation from extinction." Yet that lift is a godsend. Whole new possibilities open up in a place where Christ's alpha has arrived. Their new availability is an alpha for that place.

For instance, both the knowledge of Christ's resurrection and the eternity of Christ's reign are the alpha of a grass patch's role in something of *lasting* significance. The nation will disperse, as nations do, but its risen constituents will not. Parents and families can share this same hope. Our children will leave us just as fall succeeds summer, to join the children of other aging families and enter a springtime of their own. And someday their nests will empty, and on and on. Depressing thoughts, if mortal families just spawn more cycles of mortality. Depressing for tribes and tongues and nations too. But if those children become heirs of the Spirit and fellow heirs of God's fatherhood, they launch into a springtime that never ends (Rev. 22:2). Families, like nations, thus have a reason for being that is far greater, infinitely greater, than their own dispensable selves.

Even if a nation or a family can have no eternity of its own, it ought to be able to live with that kind of legacy and in fact rejoice in it. An alpha-nation can help nurture sons of the Kingdom. If it can't embrace the joy of raising children for another's sake, well, that's idolatry.

But there's joy in more than that. A nation can also reap some of the spiritual fruit from what the Word has sown. Every people has a set of cherished goals and has developed ways of life to strive for them. Classical Greece developed the language of virtues, in which *epithumiai* had both positive and negative places.[25] Hellenized Israel assimilated its vocabulary for the human virtues it prized. China had Confucian and Taoist counterparts. And so on. Through Jeremiah, God told Israel in exile to seek the peace of its captors' city (Jer. 29:7). Christians are in much better position to bless than exiled Israel because new humanity bears the differently virtuous fruit of the Spirit. For instance, Jesus showed something Aristotle could not see: that humility is a virtue, indeed that the Beatitudes are sturdier bedrock on which to build a life than just the cardinal virtues.[26] The Spirit can weaken cultural vices and nurture a healthier set of cultural and structural virtues. And through these gifts a nation's believers can display respect for Jesus's universal lordship in their own national idiom—true tribute.[27]

God may even get the credit he is due (1 Pet. 2:12). Daniel and his friends came to be appreciated, for a time anyway, as the gifts they were to the welfare of Babylon (Dan. 3:28–30). Christians should never *expect* that Christ's virtue in us will gain such social favor from principalities and powers; we should expect war from them in response to the peace we bring, and remain always prepared for it (Eph. 6:10–20). But sometimes recognition does come Christ's way, and it's glorious.

In fact, a nation can experience a critical mass of change or renewal to such an extent that its own national character changes.[28] There will still be weeds

25. Giles Pearson, *Aristotle on Desire* (Cambridge: Cambridge University Press, 2012).
26. See Peter Kreeft, *Back to Virtue: Traditional Moral Wisdom for Modern Moral Confusion* (San Francisco: Ignatius, 1992).
27. For one delightful example, see Thomas Cahill, *How the Irish Saved Civilization* (New York: Doubleday, 1995).
28. Some, wary of Christendom and Constantinianism, deny the very possibility. Yet such changes have manifestly happened in Christian history to villages, clans, and even whole

among the wheat, but the society will be in some sense "Christian." Does this constitute an alpha? Maybe. By the time that nation has dispersed, its metaphorical epitaph might speak of that point of conversion as the nation's defining national moment. Marriages, families, and friendships certainly have such alphas. The nations of Christendom have tended to think that way about themselves. However, the analogy seems too weak to hold. Nations have much longer spans than individual marriages, families, and friendships. Over decades and down centuries, once solidly Christian nations and their once secure Christian institutions have seen stark reversals in faithfulness. A people's Christian character can hollow out to a bare husk of its former self. It can metamorphose into a demonic parody. It can be swept away in all but name. In fact, apostasy can mushroom even within the church, as Galatians 1, 1 John 2, Jude, and 2 Peter 2 all testify. It is mistaken even to dream of an alpha-Rome, alpha-Byzantium, alpha-Russia, alpha-Geneva, alpha-America, or alpha-Korea enjoying a permanently renewed life. The sudden and repeated reversals of Daniel 1–6 are instructive: under and after the seemingly decisive conquest, the civil war always rages on.

## Catholicity: Nationhood sans Frontières

I have so far discussed the gospel's impact on a people as if it existed in isolation, but "the nations" obviously do not. The Kingdom's new strain of seed was first sowed in Israel, but never *merely* in Israel. From the beginning, the Messiah's impact was both multinational and international. We have already mentioned mercies to foreigners in Luke 4. The other three Gospels agree in their own ways: crowds early in Mark's narrative came from gentile as well as Jewish territories (Mark 3:7–8), and John's Gospel mentioned Greeks coming to see Jesus (John 12:20–21). In the Gospel of Matthew, Jesus's first worshipers were wise men from the East, a judgment on every single Jewish sage's failure to discern or celebrate the time of their own redemption;[29] and the wise men's visit led to the holy family's exile in Egypt (Matt. 2:1–15). The missional scenario that unfolds within one patch is also going on in others.

No world is an island. Every people is constantly negotiating relationships with partners, allies, and rivals. Fields of grass seed new colonies through wind, water flow, and animal migration. They compete and they cross-pollinate. Nations interrelate too: some a lot, some barely at all. Moreover, they (like

---

peoples. To deny it categorically is to deny the Spirit's power and work and fruitfulness, something Jesus emphatically warned against (Matt. 12:22–32).

29. Luke, by contrast, highlights a faithful remnant's much clearer vision (Luke 1:38–2:38).

plants) interrelate with others *as others*.[30] Our age tends to treat globalization as a new historical situation. We develop in contexts with an unprecedented volume of outside influences, and our generations gap and miscommunicate more than before. Our peoples intermarry, migrate, and cross national boundaries far more than before the industrial revolution. So our kids inevitably grow up in "third cultures." The level of this change is new, but its nature isn't. Interaction and change are as fundamental to nations as they are to the grasses of the field.[31]

Jesus has an alpha in store for relationships among nations. He is leading his side of the civil war in each nation where his gospel is heard. They are all local theaters of one grand conflict, whether they know it or not. So the gospel of his Kingdom is already a kind of omega to international confusion and disintegration in that it is the alpha of a new level of common opposition. Jesus coordinates his side, while the old world's outcast ruler coordinates the other (Eph. 6:10–12). As we saw earlier, Christ's ministry drew together the powers of the cosmos under their ruler to defend against his Kingdom's approach (Luke 23:12). Gentiles played secondary but prominent roles in that conflict and were implicated in its course and outcome. And they have been increasingly drawn in as Jesus sends his witnesses to the ends of the earth to testify to his rule and return.

But his gospel is an international omega at a deeper and more lasting level, in that his church straddles national distinctions and animosities. The offensive tactics of Jesus's warriors are prayer and the apostolic Word of God (Eph. 6:17–18), and their ground strategy is peace (6:15). The product of the Spirit's work among them is fellowship—fellowship across all the human differences that disciples sacrifice.

Those differences do more than distinguish nations; they distinguish people within nations in whole new ways. Some of these involve removing some old internal distinctions. The Torah's walls did not just separate Jew from gentile; they also separated Jew from Jew. In abolishing its commandments and ordinances, and disarming foreign nations' *stoicheia*, Jesus tore down households' interior walls too (Eph. 2:15–16). The church is a *catholic*, or universal, communion, in which all persons have a place at Christ's one table and a place in each other's lives. It's not a classless society of "masses" stripped of their specificities, stories, and present privileges. It is not just a list of "saved" individuals who have no other relevance to one another's lives, or a society whose

30. The root systems of trees and other plants favor the root systems of close relatives but compete with the genetically different.

31. However, modernity's accelerated pace of change does portend a *kind* of omega for nations but not a Christian one or one without a clear alpha.

old social structures remain unaffected while its people's spiritual destinies are radically changed. It is not a "diverse" collection of the old nations being their own selves. *He is our peace* (2:14). Masters and slaves, parents and children, husbands and wives can all walk together in love and mutual submission (5:2; 5:21–6:9). Christ's faithful church brings catholicity or wholeness to a place, altering relationships and cultural dynamics in its local fellowships. It creates a visible alternative to that local culture's status quo that outside observers can see and join—and also reject and resist. The new creation itself, its visibility, and the reaction are all alphas for that people.

Other local contexts are seeing comparable new fellowships, perceptions and misperceptions, and reactions. The two volumes of Luke-Acts masterfully portray the way the gospel's results replicate and develop beyond Judea. What came into view in the first century as it spread was both a multiplication of local fellowships with distinct local characters *and* an increasingly far-flung international fellowship of local fellowships that managed to straddle those differences. The centuries following confirmed the picture of Christian fellowship painted in Acts as spreading across wider and wider contrasts. Multicultural fellowships even survived the Great Schism and the European reformations. That is not surprising, since those disputes concerned the *character* rather than the *validity* of Christ's universal fellowship across national differences.

The international church is an alpha for nationhood. It presents an alternative (even multiple alternatives, considering those schisms) to the horns of Babel's old dilemma. Old humanity sought a kind of unity but found unity only in transgression and depravity (Rom. 5:12); new humanity is unified differently (5:18). The nations *can* be one: by repenting of making a name for themselves either individually or collectively and trusting in Christ's gift of peace. The missional church fulfills God's work of gathering the nations and the promise of Israel's unique belonging, prominence, and wisdom (Isa. 45:14, quoted in 1 Cor. 14:25).

With the emergence of the church as both a local alternative to a nation's ways and a global alternative to its foreign relations, our old identities matter a lot less. And that is an alpha for new "identities" that we can hold a lot more loosely. They can enrich us without owning us. More importantly, we can enrich them and see what God will do with them. After all, we have sacrificed them to Christ. We have released them to the Lord's disposal. And the Lord has not treated us as a conventional king would treat defeated nationalist conspirators. God has not paraded us before him in humiliation. In fact, God wasn't even that interested in *receiving* those gifts. Paul ignored that old verb in Psalm 68:19 and substituted his own because God turned out to be far more interested in *giving* gifts to empower our new lives (Ps. 68:19, quoted in Eph. 4:7–16) than having our old peoplehood mounted and put on display in his palace to show his superiority. Like the father in Jesus's parable who was more interested in his wayward son's revival than his fealty, God is focused on our new Christ-body rather than our old ethnic flesh. "Neither circumcision counts for anything, nor uncircumcision, but new creation" (Gal. 6:15).

The half-Jewish Timothy is exemplary here. Let him serve as this chapter's poster child. Under the Torah's old arrangement, his existence was a problem, a scandal, a nagging sign of the disobedience that jeopardized God's nation (Neh. 10:30). But under the new arrangement, his mixed ancestry was no big deal. In fact, it could even be an asset and a sign of the multinational church's catholicity (Acts 16:1–5).

Paul had Timothy circumcised before he visited Jerusalem so as not to inflame the civil war there between the Kingdom and the local outsiders to whom it was still a big deal (Acts 16:3). Nationhood for Paul was a powerful human reality that belonged, with all our other circumstances, at God's still more powerful disposal. Surrendering it to the Lord drains nationhood of much of its old power (Rom. 14) and empowers it anew with the gospel's power, turning its old barrier into a means of generosity and grace (1 Cor. 9:15–23).

The advent of Christ's new humanity thus changes the course of every nation it meets. It shifts the ground underneath the assumptions that shaped our cultures. My wife and I married outside our "tribes." So what? Our identity together in Christ runs deeper. As people start thinking this way, world history changes course.[32]

International cooperation in the church demonstrates God's lordship of all nations (Isa. 45:23, quoted in Rom. 14:11). I have taught in Christian contexts on five continents. In every place, I arrived and met people whom I recognized right away as my brothers and sisters. Despite our wildly different backgrounds, present circumstances, tastes, politics, and expectations, my hosts and I share "the unity of the Spirit in the bond of peace" (Eph. 4:3).

Here I need to anticipate an objection and get something off my chest. Every time I write something cheery like this, a chorus of old voices in my head tut-tuts it and issues stern reminders of the blindness of privilege, the naïveté of cultural imperialism, the emptiness of words without deeds, the need for a hermeneutic of suspicion, and on and on, rehearsing the litany of qualification and skepticism and consciousness-raising, and encouraging

---

32. Among other things, something like the United States becomes a possibility, even if unity in Christ is no longer as common a rationale for how we marry today.

if not bullying me to pass it on every chance I get. I regard that as a tragedy, because even if their points are valid, the voices have trained me in doubt rather than faith, and in this case they threaten to drown out the voice of Paul. He was well aware that "the days are evil" (Eph. 5:16), that Christians indulge in vices and forfeit their eternal inheritance, that they are prone to impose their cultures on one another, and that people occupy positions of power who are oblivious, negligent, rebellious, and abusive. In fact, he experienced those disappointing realities rather severely, and knew his readers experienced them too. Ephesians 5:3–6:9 is right there in the text for all to read. Yet Paul's warnings do not *qualify* what the other passages claim. They *apply* it. They motivate us to strive for "life worthy of the calling" (4:1) to join Christ in his perfection (4:13) even while we endure each other's present imperfection. The suffering apostle knows the way through the world's evils better than modern masters and disciples of suspicion.

In my travels, my hosts and I work together in the Spirit across our incompatibilities toward our common goal. Sometimes it's a strain. Sometimes it's downright discouraging. Sometimes I'm pretty sure that the culture of my partners is hampering our efforts. Occasionally I realize the same is true of me. Yet our cultures and peoples are not why we are gathered; the mystery of Christ is (Eph. 3:4). "The power at work within us" can help us interact in "lowliness and meekness, with patience, forbearing one another in love" (3:20; 4:2). When that happens, we catch a vision of something greater than any of our peoples' legacies, something whose value far surpasses even the unprecedented knowledge we gain of one another. We become Timothy. And we come to realize how trivial both circumcision and uncircumcision are compared to new creation. Pursuing the mystery of Christ allows us to see beyond today's grass patches like the final shot in *A Bug's Life*. We see past the usual goals of "homogeneity" and "diversity," because new creation's catholicity leaves both those visions far behind. And as that realization spreads, it too reshapes world history, at least as the church tells it.

## Conclusion

The findings in this chapter are more modest than the others. Jesus is not an alpha of immortalized, glorified resurrection-nations that live forever. Does that leave you disappointed? Relieved? Excited? I myself am a little surprised. I did not expect such a humble prognosis for peoplehood. I'm pretty sure that's because I live and work in a context that cherishes cultures. Not with the zeal of a patriot, which in academic circles tends to be not just passé but suspect, but with the ardor of an anthropologist. Academics declare world heritage sites and build museums (and libraries, which are museums of a sort).[33] We like to hold on to the things we value. When we can't, we at least try to immortalize them in a historical record. It feels wrong for them just to slip away.

This book is about the past and the future, and their turbulent intersection in Jesus Christ. The past and the future are dear to the human heart. And in matters of the heart, we have to beware the temptation to sentimentality. People tend to eternalize the things we are attached to. Families eternalize their beloved pets. Romantics eternalize their relationships and marriages. Nationalists eternalize their cultures and territories and iconic mountain-tops. Urbanites eternalize their cities, Vikings their mead halls, cowboys their prairies. Mormons eternalize nuclear families. Intellectuals eternalize knowledge, with or without libraries. Photographers eternalize images. Hegelians eternalize history. Racists and identity politickers eternalize their flesh. We desperately want not to have to let go of these cherished things, and that tempts us to project them eschatologically. A lot of "Christian eschatology" is not actual knowledge but speculation founded on sentimentality and then shored up with theology.

That is covetousness, holding on to what belongs to another. The risen Lord holds every present and future (Eph. 1:21). He calls us to release the things we hold dearest, in faith that he is their rightful and wisest trustee. "Whoever of you does not renounce all that he has cannot be my disciple" (Luke 14:33). Besides, we take nothing with us anyway (Eccles. 5:15; 1 Tim. 6:7), and only what *God* raises lasts forever. "Heaven and earth will pass away" (Mark 13:31). "Remember not the former things, nor consider the things of old" (Isa. 43:18).

Jesus's resurrection is the source of any firm insight we have into creation's apocalyptic end and beginning. Any further speculation is just more of the same "wind of doctrine" and deceitful human cunning that Jesus was sent to deliver us from (Eph. 4:14). The future's many unknowns are tests of our faith.

They should not be difficult ones. Consider the testimonies of converts in newly evangelized cultures. Do they want to go back to the way their grand-parents lived, or are they grateful for deliverance from dominating powers and eager to face the unknowns that lie ahead? Do they need their cultures to be preserved or perfected, or are they content with the Holy Spirit and ready for

---

33. For the record, I *like* museums, libraries, and UNESCO World Heritage Sites. But I think it's fine if they don't last forever or rise with the saints at the resurrection of the dead.

Jesus to return? Or think of how voices in the New Testament characterize their own cultural heritages and prospects. Ponder passages such as Acts 7; Romans 1:18–2:24; Philippians 3:2–16; Ephesians 2:1–3; Titus 3:1–7; Hebrews 12:18–24; 1 Peter 4:1–6; James 5:1–11; and Revelation 22:10–17. Do these people sound nostalgic?

# SEVEN

# Jesus—the End and the Beginning of a Life

When you were *slaves of sin*, you were free in regard to righteousness. So what advantage did you then get from the things of which you now are ashamed? The end of those things is death. But now that you have been freed from sin and *enslaved to God*, the advantage you get is sanctification. The end is eternal life. For the wages of sin is death, but the free gift of God is eternal life in Christ Jesus our Lord.

Romans 6:20–23 NRSV

In every chapter's domain, Jesus Christ's life has been decisive. He towers above the rest of Israel and the other nations. He alone brings humanity and the cosmos to their newness of being. He is definitive even for God. He is the nexus of all things.

Naturally, that applies to the personal domains of individual human lives. Jesus is the omega and alpha of a life like yours and mine. Each finally falls and stands in relation to *his* life. Christ's omega and alpha play out profoundly—perhaps most profoundly—one life at a time.

That claim begs for a definition. *What is a life?* The question is easy to ask but vexing to answer.

A human life has a timeline. Every new school year, our kids would come home complaining about how they had to put together *another timeline* of their lives. It felt repetitious. Yet it proved surprisingly challenging. As they progressed through elementary school, the length of their lives grew, the requirements became more complex, they became more sophisticated storytellers, and the exercise became even less straightforward.

I have now reached a half century, and several years ago as part of an exercise I sketched my own timeline. I now see better than I did as a child that my timeline extends beyond the apparent end points of conception and death. It has a kind of preexistence in my local, cultural, and parental contexts—how my parents met and bonded, for instance. And it will have a postexistence: a fading legacy in neighbors' and descendants' own fleeting lives and memories, and a permanent one in its resurrection, judgment, and eternity. It also crosses over to the timelines of other persons and contexts. As human timelines tangle and weave together, where does one end and another begin? The more we look, the more we see, until our account threatens to collapse from its own sheer size. Blades of grass are one thing, human beings another. How does one define such a thing as a life?

### What Is a Life For?

Fortunately, a more fundamental question is also more manageable: *What does a life mean?* What is the telos or goal of it? What is a person for? If we learn the answer, we may discover not just what a life is, but what a *good life* is. After all, Jesus claimed that he came to bring it (John 10:10). He gives our usual answers the substance they need.

Many Protestants answer the question by appealing to the first line of the Westminster Catechism: "What is the chief end of man? To glorify God and enjoy him forever." That's true, but by itself it's too vague to be very helpful. It is really an introduction to the rest of the catechism rather than a stand-alone answer. After all, Muslims seek to glorify and enjoy God eternally too, without recourse to Christ. We need specificity. Jesus provides it in the particular way his life glorifies the Father (John 12:28) and shares his joy (17:13).

Then there is God's "creation mandate" in Genesis 1:28: "Fill the earth and subdue it; and have dominion." Is that our purpose? We're certainly doing it. Yet we seem to multiply and rule by instinct rather than conscious obedience. Moreover, we tend to do both of these things sinfully, even using the mandate to justify our immoral actions. We need clarity. Jesus supplies it by how he has filled all in all (Eph. 1:23) and how he reigns at the Father's right hand. He captures the spirit of Genesis 1:28 and rescues it from our misconstruals.

Or consider the widespread conviction that heaven is our goal and destination. Books on heaven have enjoyed great success in the past few years. The best sellers often rely on testimony that is hard or even impossible to verify, or facile readings of elusive biblical images. Here too Jesus supplies not just specificity and clarity but surprise: first in his resurrection appearances, which indicated what our future bodily lives will be like, and second in his ascension to reign in heaven, the center of all power. From the Lord's capital he displays the beatific character of his rule through characteristic signs and wonders, promising to return and promote his faithful and prepared servants to inherit that Kingdom and reign with him.

By every measure, Jesus Christ displays the good life and its meaning. If keeping the covenant of Moses distinguishes the good life (Deut. 30), then Jesus personifies that fulfillment. If it's the life of worship (Psalms), then he is the consummate subject and object of the Psalter's worship. If the good life comes down to faithful servanthood in the face of suffering (Job), then Jesus sets the standard. Is it wise righteousness in the face of temptation (Proverbs)? Contentment and dutiful fear of the Lord in the face of life's manifest vanity (Ecclesiastes)? Loving union that overcomes the trial of separation (Song of Songs)? Perseverance under persecution (Daniel)? Restoration and renewal after purifying judgment (the Prophets)? By all of these biblical measures and more, Jesus lived the good life. This is the apostles' consistent and steadfast testimony.

What an extravagant pile of claims. How did the apostles come to such conclusions? Well, as Jews they were raised with all these standards and with Scripture's judgment that all people had fallen short of them. Then they encountered Jesus, a life that wasn't falling short. And then, at some point early in their mission, the frame of reference flipped. They came to see these other standards of the good life in terms of Jesus's own, even higher standard. Jesus didn't just *have* a good life; he *was* the good life (John 14:6). All these gauges of his goodness both derived from him and anticipated him (Col. 2:17; Heb. 10:1).[1] The apostles came to see that his life didn't become good by fulfilling a set of requirements; God alone was good (Mark 10:18). The good life, and the goodness in their lives, was somehow proceeding from Jesus's life, which was God's own.

Our task in this chapter is not just to describe or explore that good life. There is no point in discussing it without focusing on its hinge.[2] Jesus calls anyone who would follow him not just to admire him but to take up his or her own

1. How could they both come from him and lead to him? That's easy: he was their alpha and omega.
2. Neglecting that hinge is what many so-called lives of Jesus do when they reject the historical circumstances, reality, and significance of his crucifixion and resurrection. Such treatments did not begin in the Enlightenment. Since antiquity, Judaism and Islam have both employed the same kind of revisionist storytelling in responding to the good news.

cross first. That is the necessary price of saving one's own life (Mark 8:34–35). So we need especially to investigate how a life ends and begins anew—first in Jesus himself, then in us too, as his death and resurrection express themselves in us as saving grace.

## A Baptismal Life's Ending and Beginning

For thirty years Jesus lived a quiet life in obscurity. The Gospel writers tell us next to nothing about those thirty years of faithfulness. An ordinary life, apparently with not much to report. And then came a turning point, at around the age of thirty, when Jesus emerged as a follower of John the Baptist.

The Baptist was something like a revivalist: a prophet called to bring Israel back to the faith of the covenant of Moses, "to prepare the way" for its eschatological restoration (Matt. 3:3; cf. Isa. 40:3). When his timeline intersected with Jesus's, he was offering a baptism of repentance for the remission of sins. In Mark's and John's Gospels, this is how we first hear of Jesus: as one of the ones who set aside his earlier life and accepted that baptism, offering himself to God for the remission of sins. That is a surprising place to be introduced to a sinless Christ. He's not the type one expects at an altar call. What was he doing repenting?

Jesus's baptism was an overture—the opening movement that plays all the themes we hear throughout the rest of his life's performance. Overtures attune audiences to coming melody lines. John's baptism was a gesture of self-sacrifice in which Jews could surrender themselves to the God of Israel, to restore both their own lives and their whole people. Jesus's baptismal self-offering invited that forgiveness and restoration. That melody played on right through his life to the cross and beyond.

John's movement was popular. Whole crowds were offering themselves alongside him. What distinguished Jesus's act from all of theirs?

Its unique outcome introduced another theme that persisted right through to Jesus's resurrection and ascension. After they all had been baptized, heaven opened and the Holy Spirit came down to rest on him as a voice from heaven quoted the royal words of Psalm 2: "You are my beloved Son; with you I am well pleased" (Luke 3:22 ESV). What Jesus alone received at the Jordan was affirmation and transforming empowerment. C. S. Lewis described Jesus at his baptism as "the perfect penitent."[3] He repented—not for sins of his own, but on behalf of his people—and received a new start of forgiveness, assur-

---

3. C. S. Lewis, *Mere Christianity*, rev. ed. (San Francisco: HarperOne, 2015), bk. 2, chap. 4.

ance, and decisive anointing. The Father's gift of the Spirit inaugurated the roles Jesus had been sent to take on as the Lord and pioneer of new creation. With that new life came an omega to even that good but undistinguished life he had led for those thirty years.

Jesus served his Father on behalf of the others in his midst, and his capacious life-performance overflowed into theirs. Once Jesus received John's baptism and the Father and Spirit made it *his* baptism, the frame of reference flipped, and Jesus's cross-and-resurrection-oriented life became baptism's defining quality. It could no longer remain *John's* baptism. Our Christian baptisms are baptisms *in Christ*. Through his grace, *we* are accepted and affirmed by the Father. *We* are an offering that is consumed and buried with him in victory. *Our* bodies are empowered with his Spirit, glorified with his glory, and raised to a qualitatively new life. If his baptism both foreshadowed and inaugurated the end of his good but old life, then sharing baptismally in his death ends our bad lives. As Jesus's baptism is an overture of his ministry, by grace a disciple's life becomes a reprise.

## Baptism's Forerunners

The themes that are playing in Jesus's baptism go back further in Israel's memory. Several Old Testament episodes that echo in his baptism narratives convey what ends and what begins there. They foreshadow the altered circumstances for the cosmos, humanity, Israel, and the nations that earlier chapters have already examined.

Luke's depictions of John the Baptist echo the scene in 1 Kings 18 of Elijah and the prophets of Baal on Mount Carmel, or at least hint at it. Israel was in a desperate state of apostasy and terminal decline. God had supplied a prophetic leader to turn their hearts back. Elijah—and John—offered a sacrifice in water. Elijah offered a bull on a restored altar; Jesus offered himself gratuitously to fulfill all righteousness. God wholly accepted both with fire. Both of these heavenly affirmations, as well as the Father's acceptance of Jesus on the cross, convinced witnesses that YHWH is the living God of Israel and revived their hope—yet only intensified persecution from Israel's leadership. God broke his silence at Mount Carmel, the Jordan, and Golgotha, and each time he pierced the tyrannical power of darkness.

Earlier we looked at Psalm 2, which the Father directed at his Son at the Jordan. The psalm envisions rage and conspiracy against God's reign from all quarters. That is what royal life could feel like in David's day, and in Christ's. God reminds the psalmist's enemies of the day he installed his anointed one on

Zion as king. The Lord bequeathed the whole earth to his messiah and commissioned him to reign, to quell rebellious powers and bless faithful ones. That coronation's new beginning signaled a coming end to their old shenanigans.

The events recorded in 1 Kings and Psalm 2 did not constitute an omega and alpha for Israel. God's covenant people soon resumed their downward course into apostasy and exile. Nevertheless, in them we glimpse the altered life of the one to come.

We already reviewed Isaiah 61, the passage Jesus began to read in his hometown synagogue after returning from forty Spirit-guided days in the wilderness. Those forty days followed his baptismal anointing with the Holy Spirit as his Father's servant. He returned in that Spirit to proclaim God's good news to sufferers of every kind. His neighbors both recognized Jesus and wondered at his remarkable change. Something was different, so shockingly different, in fact, that his new behavior and message filled them with murderous and conspiratorial rage (Luke 4:14–30).

Disaster for Jerusalem is the backdrop of Zechariah 12–13. A note of persistent conflict runs through this triumphant and hopeful scene. After the city's suffering and protection, God has promised to strengthen the house of David with God's own strength, send a spirit of compassion, and open up a cleansing fountain for the people, the land, and the house of David. This gift—Pentecostals will call it "Spirit baptism"—will provoke witnesses to mourn, like a lost firstborn, the one they have pierced. Is this victory or defeat, good news or bad? God's cleansing has come through violence; God's strengthening has come through conflict. Even in the midst of the deliverance, a prophet suffers shame and rejection; a shepherd is stricken and his flock scattered; two-thirds perish and the remnant are refined in fire. The old and unsustainable order is clearly passed, but woes await the new order's heir and his followers.

Finally, Ezekiel 36:16–37:14 looms over Jesus's baptism too. The passage features two scenes. In the first, God's people and their land have been defiled with idols and violence. The resulting exile has only made things worse, disseminating God's profaned name among the nations who were meant to learn better. The prophet's message is that God will take the initiative and act to hallow his name. He will gather them. He will wash them. He will give them a new heart and spirit, and he will bestow his own Spirit (36:26). And he will restore them to abundance, rebuilding, and fecundity. Then the second scene opens to a vision of Israel as a field covered in dry bones. Not freshly slain corpses or a maintained graveyard, but the long dead, dismembered, parched, exposed, scandalous relics of an extinct people. God reassembles them, reverses their decomposition, and breathes into them his own Spirit. Both visions concern the same restoration. Water and Spirit accomplish in the first what the Word and Spirit accomplish in the second. Deadly idolatry and violence in the first are sheer death in the second, and bounty and blessing are sheer life.

## One Way, Not Two

In taking on a human life, the Second Person of the Trinity took on all of this. His one life appropriated both sides of the transformation these texts anticipated. *He* became sin (2 Cor. 5:21). *He* became a curse (Gal. 3:13). His life was every human life: apostasy, conspiracy, violence, rejection, oppression, decline, poverty, illness, dissolution, profanity, loss, shame, and extinction. Sinless Jesus *was* the exception, or would have been; yet there he was at the Jordan and then hanging between thieves at Calvary, offering himself alongside all the rest, one of us, one for us, handing over to the Father every different life he could have enjoyed instead.

*He* received the crown of glory, honor, and absolute superiority (Heb. 1:4; 2:9). His life was holiness, anointing, release, healing, prosperity, revelation, triumph, spirit, glory, power, dominion, and posterity. This is a human life too. Jesus *is* the sole exception to the rule of human failure. However, though this is one life, it is not *only* one: behold his people there too, at table with him as he shares his body and blood, then reigning forever with him on his throne, a multitude beyond measure (Rev. 3:21; 7:9–10).

Both of these lives are equally shocking: that the only righteous human being would be numbered among transgressors, and that transgressors would gain his righteousness as their own. Moreover, they are one life, not two.

But why should this shock us? It's all perfectly consistent with the divine character of the one who lived it. Jesus's eyewitnesses perceived the God of Israel in him and bowed their knees in worship without feeling any temptation to give up their Judaism. They knew who he was; the sheep knew his voice. "In this the love of God was made manifest among us, that God sent his only Son into the world, so that we might live through him. . . . So we know and believe the love God has for us. God is love" (1 John 4:9, 16).

Deuteronomy, Proverbs, and Psalms all describe two ways to live. We can pursue life or death, wisdom or foolishness, righteousness or wickedness. That's true. But we're inclined to draw wrong inferences from this obvious empirical truth. We gather that our task is to take the right way and shun the wrong one. Entire religious and philosophical traditions have made the same mistake, even Jewish and Christian ones.[4] Jesus didn't.

---

4. This is ironic, since the chapters that follow Deut. 30 indicate that Israel will not in fact divide itself into two such groups but that Israel will as a body experience sin, death, and exile

Chapter 5 discussed Moses's rhetoric of two ways, death and life. Israel traveled both, and Jesus further clarified its true meaning. He didn't tell us that we could *either* save our life or lose it. A life's alpha hangs on its omega: I can only save my life *by* losing it because of him, or else I'll lose it in my very willing to save it (Mark 8:35). You and I do choose, but we don't choose life *instead of* death; we choose death in order to gain life. The storm of evil is unavoidable—Augustine affirmed that through his doctrines of original sin and total depravity—so the way of Jesus didn't steer around it. Instead, the Father led him right for its heart. Jesus—the life, wisdom, and righteousness of God—became death, foolishness, and wickedness for us, so that you and I can become life, wisdom, and righteousness. The only way was the way through, the way of the cross.

Gnostics and spiritualists misunderstood the Kingdom as a faraway destination. Avoiding evil's storm, they thought, involved escaping from the present world. By contrast, Zealots supposed that the Kingdom would invade the present world, flooding and transforming their surroundings and dispelling the tempest. Jesus's way confounds both. Like the exodus, the Kingdom's advent involved *both* God's invasion into the world *and* a migration out of the world and into it. On the one hand, it was and remains a revolutionary movement, like the invasion that began in faraway Mount Horeb and arrived among the captives (Exod. 3:1–10). Like the dark world it invaded, the Kingdom can be resisted but not avoided. On the other hand, the Kingdom was and is a migratory opportunity that locals miss if we don't enter it while we can. We have to apply the blood to our doorframes, keep the Passover, and exit—*tonight*.

Want a more familiar parable of invasion and migration? Imagine a fashion trend that started in Paris or London and has now made it to my town and circle of acquaintances. It too can be resisted, but not avoided. We can abandon our old wardrobe and embrace the fashion trend while it's here, or we can let it pass. It won't wait for us.

The Kingdom's ambassadors issue three main commands to anyone in earshot:

*Behold*, stop just living "under the sun," and look at what has appeared from beyond.

*Come* and gather in God's now present midst.

*Go* from life's old bonds and forsake whatever doesn't suit our new freedom.

---

and then forgiveness, renewal, and restoration. Even in the Torah, the way to life proceeds through the way of death, not around it.

Medieval spiritual theology developed these commands into the illumina-tive, unitive, and purgative ways of salvation.[5] We travel them personally even as the Lord also directs them to humanity as a whole (Rev. 22:17). The Kingdom changes our lives simply by invading our horizons with its news and commands (Matt. 10:14–15), and it further changes our lives if we heed them (10:7–8).

Let's look at what ends in such lives and what begins. In a way we have already been doing this in our earlier reflections on Mary, Jacob, Paul, and Timothy.[6] This time we'll focus on Simon Peter. When Jesus invaded his old life, Simon Peter beheld, came, and went. He received a new life and a new name to suit it.[7] Simon Peter exemplifies a number of ways that Jesus is the omega and the alpha of a life. We will focus on several in turn.

## Ended in Baptism, Baptizing with the Holy Spirit

First, Jesus's baptism overflows into others' lives. *Jesus and then Peter were put to an end in baptism, and both became suppliers of the Holy Spirit's life-giving baptism.*

John the Baptist saw his era in omega-and-alpha terms. God was felling the old fruitless trees; Jesus would be left standing. Jesus would inaugurate a baptism of Holy Spirit and fire to gather the Lord's wheat and burn the chaff (Matt. 3:5–12; cf. Isa. 30:26–28). There was no point in taking John's old trail once Jesus had blazed the Father's new one.

The Gospel of John indicates that it was through John the Baptist that Jesus met Andrew and through him Simon (John 1:35–42). Perhaps Simon was a fellow disciple of John along with his brother. Perhaps he was just a fisherman whom Andrew pulled into Jesus's vortex. In any event, on meeting Simon, Jesus treated him like wheat, not chaff. The Lord bestowed a new life on him and announced that his old one would be ending (Matt. 4:19; John 1:42).

It didn't end all at once. Peter is as famous for his foibles and failures along the way as he is for his final stature as the church's first leader. The stories of his stumbles, triumphs, martyr's death, and vast legacy appeal to Christians who relate to his slow and faltering transformation. What Paul said about himself could be said just as truly of Peter: "always carrying in the body the

---

5. The sequence of these ways is not important here. They tend to intertwine anyway.

6. Chapter 3's personal focus, the ruler of this world, is not on the list because Jesus is the omega of his rule but the alpha only of his expulsion and exile. That's not much of an alpha.

7. Simon's old name and his new one (Cephas in Aramaic, Peter in Greek) signify his original name and his Christ-bestowed office in the church respectively. As Paul's two names mainly signify his two primary cultures, Hebrew and Greco-Roman, so do "Cephas" and "Peter."

death of Jesus, so that the life of Jesus may also be manifested in our bodies"
(2 Cor. 4:10).

Readers of the Gospels endure the painful death of Simon's old way of
seeing. Andrew had told him that he had found the Messiah, and Simon came
to agree. But then he rebuked Jesus for announcing that the Son of Man
had to suffer and be rejected before rising again, and he was rebuked in turn
(Mark 8:31–32). Their dispute concerned precisely the substance of Jesus's
baptism: dying as a servant of all (10:38–45). Jesus was not the Messiah that
*Simon* Peter had expected. Had he known, would he really have left his old
life to follow him? He was, after all, still the old Simon.

Simon *Peter*'s theology, though, had room not only for a suffering Messiah but for a life of suffering with the Messiah. This perspective took time
to develop. Peter needed some lessons and reminders along the way. Jesus
repeatedly announced the necessity of his "baptism" of suffering and death.
After his resurrection, he gently but firmly refocused Peter on his vocation of
pastoral care and mission (Acts 1:6–9; John 21:1–17). Long afterward, fellow
servant Paul confronted him when he forgot the cultural cost of discipleship
(Gal. 2:11–14). These lessons worked. The flame of Simon's old life dimmed,
sputtered, and died. The man who had once faced off against his own Messiah
became willing to be led where he didn't want to go.

It wasn't just Peter's worldview, context, and community that changed.
Peter changed. Christ's baptismal life of suffering and triumphant faithfulness
was the one he ended up living (Acts 5:40–41; 1 Pet. 3:14–18; John 21:18–19).
His will changed in a number of ways, which we will explore below. What
slowly snuffed his stubborn self-assertion was a new life of faith that matured
into resilient hope. The old gave way to the new: first for Jesus the leader and
then for the followers who belonged to him (Rom. 5:17).

The baptized Messiah became the Holy Spirit's baptizer, giving life to
all who call on the Lord's name (Luke 3:16; Acts 2:33). So did Peter. On
Pentecost, as all the apostles spoke in tongues of Jesus's signs and wonders
and mighty deeds, Peter stepped forward to speak thus to the whole crowd
(Acts 2:11, 14). He stepped into Jesus's life-giving role as healer (3:6–7),
Spirit-baptizer (2:38; 8:14–17), and world-transcending authority (Matt.
16:19; 28:18–20).

My choice of exemplars invites a skeptic's objection. Sure, *Peter* underwent
that transformation, but isn't Peter an outlier rather than an exemplar? The
supposedly new lives of many Christian leaders look no different from their
old ones. Some of them look even worse because of what they do with the
power they gain. Instead of dying slow deaths like Peter's, their old lives go
underground and thrive under the cover of fake new ones.

The church arrived at a twofold answer to this. As the Constantinian era dawned, sacramental theologies developed to assure the church that immoral and disingenuous leaders did not jeopardize their flocks' salvation. Jesus was still their *ultimate* shepherd, working through their ministries despite their own contrary character. The reassurance was valid, but it came at the cost of greater and greater laxity toward those compromised leaders. As for all the Christians in the pews with "alpha" lives that barely differed from their "omega" lives, theologies of grace and election arose to explain that too—or explain it away. Perhaps these people were never saved in the first place; perhaps their renewal awaited in purgatory. Meanwhile, monastic vocations arose to pursue the personal transformation available to those few who were willing to be remade as "eunuchs for the Kingdom of God" (cf. Matt. 19:11–12).

These answers provided a rationale for minimizing immorality's impact and trained the church away from applying baptismal regeneration radically to all believers' lives. If the grace and the ministries are still valid, what difference does character really make?

Jesus warned of wolves in sheep's clothing (Matt. 7:15). The church's history confirms his prophecy in spades. Unethical leaders have ravaged his church. Christian immorality has been one of the more historically compelling arguments against the gospel's validity, or at least the validity of a certain construal of it.

Better construals involve, among other things, proper respect for what baptism signifies. Public faces, professions of faith, and even teachings are not enough; only those whose lives reflect the Father's baptismal will are true disciples and disciple-makers (Matt. 7:20–23). That insight fueled the Radical "Anabaptist" Reformation. A wolf dressed as a sheep or a shepherd (John 10:10–11) is not just a pretender but a predator. There is more to Christian leadership than the clothing of office. So Paul warned the Corinthians that a little immorality will spread and ruin Christ's whole blood-cleansed community (1 Cor. 5:6–8). All Christians share responsibility for vigilance. Our alpha involves a visible and remarkable change. As it shocked Jesus's neighbors after his baptism, so it surprised the crowds who recognized the bold apostolic preachers as the same Galileans who had scattered under pressure only a few days before (Acts 4:13). Likewise, Paul could cite his erring Galatian church's own lives to prove the power of hearing the gospel (Gal. 3:1–4). The Father requires no less. The Son demands no less. The Spirit offers no less.

So some Christian traditions have concluded that full Christian life depends on a full alpha of holiness, restoration, and even perfection—if not for everyone instantly, then at least for leaders while the rest grow into it. In the case of Holiness Wesleyans, that means justification and the "second blessing" or "entire sanctification"; for Pentecostals, Spirit baptism as well. How else would we counter the endemic rot of church immorality than by depending on these gifts from God? But several things interfere with this solution. A "holy" culture develops with outward conformity to a narrow set of litmus behaviors rather than true virtue. Or a series of supposedly qualified leaders falls from grace, sowing doubt. Or candidates for leadership emerge with a desirable skill set or a family pedigree but not the same moral markers or substance, and this tempts the tradition to overlook its own formal requirements "for results."

These unsatisfying answers beg the skeptic's objection all over again: Just what is this alpha in a person's life? If it is more than nominal or invisible regeneration by identification with Christ, then why do so few disciples gain a demonstrably Christlike moral caliber, and why is good character among the rest often still so fragile?

"Many will say to me, 'Lord, Lord,'" Jesus predicted. "And then will I declare to them, 'I never knew you; depart'" (Matt. 7:22–23). That "never" indicates that many lives never underwent the alpha they thought they had. Why are there so many of them? Jesus doesn't explain. He just warns his hearers not to be among them.[8]

For those who hear his word and do it, the four Gospels' distinct timelines all describe an alpha that arrives at once, but not *all* at once. Jesus's followers gained the character that later distinguished them only in the often painful course of their service under his rather demanding oversight. That service has a definite shape, with Jesus its source, the Holy Spirit its supplier, and the Father its goal.

Paul called the church "God's building" (1 Cor. 3:9). What is a building's alpha moment? Is it the groundbreaking? Is it the ribbon-cutting ceremony? Or is it the final construction that happens just before the ribbon cutting—or perhaps quietly, behind the scenes, afterward? Or is it some subtle tipping point in the middle when the fundamentals are in place, with or without certain finished details? *Or does it even matter?* For some purposes, timing does matter; it can be too early to move into a building, and it can be silly to let some lingering minor details change a move-in date. It can be too early to move a candidate into leadership or even into membership, and it can be awkwardly late. But does it matter *when* we apply Christ's alpha label to a believer's life?

---

8. These warnings of avoidable consequences make much more sense if salvation follows something like an Arminian logic. If it followed a Calvinist one, they would have to be something other than a warning in rhetorical disguise.

If the matter were that important, one suspects that there wouldn't be so much ambiguity and even ambivalence about it in the New Testament. Baptism is clearly Jesus Christ's omega-alpha sign, but its relationship to what it signifies is surprisingly loose. The Gospels don't agree when, or even if, the Twelve were baptized, by either John or Jesus. Surely some proportion of those many alpha-less strangers who say "Lord, Lord" are baptized. Samaritan followers were baptized, but somehow they still lacked the Holy Spirit (Acts 8:12–17), while Cornelius's house received the Holy Spirit *before* baptism (10:44–48). In each of these cases, God remedied deficiencies by supplying whatever element was lacking, or removing whatever element didn't belong.

It is clearer that disciples need reminding about our new standing in him— or, in some cases, the lack of it (John 17:12; 1 John 2:19). These kinds of assurances and warnings are valid: we do know in part, even as we wait to understand how we are already fully understood (1 Cor. 13:12), and we ought to act on that partial knowledge. If I persevere right to cross-bearing's bittersweet end, my alpha will have been the beginning of something remarkable. So a more important issue than *when* my alpha arrives is *what* I am doing about it (14:1). The substance of Christian lives becomes increasingly visible and clear as time goes on. Not totally clear, of course; only the final judgment will reveal all. But even bystanders see enough to end up marveling or mocking (Luke 14:25–33). To answer that skeptic's objection, the mockeries do not discredit the marvels, at least not in Jesus's opinion (14:34–35).

The New Testament is crystal clear that whenever our alpha does arrive and by whatever means,[9] Jesus is that alpha. Our lives' specific timelines vary, but Jesus is still determinative for their baptismal omegas and alphas (Rom. 6:1–4; 1 Pet. 3:15–22). What we flesh out in our own ways is Christ (Eph. 4:13).

## An End to Ordinariness, Beginning a Holy Fellowship

The second and third ways of exploring Jesus as a life's omega and alpha come together. On the one hand, *Jesus is uniquely foreknown and predestined, and the first of many brothers and sisters* (Rom. 8:28–30). He both proved his solitary status and gave it up to inaugurate a fellowship with fellow saints. On

9. This includes means that are effective in the absence of formal baptism. Even the sacramental church acknowledged this in expanding baptism's sacramental efficacy to include the irregular forms of catechumens' "baptisms of intent" and martyrs' "baptisms in blood." Contemporary evangelicalism's apathy about formal baptism is not healthy, but that does not invalidate God's manifest transformation in many unbaptized Christians' lives. Like Spirit-filled Cornelius, they ought to be baptized and ought to desire it; but their lives are becoming Christ-shaped regardless.

the other hand, *Jesus lived an ordinary life that yielded to the unique holiness of a saint's life* (Heb. 2:9). He gave up elements of human ordinariness and began a life of extraordinary signs and wonders, character, and glory. These two pairs only seem to contradict. For our sake, the only begotten Son entered alone into an alienated and corrupt human "community"—boundless holiness taking on commonality—in order to bring common human persons into their own as uniquely holy persons who live in fellowship with him and one another.

The alpha of our adoption has to be the omega of his solitude. In rejecting its own Lord, the world had isolated itself. It had become a vast spiritual orphanage. Bonds can develop among the children in orphanages, but they don't make up for absent parents. Jesus, the Father's only child and heir, entered alone into our isolation to break it. Pressing onward along the solitary course set for him (Heb. 12:2), he came to that self-orphaned world in sacrificial hospitality and opened his Father's family to us. The one whom only the Father knows (Matt. 11:27), and the only one ever *born* king of the Jews, took on Israel's exile and persecution, made them his own, and ended the era of *our* collective solitude.[10] The one "who alone has immortality and dwells in unapproachable light" (1 Tim. 6:16) came to the estranged and suffered our acting out, so that we lonely ones could be reconciled and enter his glorious fellowship in the Spirit.

It is remarkable how unremarkable much of his earthly life was. Biographers pore over the earlier lives of people who become famous, looking for the key events that shaped them. Not Jesus's biographers. Two Gospels describe an extraordinary birth and infancy, and one relates a telling moment when Jesus was twelve, but that's it. Most of his first thirty years were like yours and mine: undocumented, and presumably rightly so. I wonder, Would focusing readers' attention on those years have encouraged readers to single out Jesus from among the rest of us, opening up the very space his unremarkable life among us was meant to close? For two millennia, speculators have filled in those gaps with apocryphal accounts of an extraordinary childhood, years with the Essenes, a trip to India, and so on, and readers have eaten them up. We can't help but suspect that such space between Jesus's life and ours just *has to* exist. I suspect that we're better off not knowing.

10. The Gospel of Matthew develops this theme powerfully. Its infancy narratives emphasize Jesus's royal lineage and birth in Bethlehem, then his exile to Egypt and refugee status in Nazareth under the threat of persecution when the King settled down into those quiet decades of life under the regime's radar. All along, though, the "formula quotations" ("this took place to fulfill what was spoken of") see Jesus's ministry in terms of an impending *return* from exile on Israel's behalf.

Whatever those years were like, he left them behind decisively. The only Son's determination to live that ordinary, estranged life for us and then leave it was shared and eternal, made "before the foundation of the world" (Eph. 1:4) in the Father's will (Luke 9:35). And he was uniquely able to fulfill it (Rev. 5:2–5). Nikos Kazantzakis's *The Last Temptation of Christ* speculated that the final and strongest temptation Jesus faced was to hold on to his ordinary life, marry and have children, and die of old age. There's something to that. The devil tempted Jesus in the wilderness with good things: sustenance, power, and protection. Ordinary life is a good thing too. There's nothing demeaning or inferior about it (1 Cor. 7:28). In Jesus's hands, how could there be? Yet by the time Jesus was getting arrested and crucified, such a "temptation" could be no more than a fantasy. The Trinity's baptismal overture had already sounded. His omega and alpha were irreversible. Aborting his mission midway could not have returned him to where he was before; his final state would be far worse. He said the same about abortive followers (Luke 14:25–33; 2 Pet. 2:20). If he were indeed tempted to back out along the way, it could only have been a flash of regret, not a realistic temptation. As the Indian hymn says, "No turning back."[11]

What ended in the course of Jesus's mission was *both* his solitude, because his messianic work was producing brothers and sisters who could follow him on the way (John 13:36), *and* his ordinariness, because they entered together into a new holy life. His old, incognito life had to end in the dawning of his new life as the head of the communion of saints. Two separate worlds, one ordinary and one eternally mysterious, came apart in order that a new one would come together.

The saints in that communion are different than before, having sacrificed their own conventional lives. This is not to say that they take on spectacular careers; many do not. But they will. It is not to say that they gain fame and glory; the lives of many remain unseen by more than a few ordinary eyes. But their deeds will come to light in the sight of all.[12]

These new persons don't leave behind the personal qualities that made the old persons who they were. Their personalities don't disappear as if they

---

11. Simon Marak, "I Have Decided to Follow Jesus," quoting Nokseng's final words in the face of persecution.

12. Church history has repeatedly anticipated this. Many of the developments that changed the world went unnoticed at the time. The Roman Empire wasn't transformed because some emperor turned everything around. The ground changed *underneath* the empire over centuries. Sensibilities were being changed regardless of its leaders' agendas and even despite them. The real change happened a life at a time, a family at a time, a village at a time, and at what would have looked like a pretty slow pace. Jesus had said it would be like that: the Kingdom of God is like yeast, or a seed, or money earning a return—something we can't just stand around watching because we won't think we're seeing anything. But what we aren't seeing is epochal.

were assimilated into some dehumanizing cult. Nor do their peculiarities and quirks fall away to leave some kind of pure, divine rationality. Saints are still gloriously human—more *gloriously* human than ever. The stories of saints confirm that they are *more* personal, more their own selves, because their fellowship with Christ sets them free from the powers that had distorted and arrested their spiritual development, and resettles them where they can flourish. Yet these new and unique creations somehow still image Jesus Christ, who heads them. It is by being who they are that they display the character and work of the Triune God.

Peter is instructive here. His background was pedestrian. When the Gospels introduce Simon, he has been nothing but a face in the crowd. His father's name was Jonah or John. Simon was a fisherman from Bethsaida in Galilee who spoke like a local. He owned his own boat, so he was not destitute. He was married to a woman from Capernaum and maintained family connections with her family and his brother Andrew, so he had a support network and was depended on. Nobody special; just a guy. There's not much to say about him. Conventional. Salt of the earth.

And a guy who was ready for a messiah. Not actively searching, perhaps; but like Jesus's other early disciples, ready to give up the life he had built in that precarious ancient society for the chance of something more (Mark 1:16–20). He was a conscious part of that Jewish world that knew it was mired in old lives too distant from God and from one another and needful of God's intended future. Simon wasn't out to build that future himself. He wasn't one of the Pharisees working hard to cultivate God's holiness throughout Israel, or the Zealots waiting to take matters into their own hands and bring a revolution, or even necessarily the disciples of John the Baptist who were preparing for God to do something new. He spent his days fishing. But when the future called, he stepped into it.

And stepped into a disorienting situation where his conventions no longer applied. Christ's Kingdom cultivated a different kind of life. It involved new authority, relationships of peace, servant leadership, beatific standards of conduct and outlook, lavish grace, imagination transformed by events and signs and parables, expectations of sacrifice, and hope for eschatological promotion to even greater responsibility. A different world.

Among all the ways such conditions can transform a life, let's focus on one pertaining to the fellowship Jesus pioneered. Simon's old life was a typically provincial one. He had a Galilean accent. He never ate anything unclean but respected the diet and practices of his local culture. The Kingdom opened up a whole new life. Through Jesus he encountered tax collectors, Zealots, Pharisees, outsider women, outcasts, southerners and urbanites, Samaritans, gentiles, Roman officials, Jewish pilgrims from throughout the Roman world, magicians, wealthy businesspeople, fellow church leaders and missionaries from across the empire—you name it. And he forged Christian bonds with many of them as brothers and sisters and fellow workers. He did not just *meet* these kinds of people; the gospel opened him up to extend Kingdom hospitality to them, to enjoy fellowship with the disciples among them as fellow saints, and to exchange gifts the Spirit offered them—to become a new kind of human being like his master.

The man who embraced Jesus's new name for him became Jesus's principal spokesman. He was likely the principal source behind Jesus's first biography, the Gospel of Mark. There Peter's old self is portrayed in painfully humbling terms. Yet Mark's Gospel is no exercise in regret or self-absorption; it is the grateful and self-effacing tale of an emancipator told by one of the emancipated, who was freed from his own earlier self as much as anything, and who still seemed amazed by it.

Peter is also the likely author (or at least principal source) of 1 Peter, the New Testament writing that seems most aware of the many currents running through the diverse and far-flung Christian churches of the first few decades.[13] The once-provincial fisherman from a Palestinian backwater was now anything but. His ministry embodied openness to others (Acts 15:7–11). On Pentecost he was the first to invite Jewish pilgrims from across the empire into Christ's Kingdom (2:39). Along with other first-generation leaders, he was receptive to the needs of excluded Hellenistic Jews in the young church (6:1–7).[14]

In a word, Peter's new and holy life was "catholic." It expressed the universality of Christ's fellowship of holy ones, among whom the Spirit makes no distinction (Acts 10:34; 11:12). Peter was actively aware of different kinds of Christians and honored them as brothers and sisters. He encouraged their service as fellow heirs of Christ's Kingdom. He strengthened the fellowship network that straddled the Greco-Roman world and beyond.

Well, you might say, of course the church's leader does that; it is a leader's job. Yet Jesus made catholicity the ethos of his whole fellowship (John 17:20–23) and called all his disciples to express it (13:34–35) in their own personal ways.[15]

13. Luke Timothy Johnson, *The Writings of the New Testament: An Interpretation*, rev. ed. (Minneapolis: Fortress, 1999), 480–81.

14. Sometimes he was accommodating to a fault, for instance when in Galatia he let consideration for Jewish sensibilities interfere with obligations to the whole church and its whole gospel (Gal. 2:12–13).

15. Miroslav Volf's *Exclusion and Embrace* (Nashville: Abingdon, 1994) refers to the Spirit's creation of a "catholic personality" with "space to receive the other" (51).

What Peter lived out, others did too and commended "to all the saints." Paul encouraged sacrificial consideration for others in his letters to Rome (Rom. 14–15) and Philippi (Phil. 2:1–5) and to Philemon. The Letter of James demands that wealthy and poor worship as one and care for one another. And so on. Jesus's character became the apostles', and his apostles bequeathed Jesus's character to their fellowships as well.[16]

Saints' lives help us get at catholicity's personal shape. Mother Teresa is legendary, of course, for including everyone in her life and in the lives of her sisters. As Christian and Muslim armies battled, Francis of Assisi traveled to Syria to preach the gospel of peace to a sultan even after being beaten by his soldiers.[17] Corrie ten Boom harbored Jews and members of the Nazi resistance during the Holocaust, and extended mercy to Nazi collaborators after the war. But these superheroes beg the question of whether such qualities are exceptional, so let me turn to a much more mundane life I know better: my own.

Teaching Christian theology to a variety of students, I came to a place where I value all of them: artists, athletes, scientists, pragmatists, apathetic undecideds, overachievers, musicians, techies, entrepreneurs, activists, slackers, geniuses, average folks, strugglers, dropouts, sexual minorities, Pentecostals and charismatics, high-church Catholics and Orthodox and mainline Protestants, fundamentalists, megachurch evangelicals who don't know whether they belong to a denomination at all, skeptics, Buddhists, prom queens and social stars and outcasts and meek invisibles, international students and ethnic minorities and "third culture kids" and "monocultural" white evangelicals, sufferers of learning disabilities and psychological disorders—really, the whole range. I wasn't inclined to value them all when I was a child, an adolescent, a college or graduate student, or even a beginning teacher. But years of interaction with my actual and potential brothers and sisters in Christ, structured by the Kingdom's rules, have opened me to seeing them that way.

I serve on an interdenominational team of volunteer chaplains with the local jail ministry in town. Every month or so I go to a particular dorm and

16. The church's typical worship practices symbolize its catholicity: for instance, one communion table for all, no preferred seating, prayers for other churches and nations, hospitality to outsiders, multilingual services, support for cross-cultural missions, and community outreaches. Or they fail to. Offenses against catholicity such as private baptisms and masses and chapels for the rich and powerful, assigned and paid-for seating, prayers and assistance for one's in-group to the neglect of the out-groups, outright segregation, and the like, display our old selves rather than our new selves, and then we stand under the judgment of our own alpha language (1 Cor. 11:29). So do our behaviors outside church that fail to align with our ritual catholicity.

17. Bonaventure, *The Life of Saint Francis of Assisi* (New York: Dutton, 2013), chap. 9.

meet with the prisoners there. Many are Christians; many are fighting (and not yet winning) battles with addiction; some are psychologically unstable; they have lives and pasts and relationships I do not relate to and would not wish on anyone. And we rejoice together in how we are the Kingdom's actual or potential fellow heirs. We discuss how we are all failures who have brought suffering as well as blessing on others. We especially focus on the ethical passages of the New Testament, because we all know we need to be better if we are to be the blessings on others that God has called and equipped us to be. This is not the kind of thing I ever imagined doing at the time of my conversion, nor would have desired. I come from a different world from practically all of the prisoners. But I am not *going* to a different world than they are, because our lives all have the same basic baptismal shape. After a couple of hours I leave them behind, walk out of the cell blocks, and drive myself home to my family; but while we are together, we pray with genuine gratitude for the opportunity to gather in Jesus's name around a Spartan metal table and celebrate our fellowship. I usually enjoy that time more than that morning's conventional church service.

As I write, I am on sabbatical, traveling abroad with my family to teach in Christian institutions around the world. I have taught Ethiopian evangelical and Tewahedo Orthodox church leaders in Ethiopia, eastern European undergraduates of every kind of Christian tradition alongside an atheist and agnostic majority, Chinese house-church students in the Philippines, and multidenominational evangelicals from across South and East Asia. I've taught and preached in monocultural and multiethnic classrooms, churches, and chapel spaces on campuses both lavish and high-tech and antiquated and dilapidated. In every context I immediately recognize as brothers and sisters my students and fellow faculty, despite the cultural chasms that distinguish us and would otherwise separate us. We belong to Jesus, and we face a common future, so from our different locations we are facing in the same direction and walking with the same Lord to our eternity together. The friends and acquaintances I've made range from indigenous citizens, expatriates from America and other countries, scholars of mixed ancestries and mixed marriages, "tribals" who are marginal and oppressed in their own countries, and Muslim-background believers and Korean-Americans, who are minorities wherever they go. And I've traveled in bursts as a tourist to Christian as well as stubbornly non-Christian destinations in western and eastern Europe, Japan, Vietnam, and Cambodia, worshiping with strangers who share our common joy, hope, and inheritance.

I never imagined this kind of life before I became a Christian. I feared it when I faced the prospect of becoming one. ("Lord, please don't make me a missionary," I pleaded.) Now all I want is more of it. Catholicity is far richer—just as Titus 3 said—than the "diversity" that preoccupies the contemporary academy.[18] Its energy is different from the energy of the cosmopolis, where people brush past each other from one little social bubble to another. I know that life well, having grown up in Los Angeles. People *adapt* to such multicultural contexts. But flesh and blood do not *adapt* to the Kingdom of God (1 Cor. 15:50). My catholic life—and I confess it is still modest, immature, and incomplete—is baptismal in origin and character.

You may object. Are these changes really such a unique achievement? Won't study and work abroad produce the same qualities? Aren't I just a product of a contemporary culture that treats tolerance and openness as cardinal virtues that are available to all, and demanded of all, and that punishes and scorns those who don't display them? And haven't non-Christians outdone us? Christian disapproval of behaviors such as idolatry and sexual sin is reckoned as intolerance, closed-mindedness, and even hate—and it often *has* taken those forms. Has the world managed to attain catholicity apart from the alpha of new lives in Christ?

Some segments of some populations have achieved ethnic and cultural tolerance and even mutual regard, and that is something to celebrate (or mourn the loss of). But tolerance and respect aren't catholicity, just shallow alternatives. Cultural pluralism, egalitarianism, and relativism are demonic parodies. To different degrees, they refrain from making judgments, and therefore they refrain from offering hope or help for improving people's situations beyond lifting the burden of discrimination. If a neighbor's idolatry really is destructive, then condoning it serves no one. Tolerance and respect do make judgments. Positive ones affirm while negative ones rebuke. While Jesus demonstrated both stances toward rivals and enemies, and his faithful disciples do too, alone that does not amount to love.

Love is a universal preoccupation in both mortal and immortal stages of life. But when what humans love is darkness (John 3:19), love draws us to sin and destruction. It's a scandal that this seems to happen nearly as much in the church as outside it. But the church has still tasted the gracious, sacrificial, faithful, hopeful, victorious, infectious, revolutionary love of Jesus Christ. What a different taste it has! Love has always been God's will for just human

---

18. Teaching in all these contexts has shown me that both cultural homogeneity and heterogeneity can produce excellence as well as mediocrity. Sometimes diversity is an advantage, other times it's a disadvantage, and sometimes it doesn't seem to matter much. Its value, while genuine, is limited. Catholicity, on the other hand, is invaluable. Unlike diversity per se, it anticipates new creation and helps learners prepare for it.

relationships; God set it at the top of old Israel's agenda (Matt. 22:37–40). Nevertheless, Jesus's love is new, "a new commandment" (John 13:34), which true catholicity lives out. Jesus's love heads, unites, and perfects all true virtues and varieties of the Spirit's fruit (1 Cor. 13; Gal. 5:22–23; Col. 3:9–14). Tasting it awakens a longing for more, and a correspondingly deep disappointment (and not just among Christians) with the ways Christians settle for the old loves and their even shallower alternatives.

Tolerance, pluralism, egalitarianism, and relativism are better described as indifference—which, Elie Wiesel noted, is really the opposite of love[19]—and even regard and respect fall short. None of these demand that we invest personally in one another, let alone die to our old selves and take on new lives. While I "live and let live," I can demonize pluralism's dissenters and feel good about myself for it; I can let lost sheep wander away; I can voice approvals and disapprovals and leave it at that; I can keep whomever I want at arm's length, keeping my own head down and out of harm's way; I can neglect people who suffer the consequences of our rudderless contemporary society's confusions. That's not Jesus, it's not Peter or Paul or James, and it's not catholicity. It refuses the challenge of offering and receiving the Kingdom's *grace and truth*, which flesh and blood cannot naturally do.

One of my favorite Bible passages, from Paul's advice to Titus, embodies gracious truthfulness:

> Remind [those you teach] to be submissive to rulers and authorities, to be obedient, to be ready for any honest work, to speak evil of no one, to avoid quarreling, to be gentle, and to show perfect courtesy toward all men. *For we ourselves were once* foolish, disobedient, led astray, slaves to various passions and pleasures, passing our days in malice and envy, hated by men and hating one another; but when the goodness and loving kindness of God our Savior appeared, he saved us, not because of deeds done by us in righteousness, but in virtue of his own mercy, by the washing of regeneration and renewal in the Holy Spirit, which he poured out upon us richly through Jesus Christ our Savior, so that we might be justified by his grace and become heirs in hope of eternal life. The saying is sure. (Titus 3:1–8)

What an astounding attitude. Hearing it in our current polarized and ideologically repressive environment is like drinking fresh water. We can be compassionate to all, rather than indifferent, let alone hostile, because we can identify with wherever they are. Before we received our new lives, we lived just those sorts of old lives. So we show the same goodness and loving kindness with

---

19. Elie Wiesel, "On Indifference," *US News and World Report*, October 27, 1986.

which Christ remade ours. God's lavish grace brings personal renewal that connects us in love with people who still need that renewal.

"The saying is sure" means that this is no bold proposal from the author but proverbial Christian wisdom. We may need support to live up to it, but we know it's right. Of course, people stuck in omega-less old lives—some of whom gather for Titus's teaching and for ours—won't necessarily understand that truthful grace nor respond in kind. Pride blinds us all and seals us off. Whole cultures and subcultures, including subcultures of elites and "teachers," suffer that kind of blindness and diligently pass it on (Matt. 23:24) and denigrate the Kingdom's true representatives.[20] Often, truthful grace takes time to penetrate. So, Paul continues, "avoid stupid controversies, genealogies, dissensions, and quarrels over the law, for they are unprofitable and futile. As for a man who is factious, after admonishing him once or twice, have nothing more to do with him, knowing that such a person is perverted and sinful; he is self-condemned" (Titus 3:9–11). This attitude is neither hate nor indifference. After all, *we ourselves were once* the same way. That quarrelsome person may yet change (and we may not have changed as much as we like to think). Paul's directions reflect humility and patience with the limits of one's own power and role in the remaking of other people's lives. After all, he surely remembered that back when he had every Christian on the run, Jesus intervened personally to demolish his pride and set him on his new course. Though self-condemned, he was still in Christ's reach. So as a Christian he never stopped praying and contending for the ethnic brothers and sisters with whom he would even have traded places (Rom. 9:3–5).

### Obedient Servant to the End, a Servant-Leader's Eternal Living Sacrifice

Our fourth topic concerns the revolutionary overflow of Christ's sacrifice. The Son didn't just take on a mortal life and sanctify it; he handed it over for others to put to its appointed final end. Jesus loved the Father with a sacrificed life. He expressed his love with supple but firm obedience to the Father's will, right to the cross. His death was an omega-sacrifice: the kind that can only be given once. And just as Jesus's old life concluded in his new one, so *his omega-sacrifice led to a new sacrifice, a living sacrifice, which can be given forever.* That is our next topic.

20. Is this not the situation in the secular West, whose cultured despisers have subjected Christianity to singular criticism for centuries—straining out gnats, Jesus might say, while swallowing one ideological camel after another? If so, then Titus points the Western church's missional way forward.

Why does the end of a human life span matter theologically? Why do we put spiritual weight on one's standing at the time of death, and on the symbolic death of one's baptism? Perhaps because it honors life's sacrificial character. One way or another, we *spend* life, and we spend *our own* lives. Even vegans sacrifice life to maintain their own lives. Every new family is torn from its predecessors: "A man *leaves* his father and his mother and *cleaves* to his wife, and they become one flesh" (Gen. 2:24).[21] In family relationships, children sacrifice differently from parents, and husbands differently from wives, but they all sacrifice (Col. 3:17–4:1). Even if we spend our lives and others' lives on nothing, they still get spent. How we have spent them is who we've become.

"To dust you shall return" (Gen. 3:19): our old lives come to blood, sweat, toil, and tears. Mortal lives are oriented toward the grave's inevitable omega even as we strive to delay that destiny and work around it. Mortality conditions our whole biological existence: childhood, maturity, marrying and giving in marriage, and decline. Ecclesiastes, Job, and Proverbs are all relentlessly honest about this in their own ways. Death casts its shadow even in Song of Songs (8:6). Our weakness finally returns us to the ground from which we were taken (1 Cor. 15:43).

My culture prefers to narrate this along two main lines: triumph and tragedy. Either I can admit my weakness on the way to telling the story of how I overcame it (even just by dying), or I can make weakness my epitaph and myself its victim. Both turn weakness into a foe. Tales of triumph capitalize on it for admiration, whereas tales of victimhood defer to it for pity. Both triumph and tragedy spend our mortality, but not on what Jesus himself sought. Jesus's omega-sacrifice was his own weak life (Rom. 3:23–26). The Father put him forward—spent him, like a sin offering—for the sake of righteousness.

A whole burnt offering takes time to burn away. Jesus submitted at the Jordan to John's baptism, and later he set his face toward Jerusalem. Once there he made his body and blood an offering for his disciples' consumption, then surrendered to his Father and then to the guards in Gethsemane, then refused to defend himself in the awful hours that followed. All of these were moments of expending "the days of his flesh" (Heb. 5:5–10), consuming on others' behalf a life he would never get back. And he never has gotten back the days of his flesh. He had one mortal life to finish and one death to suffer, and he offered them wholly. He made no provision for the flesh or its desires (Rom. 13:14).

21. The process of family formation, not coincidentally, resembles the illuminative, unitive, and partitive ways in spiritual theology (Behold! Come! Go!) because a family's formation mysteriously symbolizes the church's formation (Eph. 5:30–32).

His death for us pioneered ours (Matt. 10:16–22, 38; Rom. 6:3–4; Gal. 2:20; Col. 2:11–12, 20). On his life's turning point our lives can turn too. Jesus's omega-sacrifice also expends any provision for *our* flesh and its desires. He didn't want our admiration or pity, and he didn't want his disciples to want these things either (Matt. 6:1–18). Following him, we forsake those spending patterns as well, and are freed from mortality's tyranny of passion, fear, and self-centeredness (Rom. 6:5–14; Gal. 5:16–25; Col. 3). Forfeiting our old lives burns away the reasons for recklessness and timidity and yields courage.

Jesus's omega-sacrifice changed Simon Peter in stunning ways. Peter's strong personal impulses were the stuff of leadership, and they deserve admiration of a sort. But they led to trouble whenever Peter gratified his flesh. It too took some time to burn away. Simon Peter was the one who followed Jesus out of the disciples' boat and onto the Sea of Galilee, but fear of the wind sank him (Matt. 14:28–32). He set himself against his own Lord by rebuking Jesus for announcing his omega-sacrifice (16:22–23). His bravado in Gethsemane and attempt to rescue his own rescuer through violence invited the same rebuke (John 18:10–11; Matt. 26:51). When the disciples scattered at Jesus's arrest, he shadowed Jesus nearby (Matt. 26:58), but lied and denied him when confronted (26:69–75), and absented himself from the rest of Christ's passion. He put himself first, ahead of others (cf. Phil. 2:3), and he wasn't the only one who paid the price.

Were these acts of courage, cowardice, or both? Let's call them an inconsistent and unstable combination of recklessness and timidity. It would be courage if it weren't disordered and tyrannized by sin and death. I recognize that combination in myself, and we see it all around us—and all around Simon Peter. His inconsistency and expediency weren't so different from Herod's, Pontius Pilate's, Caiaphas's, or Judas Iscariot's. Provide for the flesh and gratify its desires, and this is the kind of leader I'll become too. It's a common enough way for a man or woman of ambition to disburse one's life.

Jesus's death was the final expenditure of his one and only mortal life. Yet it didn't end the love that inspired it, because love never ends (1 Cor. 13:8). After the one kind of sacrifice came another. His service unto death inaugurated an eternal future of servant-leadership (Heb. 8:1–2). His free and full obedience to the Father proved the Son trustworthy of unequalled, unending power and glory as Lord of God's people (Phil. 2:5–11). Christ's new sacrifice is the life the Father bestowed on him in the Spirit: adventurous, Father-glorifying and Spirit-led, eternal in the heavens.

An omega-sacrifice is penultimate and small: one's limited life; all one has.[22] The alpha-sacrifice is ultimate and infinite: one's eternity, all one can

---

22. As I like to remind my students, YODO: you only die once.

become. So the former becomes the basis for the latter. This is how the end of a human life span matters theologically. We've spent all that we were or would have been. Did we spend it to obtain this or something less?

Jesus's new sacrificial life is the gracious gateway to ours. He pioneered our resurrections as well as our deaths: "You were buried with him in baptism, in which you were also raised with him" (Col. 2:12). The yield of our sacrificed lives can be something *given* more than earned: a new life, life abundant, lived even now in death's presence but no longer in its shadow.

And Peter's leadership did indeed turn a corner after he saw Jesus risen. The transformation was immediate. Throughout Acts he is decisive, steady, and wise. He led assertively in filling Judas Iscariot's vacancy among the Twelve, and after Pentecost he consistently showed courage to speak the good news boldly, prayed for more, and put it to good use in perilous Jerusalem, port city Joppa, sketchy Samaria, the multicultural Roman outpost Caesarea, and beyond.

Peter had stepped into both stages of Jesus's pioneering life: into Jesus's sacrificed days of his flesh, and into the eternal living sacrifice of his resurrection in the Spirit. Peter's courage and consistency were grounded and grew from there. His own perishable life had been reborn into imperishability (1 Pet. 1:23). He was no longer dominated by or conformed to his former passions (1:14). Jesus had freed him finally to act in realistic hope, true holiness, genuine love, and sober confidence (1:13–21) and to commend those virtues to all his fellow disciples. This is the leader he actually became. He could put others first, even enemies (2:13–17). As Jesus's love for others came from his love of the Father, so Peter's love of others came from Jesus. As a result, he finally came into his own as a full person with a full life, and he was far from the only one who reaped its blessings.

Jesus listed the qualities that suit the human subjects of God's new arrangement: deep humility, sober mournfulness, longing for righteousness and peace, sacrificial mercy, and purity of heart (Matt. 5:3–11). Paul did too: faith, hope, love, joy, peace, patience, kindness, generosity, gentleness, self-control, and the like (1 Cor. 13:13; Gal. 5:22–23). Some version of every item on Matthew's and Paul's lists appears in 1 Peter.[23] As a leader in the church, Peter

23. Namely, hope (1 Pet. 1:3), joy (1:6–8), faith (1:7), love (1:8), sobriety (1:13), fear and mourning (1:17–18), purity (1:22), mercy (2:10), goodness (2:12), submissiveness or meekness (2:13–14), patience under persecution (2:18–23), gentleness (3:4), poverty of spirit or humility (3:8), mournful and fearful tenderness (3:8), peace (3:11), hunger for righteousness (3:14), mournfulness (4:1, 6, 19), self-control (4:2–6), generosity (4:9), and blessedness in injustice (4:14). In addition, 1 Peter urges praise (1:7), holiness (1:15), confidence (1:21), sacrifice (2:5), chastity (3:2), honor (3:7), kindness (3:7), obedience to God (4:2), and hospitality (4:9) among others.

demonstrated these qualities of truly living sacrifice. He became "a fellow elder and a witness of the sufferings of Christ as well as a partaker in the glory that is to be revealed" (1 Pet. 5:1). Along with the other saints' lives, Peter's new life reflects a freed human will, less and less hampered by the flesh's vices and more and more informed by the Spirit's virtues.[24]

Christlike life has under-the-sun value as well as eternal value. Earthly life's worth is no longer constrained by mortality's imperfections (Matt. 5:46–48) and inevitable losses (James 1:9–10). For now we still live biological existences, but the Kingdom's eschatological existence enables us to live them, die, and even grieve in hope (1 Thess. 4:13). Christian lives are now built on hope of inheritance rather than fear of the grave. New birth sets our old selves free to manifest some of its intended abundance even while we labor and groan.

But gaining that freedom involves a struggle—for us, from us, and within us. Attending to that is our fifth topic.


### A Threat to Our Righteousness, Its Only True Security

All who encountered Jesus found themselves *coram deo*: facing the one true God. So he didn't just pose a threat to big things like the world's structures and the nations' arrangements. *Jesus posed a deadly threat to every life he met.* We've regarded him that way (2 Cor. 5:16) for good reason. *Yet he proves to be our lives' only true security.*

I mentioned that entering the Kingdom involves both an invasion and a migration. The Kingdom's invasion was really a recovery operation, like Normandy in 1944; but it was an invasion nonetheless. Invasions are serious threats. The King entered not just territory and principalities but hearts (Luke 2:34–35). Jesus brings a sword not just to relationships but to our own selves (Matt. 10:34–39). Herod perceived that right away. On hearing the news of a newborn king, he recoiled and slaughtered innocent children because of the *personal* threat Jesus seemed to pose (2:3, 16). After all, the men from the East, probably pagans, who arrived in Judea to worship Israel's newborn king signaled that foreign powers might someday throw their support behind a rival.

Simon Peter didn't have Herod's power to persecute, but Jesus's arrival put him on the same defensive. "Depart from me," he pleaded as he surveyed his

24. This is displayed, perhaps surprisingly, in the relinquishing of Simon Peter's old insistence on his own way, something Americans would typically associate *with* free will, and his patience and trust even when suffering mistreatment for acting righteously, something that champions of modern liberation would typically misunderstand as weakness and "mental slavery" (1 Pet. 3:14–22).

catch, "for I am a sinful man, O Lord" (Luke 5:8–9). He must have sensed that it symbolized the end of his old life, even if he didn't yet grasp the new life awaiting him (5:10).

Simon was a decent guy, and probably a relatively righteous one. He doesn't seem to have had "a history" like Levi the tax collector or Paul the persecuting Pharisee. Yet as the astrologers' tribute was a judgment on Israel's provinciality and spiritual witlessness, so that enormous catch of fish was a judgment on the struggle, scarcity, and insignificance of Simon Peter's conventional way of life. And it was only the first of many negative verdicts that Jesus would deliver on Peter's life and mindset, and ours.[25] The experience shook him to the core. Mine shook me to the core too. Falling into God's living hands is a dreadful thing (Heb. 10:31). Whether our self-image is high or low, it perishes before him, sacrificed along with everything else in our struggle with his genuine righteousness.

After the Kingdom's invasion comes migration. Simon Peter's first action as a disciple makes the change sound immediate and not necessarily that difficult: he "left everything and followed him" (Luke 5:11). But the substance took years. He was right to realize he was a sinner, but wrong to plead that Jesus keep his distance. He was right that Jesus was the Messiah, but wrong to assume the world could just receive him without striking down its shepherd and scattering his sheep (cf. John 13:12–20). He came around to appreciating God's sacrificial love for Israel (Acts 2:38–39), but even then failed to realize it extended equally to the nations (10:9–16, 34–35). In his judgments of Jesus's life, Simon Peter had relied on a wrongheaded ignorance of the Lord, justice, the future, others, and himself. That set him up—as it sets us up—for a rough transition from old to new. Peter's shifts in judgment went far beyond a conventional realization that we fall short and need a savior. His repentance involved repeated disorientations and reorientations as he came to realize that Jesus was really the judge and that he was really the one judged: radically inadequate, yet—and here dawns the alpha—radically accepted anyway through God's unfathomable grace and truth.

25. Imagine being personally on the receiving end of these lines (only some of many), either alone or with your fellow disciples: "Not seven times, but seventy times seven." "Do you not understand this parable? Then how will you understand all the parables?" "Then are you also without understanding?" "Do not rejoice that the spirits are subject to you." "Faithless and perverse generation, how long?" "Do you still not understand?" "Why did you doubt?" "Get behind me, Satan!" "Why are you afraid? Have you no faith?" "You will deny me three times." "Do you love me?" For Peter to bear all these and more, even distributed over a long time, took stamina that few of us have in our hypersensitive times. That's what it takes to be remade, then and now.

Without that alpha, being judged like this again and again would be shattering. In fact, even *with* the alpha it's shattering. Coming to face my own continuing failure as a Christian, a human being, a son, a brother, a husband, a father, a theologian, a colleague, a teacher, a citizen, a neighbor, amounts to a kind of rolling devastation of my ego. The shadow of our old lives just seems to lengthen as we travel farther and farther from its source. Maybe Peter's did too: he closes his letter with hard-won gentleness and patience, awaiting a restoration that lies as much in the future as in the past (1 Pet. 5:6–11).

But the dawn beckons closer and closer. From old life's grave rises new life, radiating outward from Jesus. The Lamb slain by usurpers was the Good Shepherd; the object of our misjudgments was the true judge (Matt. 25). This alone is revolutionary. It transforms Jesus into the object of our worship (28:16–17) as we come to see him truly. We begin to share his adoration of the Father and Spirit, and their adoration of him. This calls for a reexamination and realignment of our whole lives (28:18–20). And on top of it all, the once-judged judge shares his throne and its prerogatives with us as his deputies (Rev. 3:20–22; John 14:12; 15:16; 20:23). That high privilege calls for a thorough personal transformation to acquire as well as understand his character.

Simon had wanted Jesus to keep his distance. That's how prudent people respond to threats. But distance was the source of Simon's misunderstanding, poor judgment, inconsistency, and undependability. The real threat was elsewhere. *Satan* had demanded Simon. Jesus provided protection, restoration, and patronage (Luke 22:31–32). Our eternal lives are secure in the Father who knows all things (Acts 1:6–7). So Simon the threatened became Peter the threat (Acts 4; 1 Pet. 4:12–14). Simon the disoriented and scattered became Saint Peter holding the keys of the Kingdom (Matt. 16:18–19; 1 Pet. 5:1–4).

Ah, but here especially, isn't Peter exceptional rather than exemplary? Who else holds those keys at the pearly gates? Well, the Matthew 16 passage I just cited doesn't refer just to the apostle Peter or the bishop of Rome. It draws on Matthew 7, which also features gates (vv. 13–14), the Kingdom of Heaven (vv. 21–22), and building on rock and being overcome or not (vv. 24–27). There Jesus was addressing all his disciples. The bundles of metaphors in these two chapters all point to an end to *every* disciple's futile old life and the beginning of a new and durable one. We need to take them together to get what Jesus told Peter.

Peter himself isn't the bedrock under Jesus's church. The church's one and only sound foundation is Jesus's own word, which embodies the Father's will (Matt. 7:15–21, 24) that the Son of Man should suffer and be raised (16:20–21). This dependable material contrasts with the spreading leaven of the Pharisees and Sadducees (16:1–12). Their poor guidance, misperceptions, and deceptive tests (16:13–14) only speed people along the wide road leading to destruction. That shaky stuff is the same sand on which doomed people build that Jesus criticized in the rest of the Sermon on the Mount.

Jesus is not introducing Peter the bishop of Rome, but Peter the New. Jesus's nickname for Simon indicates that in the future he will be building on the Lord's bedrock, taking up his own cross and following Jesus (Matt. 16:24–28), and traveling the narrow path of life. Peter will receive the keys to that gate, to enter and to reach its destination. In fact, death's wide gates will not lock out the invading Kingdom's ambassadors, of whom Peter is a prominent example, or prevent emigrations of the condemned who want to leave its wide way for the Kingdom's narrow one.

Jesus was assuring the Kingdom's missionaries that they would be secure even when they are playing offense. Simon's life wouldn't be cut down like Matthew 7:15–20's bad tree. Jesus would indeed be rejected and killed, but he would rise again. His way is the narrow way; his words are the rock. Peter's allegiance to these indicates that he was now of the same tree and would yield its same fruit. Peter's new life is not exceptional but typical. We get to take heart in his example and follow it in the same confidence.

## Where Are All the Saints?

An objection has haunted me all the way through this chapter, akin to similar objections in the others. I keep raising these because they express our culture's runaway skepticism toward Jesus and disillusionment with Christianity, and they deserve a hearing and a response. Why do the lives of so many Christians look so *unlike* what I've been describing? Why is there so often so little change? Where are all the omegas and alphas? Where's the evidence?

Moderns are hardly the first ones to wonder. The early church often stipulated that only a few would be saved. Augustine got more and more pessimistic about the likely ratio as he aged, and as I age I can sometimes see why. The sheer *momentum* of the world, of sin, of every single nation and of their common efforts, of every single person and of their relationships, seems unstoppable.

It is not that the biblical picture is unrealistic. It matches the real world quite accurately. Peter admitted that his walk was a prolonged struggle *even with Jesus right there* ministering in the Spirit, delivering astonishing sermons, casting out spirits, healing Peter's mother-in-law, walking on water, feeding multitudes with their own paltry lunch, being transfigured in Peter's sight, outwitting opponents without skipping a beat, healing a woman without even realizing it, walking straight into the hands of his persecutors, dying a graceful death, and greeting Peter and the others mercifully on his return. All that, and still it was a struggle to understand and trust him.

Jesus had put it well himself: If people won't heed Moses and the prophets, what difference will a resurrection make (Luke 16:31)? The problem is not in the scale of the Kingdom's signs but in the eyes of their beholders. The truth can get through, but it can also not get through. And very often it doesn't.

Even when it does, often surprisingly little penetrates. It has been said that Christianity in Africa—one of the faith's great success stories—is a mile wide but an inch deep. It blankets rather than reforms vast pre-Christian sensibilities that run as deep in African hearts as in African cultures. That's been said about Korea too, where Confucianism pervades the ancient consciousness underneath Korea's recent adoptions of Christianity and (more broadly) modernity. It's been said about the individualist, Enlightenment, materialist United States as well. In each of these places and many more, the metaphor of uniformly shallow faith expresses genuine frustration with the limits of Christianity's transformation there. Yet the metaphor is just as frustrating to people who know deep Christians in each of these places. *Their* Christianity isn't an inch deep. A more accurate metaphor would honor the complex reality that many lives aren't transformed at all, others only shallowly, others only temporarily, and a few deeply and lastingly.

We already have one: Jesus's parable of the sower. In Mark's Gospel it follows the first events of Jesus's ministry. His remarkable signs and wonders, his call of the first disciples, and his parables of new wine and binding the strong man (Mark 1–3) all heralded a grand omega-and-alpha-style transformation. With the parable of the sower, Jesus then put the brakes on some runaway interpretations of those events. His work was never going to balloon into a dramatic uniform transformation of the whole world, like a widening circle of ripples in the pool of history.[26] The gospel's power would not create a hospitable environment for its own reception. Many of even the ones who initially responded to Jesus would revert to their old selves.

Christianity everywhere *is* an inch deep—in the ones whose soil is shallow. In the ones who have been trodden down into a sterile path or choked with weeds, it isn't even that. Yet in every place, in some people it has penetrated to the core of their lives. These new lives will touch their cultures—which,

26. The phrase is Karl Barth's, and I am being unfair to him by taking it out of context. He was emphasizing the Gospels' widening reverberations, not their uniformity. But the metaphor itself implies uniformity and has been used out of context in just that way. See Karl Barth, "Biblical Questions, Insights, and Vistas," in *The Word of God and the Word of Man*, trans. Douglas Horton (New York: Harper, 1957), 63.

after all, are patches of grass to which the shoots of these individual lives truly belong. But their cultures cannot be touched as deeply as they themselves have been touched. The Christianity of a place will always be shallower than its most transformed Christians, and deeper than its least.

This reality strains Orthodox and Catholic sacramentalism, which wants the church's grace to be more uniformly and deeply powerful as it spreads and remakes civilizations. It threatens Lutheran and Reformed theologies of the Word of God, which want the same thing for the gospel and the Scriptures. It intrudes into "Anabaptist" ecclesiology, which wants the same thing for whole communities of structured and dedicated discipleship. It frustrates Pentecostal convictions about the Spirit and sanctification, which want the same thing for the Spirit's baptism, gifts, and fruit. All of these have to fall back on some kind of explanation for missing transformation, which qualifies in some way the very thing they insist on.[27] We want more than we see.

It hurts most when we find resistance in our own children, after we have exposed them to all of these means of grace and spent ourselves in love, sacrifice, and prayer. I attended a conference in Korea where parents were invited to request prayers, and overwhelmingly they asked for prayers for their own children's conversions. This wasn't a Confucian sensibility; these parents had absorbed a sacrificial desire to bless their children rather than receive their well-deserved fealty. Their prayers were the same ones that many of us have lifted up for our churches' children in our supposedly individualistic America. At the conference, the tone of these requests felt desperate. The parents felt powerless to reach adolescents turned apathetic, seduced by diversions and ambitions and passions, disillusioned by poor teaching and examples within the church itself, and dismissive of family tradition.

Frankly, when their children and ours seem so oblivious to our desires and concerns for their spiritual welfare and so focused elsewhere, such parental zeal feels irrelevant. Does one pray for rocky soil to become deep and rich after seeds have already started withering? That doesn't seem like the direction of the parable.

After all, the point of a farmer sowing is not to "save" bad soil. That is how Jesus sometimes framed his work elsewhere, but not here. The transformation he envisioned is of the system itself: from ungerminated seed and fallow soil to mutual fulfillment. The point is to raise a harvest of fruit from the combined potential of the seminal gospel and its receptive soil. We can

27. For instance, the untransformed weren't saved in the first place; they weren't elect; they didn't have enough faith; we just haven't seen the full results yet; true conversion is inward and invisible; God honors our wills; it's all a mystery; and so on.

call that salvation, and if we do, we can further specify that it is salvation for both the seed *and* the soil, who need each other like a bridegroom and a bride.

Not all seed and not all soil is so transformed or "saved." But that was not Jesus's point. He focused his interpretation on each one with ears to hear him (Mark 4:9). Then with a different metaphor he repeated himself: light is for shining, and a lampstand is for extending light's reach (4:21–25). The system is the point. Jesus would broadcast his good news, which is for hearing, but he didn't expect the deaf to hear it. Then he would take the *next* step in his strategy: focus on those who receive it and produce a harvest that deserves an even greater investment in the future. The proportion of good soil to bad, lampstands to bushels, wasn't his concern, either then or later (10:23–31; cf. Luke 13:22–30). Where ratios are concerned, Jesus focused mainly on the rate of return among those who produced it, one life at a time (Mark 4:20). This brings us back to Peter and the discouraging day that Jesus told his parable. The disciples couldn't understand it, or apparently any of the others (4:13), so Jesus had to explain. Then had they really heard it? Did they lack ears? And that evening, he and the disciples boarded a boat, and a storm arose that exposed their lack of faith (4:40). Were they really the right kind of soil?

Peter knew he wasn't. His storytelling shows no trace of hubris. Yet the Twelve were the ones Jesus had recruited and would stick with until his return (Mark 16:7). And he taught them only "as they were able to hear it" (4:33), adapting to their hardness of hearing. He cultivated the developing system, turning the soil and supporting the word's new growth with great patience and despite repeated frustration. So who is to say that a person is too spiritually deaf to hear and take the word to heart? That's all that being good soil seems to involve. The reality of personal omegas and alphas is complicated. Soil can be either rich or barely adequate and still yield a harvest. Even when a successful harvest results, the whole system takes time and effort, suffers setbacks and disasters, and frustrates everyone.

Where Jesus wanted a hearer to focus was on *one's own system* of soil and word. I came away from that conference with the conviction that while it's right to pray for my children and others', my first focus should be my own productivity. The weeds that most need pulling and the rocks that most need removing are my own. Jesus prayed for his flock and for lost sheep, but he did a lot besides pray. In fact, he is mainly remembered for the rest. He entered profoundly into the lostness of those lost sheep, but always returned to his own flock and above all to his Father. He put his hand to his plow without focusing on those who weren't following him (Luke 9:62).

Paul didn't look back when he reflected in 2 Timothy 4 on the fellow Christians who disappointed him. John told his churches not to look back (1 John

2:18–20). The writer of Hebrews didn't look back on those who had drifted away from Jesus Christ, and advised readers that trying to argue them back in would be fruitless (Heb. 6:1–8). Peter told his audience of sojourners not to look back nostalgically on their own past behavior even in others who persist in it (1 Pet. 4:3–6). None of these passages condemn the people concerned to inevitable perdition; any and all who did repent would surely be restored. All these writers did was set aside what lay behind, so to speak, and strain for what lay ahead for them, while advising others to do the same (Phil. 3:13–21).

So the heartbreaking phenomenon of even vast numbers of shallow and temporary Christians is already part of the biblical picture. Not all migrate when the Kingdom of God invades their territory, and not all who do migrate remain. Their lives do not bear Christ's omega and alpha, at least not yet. I don't like this feature of the faith, and God seems to like it even less. I guess I can "object" that I wish reality were otherwise.[28] But it is what it is.

And doubtless for good reason. "We shall be like him" only through our right relationships with him (1 John 3:1–3). The Lord will not coerce, manipulate, or neglect us into Christlikeness. He will invite us into it, endure us into it, suffer us into it, and even suffer our refusal to accept that invitation or persist in the life it offers, all with true love (2:1–6).

Yet I shouldn't jump to pessimistic conclusions any more than optimistic ones. After all, at what point did *Peter's* life definitively express Christ's omega and alpha? It is obvious in retrospect, but not before. Along the way there were plenty of reasons for the so-called Rock to worry and doubt, and even to despair (Matt. 26:75).[29] But Jesus held onto him. Maybe that's why Peter expects some pleasant surprises on the day Jesus returns (1 Pet. 2:12), not just unpleasant ones. Only then will we see everything clearly, including ourselves.

### Death's Door?

Appealing to retrospect begs a common question that we have raised but not yet answered: Is the end of a human life span eschatologically *decisive*? Does my spiritual state at my time of death *determine* my eternity?

The medieval Catholic framework has dominated even Protestant imaginations that formally reject it: I am sacramentally maintained in a "state of

---

28. But that's more of a complaint or protest than a logical objection. And the Psalms are full of those. Complaints have a proper place in lives of faith. However, they aren't valid reasons to deny the reality of the apostolic and biblical picture any more than the disturbing implications of physics or biology are valid reasons to reject findings in those disciplines.

29. Paul sounded less than absolutely certain about his own future (1 Cor. 9:24–27), though he didn't seem anxious about it.

grace" and so participate in Christ's salvation, yet "mortal sins" (cf. 1 John
5:16) jeopardize that relationship until they are remedied by the sacrament
of reconciliation. If I die in a state of mortal sin, I seem not to have any firm
basis for hope. This is why suicide has been regarded (or at least dreaded)
as a decisive loss of salvation: because there is no opportunity for reconciliation afterward.

Evangelical Protestants commonly make one's profession of faith—
"accepting Christ as personal Lord and Savior"—decisive instead (cf. John
5:24). But then what theological significance does the rest of one's mortal
Christian life have? Perhaps, as Lutherans claim, it indicates the paradoxical
character of Christian lives that are both old and new. Or perhaps, as Calvin-
ists claim, it signals how genuine one's profession of faith was. Or perhaps,
as Arminians claim, it demands persistence in faithfulness. At any rate, a
fatal stumble at the end might not be as indicative as the broad pattern over
one's lifelong walk.

The matter of people who die without having heard or really understood
the good news of the Kingdom troubles both Christians and non-Christians.
What about beloved ancestors? Innocent and even unborn children? Generations and peoples who come and go ignorant of the gospel? People who have
followed the rays of grace and truth that are available beyond and before
Christian mission? Peter's letter includes a tantalizing detail that might speak
to the issue. "Let the time that is past suffice for doing what the Gentiles like
to do. . . . They will give account to him who is ready to judge the living
and the dead. *For this is why the gospel was preached even to the dead, that
though judged in the flesh like men, they might live in the spirit like God.*
The end of all things is at hand" (1 Pet. 4:3–7). This passage honors both the
medieval Catholic and the Protestant logics. The dead here are still judged
in the flesh like all humans. Their mortal stories have come to an end, spent
on this or that, and they have reaped the consequences. Yet news of the risen
Jesus has somehow reached them and proclaimed his victory, with spiritual
consequences that might end their old situation and lead to life. Through
the gospel of grace, he can be the omega and alpha not just of the living but
also of the dead.

Peter already claimed that the living Jesus, "in the spirit," invaded the
realm of the grave and assured its inhabitants that he reigns far above all
angels, authorities, and powers (1 Pet. 3:18–20; its phrase "made alive in the
spirit, in which he went" shows that it does not refer to a "descent into hell"
of a dead and not-yet-risen Jesus). He is their judge and Lord. This passage
is couched in apocalyptic folklore, drawing on 1 Enoch 10, so a literal sense
is harder than usual to grasp. Furthermore, along with the even more cryptic

1 Corinthians 15:28–29, 1 Peter 4:6 is an outlier. It is silent on questions involving the dead of future generations, the dead who in life did hear the good news, the dead who received a distorted or heretical gospel, and Christians who died in problematic ways. All these make it an undependable basis for generalized doctrine. It is certainly no excuse to shirk mission and evangelism! Nevertheless, in all its quirkiness it teaches one very clear thing. Without minimizing or trivializing death's role in life, it firmly subordinates death to Christ. Like everything else, death is now at Jesus's disposal. Its end is at hand too. It is no barrier to his word's reach (Matt. 16:18; 1 Pet. 1:23–25). It serves him, not vice versa.

## When Dawn Breaks

When Jesus does return, what has been modest and elusive will be anything but. All will be revealed, brought into the light, and shouted from housetops (Luke 12:2–3). The appearing or parousia of Jesus Christ will involve the appearing of him in all who belong to him (Rom. 8:29–30; 9:23; 1 Pet. 1:7). Those sown in dishonor will be raised in glory to appear with him (1 Cor. 15:43; Col. 3:4), crowned with his glory (Rom. 5:2; 1 Pet. 5:1, 4, 10; 2 Pet. 1:3).[30] Glorification doesn't sound like an understated affair.

In the life of the age to come, the alpha qualities God has been nurturing in holy ones will finally be fully at home. The parousia will be like the first hour on a job for which a person has been training for years. Peter's courage, love, and gentle sympathy won't be obsolete, like one's career achievements commemorated at a retirement party; they will be ready for presentation and full use.

Wait, is that right? Why would the saints need *courage* in the new creation? Peter's courage isn't an "omega" quality, since it belonged to his new life. But how is it an "alpha" quality if it doesn't last or need to last? It is too easy to draw a straight line along the trajectory of the saints' present sanctification that rises higher and higher to perfection. The future may not be so straightforward.

What applies to Peter's courage applies to a number of the saints' virtues. They may have been instrumental along the way to glory, but what about their roles *in* glory? Suddenly they seem like the high school awards I have packed away in a box somewhere in the garage. It felt wrong to throw them

---

30. This seems also a proper way to interpret the glory and honor of the nations in Rev. 21:24–26, since no other glory but the Lord's is worthy of that kind of attention. The glory of the nations is Christ's alpha-glory manifested among his disciples from all nations.

away, but decades later it seems odd to be holding on to them. Or here is a more disturbing analogy: What if they are like the *studying* I did, and particularly like the finals-week cramming, in order to graduate? Paul talks about straining ahead to gain the prize (Phil. 3:13–14). Is this some kind of placement test where we can forget it all once we pass? Does God require us to labor so hard to produce character qualities that are not of eternal value? Why is perseverance so valued in a temptation-free new creation? What use is sympathy when suffering is no more? And why make temporary qualities like these the criteria that distinguish the good and faithful servants who inherit the Kingdom and get promotions from the wicked servants who get the sack? What kind of glory is that?

The usual Protestant objections to works-righteousness aren't the issue here. We face the same problem even if *God* is the one graciously working in us to work out all of this (Phil. 2:12–13). Is there eternal significance in all that forming and shaping and judging and rewarding, or just passing significance?

It's good to remember that after alpha comes beta, gamma, and the rest. Paul treated spiritual gifts as of passing significance. We might call them "beta" qualities in that they reside on the new timeline but will also be dispensed with, "ended" (1 Cor. 13:8–10, my translation). By contrast, other presently available qualities such as faith, hope, and love will last. To help us understand, Paul drew an analogy with qualities along the old timeline that can become obsolete along the way: childhood, for instance (13:11). Knowledge, prophecies, tongues, and other spiritual gifts are like temporary scaffolding used to facilitate the construction of a building. In that case, Peter's courage would have been necessary during the time that courage was necessary, but not forever. It wouldn't tell us what Peter will become in his glorification.

Paul's comparison with childhood suggests a different answer, though. We do lose our umbilical cords and our baby teeth as we grow, and our ganglia pare down their unused dendrites as we mature, but childhood is a process more of gain than loss. Childhood is not a stage that a person could skip on the way to adulthood. Childhood *is the way* to adulthood. A final or placement exam that tests nothing but short-term memorization is a bad test. Courage wouldn't be like that; it would be more like a necessary developmental milestone along the way. At the same time, one doesn't extrapolate along a straight line from children's milestones to derive a full picture of their adult selves. Adolescent turbulence doesn't last, and thank God for that. So perhaps courage and sympathy are less like the gift of prophecy, which glorification makes as obsolete as baby teeth, and more like the partial knowledge that "ends" in full understanding (1 Cor. 13:12). The perfection of courage would be steadfastness, which as a divine attribute never passes away under any circumstance. Far from a pointless test or even a stage of life that is closed off and packed away, Peter's courage-turned-steadfastness would crown him eternally and characterize all that he did in his never-ending service as co-heir of Christ's endless reign. And the same is true of ours as fellow servants in the fellowship.

That is something to look forward to, and to work toward with full apostolic resolve (1 Cor. 14:1).

# Afterword

*Jesus—the End and the Beginning of the Book*

Where do we go from here, at the end of our exercise? Following the apostles who first traced the logic of what God had done in Jesus Christ and the three paths of spiritual theology outlined in chapter 7, here are three promising directions in which to focus. They do not detract from each other.

First, focus back on Jesus. Each chapter has looked at how Jesus ends and begins something or other. Without taking its eyes off of these achievements, the church has always been drawn back to the glorious achiever. He is the core of our remembrance, gratitude, union, adoration, contemplation, and allegiance. Gathering in worship is a great opportunity for us to *come and see* the one who has been changing everything.

Second, focus forward to the new omega toward which the new alpha has reoriented us. Recall the figure from the first chapter (next page).

Our new course leads away from our point of departure to somewhere else: a newly satisfied God, a perfected creation, a perceptive world enjoying the reign of its loving and just ruler, and glorified humanity, nations, and fellowship of holy persons. Instead of looking back on the old, we can travel this path in faithful, hopeful love, with service, redemptive work, mission, hospitality, and patient endurance as we *go and tell* those who have not heard the good news about what the Lord has been doing for us.

Focusing on either one should carry us to the other, back and forth. The two ought not detract from each other, though some people and some Christian traditions get preoccupied with some of these practices and lose their apostolic perspective.

Figure A.1

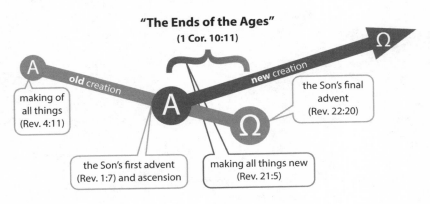

**"The Ends of the Ages"**
(1 Cor. 10:11)

old creation

new creation

A

A

Ω

Ω

making of
all things
(Rev. 4:11)

the Son's final
advent
(Rev. 22:20)

the Son's first advent
(Rev. 1:7) and ascension

making all things new
(Rev. 21:5)

Finally, we can focus on our own lives. In the introductory chapter I posed some questions. Then in the following chapters I consistently raised objections from disappointed and skeptical observers: *How different are these new things really?* The most productive place to pose a question like that is on that modest place where I least want it: myself. So it is time to *behold* what Jesus has illuminated in and around me and revisit those difficult questions. Not in an analytical way now, but diagnostically and prescriptively. They can help spur the change Jesus means to bring.

What *is* the turning point of my life, the hinge and identifier of my story? Is Jesus Christ my omega and my alpha? Is my life baptismal, dead-and-risen, Christ-shaped? *Is it?*

What has Christ put to an end? And what am I holding on to that needs to go?

What has Christ begun in me? And what am I either encouraging to grow and mature, or trying to prevent him from bringing to life?

And into which unconsidered places of life and which unimagined dimensions of reality are his missional life, atoning death, risen new creation, ascended reign, and looming return reaching into my midst and leading me?

You may want to ask yourself these questions. I truly hope you do. But my task now is to pose them to myself.

# Scripture Index

# General Index